Kate Simons, a research fellow at Federation University Australia, has lectured in literature and film studies. Her current research interests include mythology and medievalism. She has travelled widely on three continents, and in 2010 she walked the Camino de Santiago. Latterly she also walked the Old Pilgrims' Way from Winchester to Canterbury. Kate lives in Ballarat, Victoria with her husband.

For my Husband with love.

Kate Simons

MEDIEVAL WANDERS AND WONDERS: UNDERSTANDING NORTHERN SPAIN AND THE CAMINO DE SANTIAGO

AUSTIN MACAULEY
PUBLISHERS LTD.

A CIP catalogue record for this title is available from the British
Library.

ISBN 9781786291653 (Paperback)
ISBN 9781786291660 (Hardback)
ISBN 9781786291677 (E-Book)
www.austinmacauley.com

First Published (2017)
Austin Macauley Publishers Ltd.
25 Canada Square
Canary Wharf
London
E14 5LQ

Acknowledgments

In part I have written this book to acknowledge the kindness and generosity shown to me by the people of Northern Spain, in particular the network of pilgrim confraternities and the various hospitallers who work tirelessly and without remuneration in the refuges (*albergues*), where I lodged each night.

I also wish to thank Federation University Australia, in particular Professor John McDonald, Executive Dean for the Faculty of Education and Arts. Without the support of the university, and the hard-working library staff, this book would have been extremely difficult to write.

I am also in the debt of Adjunct Professor Alice Mills who patiently read the numerous drafts of my manuscript. Not only was she generally encouraging but also provided useful criticism and adroit advice.

Thanks are offered too to my editor, Vinh Tran, who has not only been helpful but also supportive and extremely patient.

Last but not least I thank my husband who accompanied me to Northern Spain. Not only did his sharp eyes extend and enrich my research, but he was also obliged to walk many kilometres at my behest. Thank you.

Contents

Preface

Steps and Mis-Steps

There was once a pilgrim called Gerald who walked across the north of Spain to the city of Santiago there to venerate the holy relics of Saint James. He came from the city of Lyon in what is now France. Though a good and honourable man, Gerald was overcome by the voluptuousness of flesh and fornicated with a certain maiden the night before setting forth on his pilgrimage. Ignoring his sin, he travelled happily for several days with two companions and a beggar man whom they met along the way. The Devil, envious of this peaceful and charitable company, approached Gerald. Disguised in charming human form the 'Evil One' explained that he was James, the very saint this pilgrim was hoping to revere in Santiago. Castigating the young man for his grave wrong-doing the night before leaving home, the disguised fiend told Gerald his only recourse if he wished to gain eternal life was to cut off the member with which he had sinned and then take his life.

That night Gerald's travelling companions, hearing tortured cries and witnessing the shocking gush of blood, were stricken with terror. They ran off, leaving the young man floundering in his gore lest they be blamed for the death. In the morning the corpse was discovered by the family in whose house the companions had lodged. The

11

dead body was taken to the church for burial. As the grave was being dug Gerald suddenly sat bolt upright upon his funeral bier. Those who were present and seeing this resurrection, fled in terror. Alarmed by their cries, people ran up and asked what had happened. Gerald explained how he had indeed died and in death he had been approached by the real, and very handsome, Saint James, as well as by Mary, the Venerable mother of God whose beauty was beyond description. Together this holy duo had returned him to life and healed his wound. Thus restored (or so Anselm, Archbishop of Canterbury is alleged to have written in the eleventh century), he was able to continue his journey to James' venerated shrine.

In the seventeenth century Domenico Laffi, a priest from Bologna who preferred travel to parish work, and Domenico Codici, a painter from the same Italian city, also walked across northern Spain to visit Santiago. They had just left Burgos and were heading towards Hontanas. It was summer and the going was hard, the barren plains not only scorched by the fierce sun, but also ravaged by an immense locust swarm. Every bit of vegetation had been devoured. In his journal Laffi claims there were so many of these accursed creatures he could hardly walk. 'At every step', he wrote, 'they rose in the air in clouds so dense that you could hardly see the sky'. The two pilgrims eventually arrived at their destination, a wretched village of a dozen or so straw-roofed hovels and were offered shelter in a hut surrounded by a strong palisade. Here they were shielded from the wolves who prowled about in packs so famished they frequently ate each other.

In the morning the two stepped out with the shepherds, taking advantage of the protection afforded by their huge sheep dogs. Before they reached the next town, Castrojeriz, they came upon a French pilgrim lying on the ground. He was dying and completely covered with locusts which were eating him. Unable to help, they prayed with the Frenchman as he departed this world. Laffi and his companion then covered the dead body with sand to protect what was left of the corpse and continued on their way to Santiago to worship at the tomb of Saint James.

In 2010 I also walked eight hundred kilometres across northern Spain. I did not encounter James or the 'Evil One', but I did meet a great many interesting pilgrims and I made several dear friends. Flying in from the African desert locusts can still threaten Spain, but now they are usually eradicated before they arrive. Today's walkers are also safe from wolves, these animals almost exterminated in the 1950s by the Francoist government. Those still found in the far reaches of north-west Spain are few, protected and almost impossible to find. When I was walking, sunburn and blisters were my greatest hazards.

For those who do not know of it, the pilgrimage walk across the north of Spain is called the Camino, *camino* in Spanish meaning 'the way'. The French provided a more romantic title. Travelling as one does from east to west, the milky stars in the heavens above seemed to direct medieval pilgrims as they walked, and so the trail was nicknamed *Voie Lactée*, 'the Milky Way'.

The Camino has been traversed since the late ninth century. Today it still crosses the same mountains and rivers and passes the same cathedrals and monasteries as it did in medieval times. Unlike other famous walking tracks, this trail does not avoid villages and towns, but seeks them out, making it easy for pilgrims, then as well as now, to procure food and lodging. Over the centuries hundreds of thousands of pilgrims have annually made the crossing, the numbers only decreasing at two specific historical points, the first during the religious reformations taking place during the Renaissance, the second because of the scepticism of the eighteenth century Enlightenment. Even then the pilgrim flow never entirely ceased. At the height of its popularity in medieval times it has been estimated that five hundred thousand pilgrims arrived annually at Santiago. Some authorities claim there were more. Though the twenty-first century is often considered a post-religious age, the walk is still popular, records showing that more than 200,000 pilgrims made their way to Santiago in 2013. In Jubilee years (the year the saint's feast day falls on a Sunday), the numbers are always much higher.

A scallop shell easily identifies a Santiago pilgrim, both in medieval times and today. Pilgrims of old were provided with this piece of insignia after they had arrived in Santiago. They wore it as they triumphantly walked home. Because we now return home either by aeroplane or train, today's pilgrims wear the scallop as they set forth, attaching it to either hat or backpack. How the relationship between shell and the Camino evolved is uncertain, some claiming it was simply because Santiago is close to the ocean and scallops so plentiful on these beaches. For medieval pilgrims who were living rough, the shells made a useful tool, used either as a large spoon or small plate, or for scooping water from rivers or wells.

I prefer the scallop explanation found in the medieval text, the *Liber Sancti Jacobi*. Here the author tells how a knight was seen riding along the beach. His horse took fright and plunged into the ocean, drowning the rider. James went to the rescue. When he was brought forth from the sea the knight and his horse were not only alive but covered in scallops. According to some this was James' first miracle and the reason why the Camino is associated with this shell.

Pilgrims of old travelled the Camino for religious reasons: to profess their faith, as a penance and means of atonement, as an opportunity to venerate the saint and his relics or to gain religious merit. Unlike those pilgrims I did not go to repent or revere. At a low ebb in my teaching career, walking a pilgrim trail seemed a romantic means by which to revitalize my flagging enthusiasms. I took leave from my university and simply went walking. In Europe it was summer. My pack was light and I found it easy to establish a walking rhythm and general routine. Each day, to avoid the worst of the heat, I would rise in the dark and burst forth to join the dawn. I found the vastness of the Spanish sky, the early morning freshness and the deep solitude exhilarating. I crossed mountains and rivers, walked through forests and tramped over the flat and dusty Meseta plains. Mostly it was dry. A few times it rained. On occasions I found the dilapidation of many of the northern Spanish villages distressing. It was also sad to note so many locked and neglected parish churches, but this bleakness was off-set by the marvellous cathedrals, mysterious religious houses and wonderful treasure to be found in museums located in the larger towns.

From earliest times pilgrims have felt compelled to chronicle their journey. I, too, had experiences and insights which I wrote down and pondered upon. In this book, however, I do not wish to share these but instead I write about what happened after I returned home. Exhilarated and sun-tanned I felt as though it had been an easy walk, in spite of tendonitis in my right knee, but I was unable to settle. On balmy evenings I would sit out with my husband, Terence, glad to have me home again and interested in my adventures. As I talked I realized that, even though I had walked a great distance, I had not fully appreciated what I had walked through. Now rested and reflective I wanted to understand why I had embarked on such an undertaking, and why as a pilgrim. What was significant about pilgrimage in medieval times and how, if at all, does pilgrimage differ today? What does medievalism really imply and what was it like to live then? In the physical euphoria of rhythmic motion what had I failed to observe in northern Spain and what splendid gems were still to be discovered in the many museums and cathedral chapter-houses I had blithely walked by?

My reluctance to renew my teaching contract made me realize that what I really wanted was to return to Spain. I tentatively broached the subject with Terence and, to soften the blow that he might once again be abandoned, invited him to join me. I expected my invitation to be declined, my husband being a quiet, peace-loving man, so I was astonished by his enthusiastic acceptance. Terence's eagerness was contagious and spurred me into action. I enrolled myself into a course of Spanish language classes. I bought books and began to study church history and medieval art. Terence tended to his travel documents and purchased a backpack and appropriate clothes. We did not intend to walk as pilgrims, but planned to stop off at a number of strategic places along the route and take time to absorb the atmosphere, appreciate the architecture and ecclesiastical treasure, as well as contemplate on medieval sensibility.

As opposed to pilgrimage, the trip was to be a cultural and historical quest. This meant that we would utilize public transport and find ourselves accommodation in guest-houses and pensions. Terence agreed to all my suggestions. Having experienced a Spanish summer I suggested we arrive in the spring. Two years later we set off. In this book I refer to my Camino experiences, but mostly I chronicle what I found out about pilgrimage and the medievals who had also walked this amazing trail.

Works cited in this prologue

Bentley, James. *The Way of Saint James*. London: Pavilion Books. 1992.

Coffey, Thomas F, Linda Kay Davidson & Maryjane Dunn, trans. & eds. 'The Miracles of Saint James', *The Liber Sancti Jacobi*. New York, NY: Italica Press. 1996.

Laffi, Domenico, trans. James Hall. *The Diary of a Seventh Century Pilgrim from Bologna to Santiago de Compostela*. The Netherlands, Leiden: Primavera Pers. 1977.

Rabe, Cordula, trans. Gill Round. *Camino de Santiago: Way of Saint James from the Pyrenees to Santiago*. Munich: Rother. 2007.

1

All Things Bright and Grisly

The shimmering casket lay at the end of a short underground passage. It dazzled, radiating life and astonishing energy. I was astounded. Could old bones really do that! For several moments I was overwhelmed. Overhead a religious service was in progress and, because James' crypt is directly under the cathedral's high altar, the priest's sonorous incantations were muffled and uncannily suggestive of something supernatural and vaguely threatening.

I was one of hundreds who, over the past weeks, had walked across the north of Spain and then waited in the searing sun outside the Cathedral of Santiago de Compostela in order to view the remains of Saint James, a Jewish fisherman from Galilee, son of Zebedee and in time, favoured disciple of Christ. I felt jaded and uncertain why I was enduring this blazing heat. There was little chance that the bones contained in the cathedral crypt could possibly be genuine. I was therefore unprepared for the rush of emotion I had felt when I eventually looked into that narrow passage. Once more in the open I quickly recovered, recalling the well-known fact that medieval builders deliberately designed and constructed cathedrals to rouse not only admiration, but also to provoke veneration. Was all my astonishment simply the consequence of a clever trick?

The installation of a well-promoted saint was an added bonus for both the medieval laity and the church. Travellers visiting a sanctuary in medieval times believed that reverencing a saint's exhumed bones would improve their chances of salvation, while the church authorities became wealthy on the dues and generosity of patrons and pilgrims. Shrines had therefore to be impressive, providing a sense of wonderment as well as convincing the beholder of the saint's holy presence. In an atmosphere calculated to provoke veneration, miracles could also happen. In great gratitude there would be big-hearted giving. The authorities in Santiago had done well in deluding not only the medievals, but also myself. This was my thinking as I stood in the cathedral square after my visit to the tomb. At that point I did not understand about the cult of the saints and the significance of old musty bones.

As I walked the Camino I had paid little attention to James and his rise to fame, finding it incredible that a Palestinian Jew could make his way to Spain at the start of the first millennium and there generously leave behind bones that were apparently capable of wonder-works. My early Anglo-Catholic religious education had claimed the saints as 'real', but the Anglican Church has long since sanitized these beings, securely locating them in heaven. Without earthly relic evidence, saints cannot disconcert Anglicans. In Santiago, however, I found the focus on the on-going corporeality of James fascinating but also somewhat unnerving. Doubting the authenticity of the bones, I was prepared to distance myself from the phenomenon. However, if you wish to travel in Spain as a pilgrim this is hardly possible. The saints and their bones are too important, but it was only when I returned to Spain and was travelling with Terence that I found out just how significant they really were.

Our first real encounter with holy bones came soon. We had landed in Madrid. Before journeying northwards we spent a few days in this city sight-seeing and recovering from jet-lag. Having visited the Royal Palace, we called in to the Royal Monastery of the Incarnation. This monastic house had been established for the internment of noble women: unmarriageable daughters, widows and poorer royal relations. King Philip III's wealthy Austrian wife had founded the monastery, donating money for the building as well as purchasing a vast number of relics which she believed would safeguard the inmates and ease their eventual journey into the afterlife. Displayed in a room adjacent to the chapel, the reliquaries are now available for public viewing, the royal women no longer in residence. As a twenty-first century observer I was astonished at how much value had been placed upon these bones and marvelled that such bizarre objects could not only be expected to shield, comfort and empower, but that they were also revered. At this point I was somewhat cynical.

Many of the reliquaries were sealed, the contents remaining a mystery. In others, the grisly bone was plain to see, though not always easy to identify. Arm bones were an exception. Inserted into a specially constructed replica arm hollowed out of wood and richly decorated, the radius or ulna was uncannily displayed through a cut-out lattice. The prize relic in this collection was a phial of the solidified blood of Saint Pantaleone, a fourth century martyr whose eventual rise to sainthood occasioned many miraculous healings. It is difficult to fathom how, at the time of his death in the fourth century, the authorities of that time knew his blood would be needed in the sixteenth. I also wondered how it had been preserved. We were told, too, that even in the twenty-first century the phial could still manifest its miraculous properties, the blood reputedly liquefying for twenty-four hours each year on the saint's feast day in July!

The abundance of bones made me feel queasy. Terence was surprised by my dis-ease. As a small child he had been raised by his Roman Catholic grandmother. Frightened of the dark, he had kindly been supplied with a night-light in the form of a foot-high plaster Christ. The chest region had been hollowed out and the cavity fitted with a red electric bulb. Whenever Terence woke he could see this light pulsating in the dark. He said enduring this for several years had been sufficient to inure him to a few non-illumined and innocuous medieval bones. I could not agree. For me they were not only grisly but also somehow uncannily animated. Even though they were now little more than museum pieces, it seemed as though they may still have been secretly worshipped.

I was not troubled by all the relics we viewed on the Camino, finding at least one bone particularly poignant. Terence and I had arrived in Estella and had walked to Irache, a very old Benedictine monastery on the outskirts of the town. New postulants not forthcoming, this house has now ceased to operate as a religious order, but its winery still flourishes. We intended to visit the famous wine fountain established almost a thousand years ago to raise the flagging spirits of passing pilgrims and still flowing today. Having procured a small sample we shared a picnic lunch in the monastery grounds before entering the church. The Benedictines have always been renowned for their great wealth, rich ecclesiastical treasure and the power it wielded, but in the Irache basilica all this had been removed. Remaining, however, was one small relic demurely hanging on the wall of the chancel and not easily noticed. The bone was tied to a sparsely decorated and rather dingy cushion. What were the affluent Benedictines doing with this modest relic? I wondered, too, what devout monk had been inspired by this one small, dried-out bone. Had it performed any miracles and why was it now abandoned, its story lost in time? It seems royalty and the rich are recorded in the annals, but the humble monks' tales too often remain untold.

Towards the end of our journey we viewed another splendid relic collection, this time in the cathedral museum in Santiago. Where I found the haphazard display in the Royal Monastery in Madrid somewhat off-putting, possibly because of the vast number of bones, those in Santiago are tastefully organized in a very lavish Baroque chapel, each one carefully placed in a very tall, commodious retablo erected above a golden altar.[1] A stout ironwork grille separates the public from the display, impeding close inspection, but it was obvious the reliquaries shown in the altar backdrop were deeply encrusted with ornate jewels. Undoubtedly they were valuable, but I found these bones bereft of mystery and no more than obsolete museum exhibits remote from the saints of whom they had once possibly been a part.

Of all the Spanish saintly relics, the ones that really concern the Camino are those supposedly belonging to Saint James the Greater, one of the three apostles most loved by Christ, and also martyr, powerful wonder-worker and patron saint of Spain. Initially I found his story perplexing. In the Bible James is described as a fisherman born in Judea. In the 'Acts of the Apostles' it is recorded that after the death of Christ, King Herod had James beheaded by a sword-wielding executioner. Tradition has claimed him as the first of the apostles to have been martyred for his faith. So how was it that this

---

* In Spain a retablo is a large, very ornate backdrop erected behind and above the high altar.

23

Aramaic-speaking Jew from the Holy Land came to be in Spain?

The answer may be found in a directive issued by Christ a short time after his resurrection in which he bade his disciples, 'Go ye therefore and teach all nations, baptizing them in the name of the Father, and of the Son, and of the Holy Ghost' (Matt. 28: 19). As a missionary, James is said to have chosen Spain. How he got there was something of a mystery. However, having arrived he was apparently unsuccessful in his proselytizing and, again obeying Christ who told his disciples not only to walk away from those who would not listen but also to shake the dust off their feet (Matt. 10: 14), he returned to Palestine where the beheading took place. Then, so the legend goes, a few of his loyal disciples laid his body and decapitated head in a stone boat and all were borne away over the ocean. Without rudder or sail, the martyr's corpse eventually returned to Galicia, a small kingdom in the far northwest of what is now Spain, seemingly helped there by angels. After a 'few difficulties', he was buried.

With the passage of time, the exact location of his grave was erased from the memory of the locals. Then, one night eight hundred years later, a simple shepherd called Pelayo was watching over his flocks at night and saw the falling of a particularly bright star. His curiosity aroused, he investigated and found the apostle's forgotten grave. James' bones were exposed and declared genuine and a church built in the place where his body had been found. I read this version of the story in Cordula Rabe's walking guide to the Camino before I left home to undertake the pilgrim walk. Clichéd and fantastical, it is hard to take this tale seriously.

Further reading upon my return from Spain did not alleviate my scepticism. I discovered Rabe's 'few difficulties' related to Lupa, a formidable ninth century Galician Queen. She was outraged by the disciples' story and not only refused their request for burial ground, but also imprisoned the whole mob. Another helpful angel organized their release, but James' escaping followers were pursued by prison guards. Again the angel assisted, this time by collapsing a bridge. The guards, who were crossing at that point, were all drowned. Naturally the disciples made it safely to the other side. Thinking the queen would heed these miraculous happenings, they returned to the palace and once more asked for a burial plot. This time the queen seemed friendlier. She bade them go into the mountains and there harness a number of bulls. Knowing the animals to be wild and uncontrollable, she had anticipated the bloody removal of this tiresome band. However, her plan was foiled. The bulls, beholding the wonder of James' holy casket, became as meek as lambs and allowed themselves to be yoked and the whole party returned intact. This time the queen was impressed. Not only did she now believe the disciples had been divinely brought to Galicia, she also converted to Christianity, had her palace consecrated as a church and then became a 'good woman'. Of course James was allocated burial space.

There are numerous renditions of this story and they differ only in minor details. Where the popular version claims Pelayo as a shepherd, more academic texts assert he was either a monk or a hermit. These works also dismiss the 'shepherd watching his flocks by night' cameo. Some include heavenly music and the one bright star is sometimes augmented by many smaller flickering ones. Galician tradition also claims that James had initially arrived in Spain at Iria Flavia, a small Celtic port on the west coast twenty-three kilometres from where Santiago stands today. Upon arrival his boat had been moored to a large rock and the disembarking James set forth from this point to spread the Good News. It seems the angels responsible for returning James' body again chose this same spot.[2] When the location of the grave was revealed, possibly in the year 830, the bishop of Iria Flavia had been Theodomir. Suspecting a miracle had occurred, he recommended fasting and three days of prayer before further investigations were carried out.

In due course a shrine was found in the underbrush, as well as a sarcophagus placed beside a small altar. A parchment, unspoiled by eight hundred years of weather, identified the coffin and bones within as those belonging to James. When the casket was opened, the remarkable Theodomir could recognize the bones! Of course they became holy relics and in a short time were able to perform miracles. This provided further proof of the bones' authenticity, as well as legitimizing the claim made in the ancient document. Almost instantaneously James' fame as a miracle-maker spread. From all over Europe pilgrims flocked and, for more than a millennium, made Santiago a major pilgrim destination rivalled only by Jerusalem and Rome.

The twelfth century text, the *Liber Sancti Jacobi* (the Book of Saint James), extends James' story. This is a five-volume Iberian anthology written to provide pilgrims of the time with background detail and advice. Book Two contains the miracles wrought by James after his long internment and elevation to sainthood. The stories are supposedly accounts of people who had witnessed, or been the recipients, of his wonders. The tales make entertaining reading. The unknown author claims that while James accomplished many more such marvels, only

---

[2] Somewhere round the tenth century the name of this small settlement was changed to Padrón, Galician for 'big stone'. A church was built at this precise point, the mooring stone located beneath the high altar. It can still be seen today.

twenty-two of the best were recorded. On the surface it would seem the purpose behind the stories was to advance James' reputation. Already, from all over Europe, pilgrims, in the hope of receiving succour or relief, were enduring the arduous journey to reach his tomb.

The twentieth century medieval scholar, Klaus Herbers, has a particular interest in these tales and reads them against a much broader historical backdrop, believing the real drive behind the idea of James as a miracle-maker had much weightier political and military significance. It was always advantageous to have a lucrative cult-following, but at that point in Spain it was essential for James to be established as a powerful warrior-saint capable of protecting the people of Galicia in time of war. The adversary was already on the door-step. Having invaded Spain in 711 AD, the Muslims had been contained in the south. Now they were slowly infiltrating and threatening the previously independent north.

In ninth century Galicia the turmoil occasioned by the Moors' intrusion was also exacerbated by territorial quarrels between the various northern kingdoms. As well there was interference from beyond the Pyrenees. As a consequence northern Spain was a moil of unrest. In order to hold the north together it was necessary to fabricate and launch a strong focal idea round which an army could rally, remain resolute and march forth. Such a story was easy to formulate, James having had a saintly precursor who had already established the pattern. This was Martin of Tours, another soldier-saint who had been protector and patron of Galicia two centuries before.

In life Martin had been a steadfast man whose greatest desire was to follow Christ and help the downtrodden. However, as the son of an officer in the Austrian Imperial

Army, he was made to follow in his father's footsteps, serving as an elite cavalry soldier. But Martin had no taste for military life. The incident for which he is most famous is probably no more than a legend used to illustrate Martin's generosity towards the poor. The story tells how Martin, riding by on his magnificent military mount, caught the pleading eye of a beggarman cringing in the snow. His heart was smitten. Dismounting, the saint removed his white lambskin cloak, a garment of the household guard, and, using his sword to hack it into two, he shared the garment with the beggar.

After serving his time in the army Martin fled to France and took up holy orders. Before he died he fulfilled his desire to serve the poor and submitted the remainder of his life to the will of God.

In the sixth century, two hundred years after the death of Martin of Tours, another Martin, Martin of Braga (a town in northern Portugal), arrived in Galicia with a relic belonging to Martin of Tours. Martin of Braga's missionary zeal won over the Suevic people, a Gothic tribe who inhabited Galicia at this time. A threatened race, the Suevics were eager to accept the protection they imagined Martin of Tours could provide and embraced this saint. For a while all went well. Then, because of political and religious re-shuffling between Galicia and Gaul, and the devastating destruction of the fragile Suevic kingdom, Martin was deemed lacking. As a passive elitist with no taste for battle, it seems Martin may have been too gentlemanly for medieval Spain's more aggressive needs and so he and his relic were deported. The position of patron saint fell vacant. Clearly the new saint had to be mightier. Not only was an apostle chosen but one of the three most favoured by Christ. Herbers points out how the Compostela's resourceful ninth century clerics and supporters exaggerated and remodelled the miracle tales in their endeavour to establish James' power and promote his reputation. In a short time the stories were circulating and James became eminently eligible for the role.

The Battle of Clavijo was James' inauguration as Spain's warrior saint. As the tale goes, Christians had long been obliged to pay the Muslim invaders an annual tribute of one hundred maidens, but in the year 844 Ramiro I, King of Asturias in North West Spain, suddenly dug in his heels and refused to pay. At this point James supposedly stirred from his long confinement and appeared in a dream to Ramiro who, like other leaders of the time, was also having difficulty in generally fending off these very demanding Moors. In the dead of the night James explained to the fraught monarch that Jesus Christ had entrusted Spain, and its virgins, to him to watch over and protect from the enemies of the true faith. Accordingly on the following day James promised to ride into battle with the king mounted on a powerful white charger, flying a white standard and brandishing a great shining sword. This he did. Though ethereal, James was stunningly successful, helping Ramiro to the first decisive counter-Islamic victory. As a peaceful preacher in earlier centuries James was quite ineffective, but now as a militant Moor-Slayer he was a triumph.

On my second visit to Spain I took Terence to visit Clavijo, sixteen kilometres south of Logroño. It is also the site of an ancient castle constructed on a spectacularly sheer rocky outcrop in the Laturce Mountains. John Brierly's guide book warned that this edifice is now no more than a 'sombre ruin', but I found it superb. Only the central tower and a sizable stretch of buttressed wall remain. The entrance is small and has the Islamic horseshoe arch. In all probability a heavy wooden door would have backed this opening. There is no evidence of the original path leading to the castle and our scramble up was strenuous. The stronghold overlooks a spectacular plain now cultivated to look like a vast agricultural patchwork, certainly large enough to accommodate two huge armies with their horses and the mighty James mounted on his splendid charger. Distant blue mountains circle the plain and would have contained the fighting. In the blast of a bracing wind and through the wafting early morning mist it was easy for me to hear battle cries, the clang of mighty swords and roars of triumph.

What a pity contemporary scholars claim this particular campaign never took place. To me it seemed so real. However, sitting on a triple frontier between the once confrontational kingdoms of Aragón, Navarra and Castilla/León, these plains would certainly have been witness to other less exultant military clashes.

The inauguration of James as patron saint is remarkable, given that there is practically no evidence that he had ever visited or preached in Spain. One or two early church documents exist which suggest an apostle had been to the peninsula, but these documents name no specific person. Clement of Alexandria, a Christian theologian writing towards the end of the first century, and Eusebius, a Roman historian who became bishop of Caesarea in 314, both discuss James' work in the years between the death of Christ and his own martyrdom, but in both cases the saint's jurisdiction is limited to Judea and Jerusalem. An early literary work also records James as a preacher but spreading his message only in Judea and Samaria. The first hint that James might have gone to Spain is recorded in a late sixth century collection of stories about the lives of various saints, but scholars today doubt the authenticity of this reference, believing certain critical words had been corrupted in order to make this claim. However, because of this unreliable document, the idea that James had travelled to Spain took hold. As a would-be patron he was mentioned in some commentaries and in a few literary works. In the eighth century the monk, Beatus of Liéban, wrote a famous hymn to James addressing him as,

'Oh most worthy and most holy apostle,
Shining golden chieftain of Spain,
Be our protector and patron on earth,
Warding off ill,
Be our celestial health...'.

Today, every time the huge thurible is swung in the Santiago cathedral, these ancient words are still recited.[3]

In Spain the political expediency of having a patron saint was not restricted to James and his ability to protect the north. Domingo de la Calzada is another saint who was sufficiently powerful to assist. On the Camino Saint Domingo is well known because of the delightful story in which he miraculously resurrects a rooster and hen. It was a miracle apparently performed to bring justice to a young man who had been wrongly put to death for a crime he did not commit. The story is not particular to Domingo, but is a retelling of a miracle originally attributed to James. According to the *Liber Sancti Jacobi* some rich pilgrims on their way to Santiago arrive at an inn in Toulouse in France. The innkeeper, a greedy and unscrupulous man, wanting the pilgrims' riches for himself, inebriates them and then hides a valuable goblet in the bag of one of the young men. The following day he has the party followed and detained. A search exposes the goblet and the young man is tried and committed to the gallows. As he hangs James holds him aloft, so preserving his life. On the return

---

[3] A thurible is a metal censor suspended on chains in which incense is burned during religious services.

trip the boy's father, also on the pilgrimage, decides to visit the gallows. There he finds his son alive, still supported in the arms of the saint. The innocent victim is freed and the innkeeper is hanged in the boy's place. Saint Domingo's biographer appropriated this story but made opportune changes.

In the second telling Saint Domingo replaces James as the wonder-worker, both saints seemingly capable of sustaining life. The site of the miracle changes from France to Spain, specifically to the town of Calzada in the district of la Rioja. The piety of the young man is emphasised. A promiscuous female servant, trying to creep into his bed at night, is spurned. Indignant, she is the one who hides the goblet in his bag. The author then extends the story with the rooster and hen add-on. The judge who had tried and committed the young man is patiently waiting for his evening meal, inspecting the two birds as they roast in the flames. As he watches he is approached by the young man's parents and informed that the boy is miraculously still alive. The disbelieving judge ridicules the parents saying he would sooner believe the poultry roasting on the spit could live. At that moment the two birds instantly grow feathers, fly from the fire and the cock starts to crow.

Circulation of this amended story first began in the late eleventh century during the reign of King Alfonso VI. This was the time of the Gregorian reforms, a mandate from the papacy demanding that all Europe be liturgically unified.[4] Alfonso used this ultimatum to benefit his own project—the uniting of the kingdoms of León, Castile and Galicia. By bringing these monarchies under the crown of Castile, Alfonso wished to counter the rivalry instigated by his father, Ferdinand I, when he split Castile, granting

---

[4] I expand upon the Gregorian reforms in Chapter 5.

to each of his three sons a portion of Spain. No matter the era, change is always difficult, and in the north of Spain both the Pope's decree and Alfonso's enterprise were resisted, the people wanting to retain the Mozarabic liturgy inaugurated by the Christian Visigoths, as well as maintaining political autonomy. While dealing with these problems Alfonso was also being pressured by the Cluny Benedictines from France who wanted the way to Santiago opened and made secure.[5] Domingo played a vital role in this political moil, not only by opening the Pilgrim Way, but also co-ordinating and promoting the necessary infrastructure to unite Northern Spain.

Javier Pérez Escohotado has meticulously researched this saint, consulting official civil documents, the many confusing histories and other popular literature of the time and has established that Domingo's dates did in fact coincide with Alfonso's reign. Many of the biographical details in the various official records are contradictory except for Domingo's application to become a monk which was refused on the grounds that he was not intelligent enough, possibly because of a reluctance to deal with Latin. Some records claim he had no education at all but, when it was demanded of him, Domingo proved a talented engineer, designing and building roads, bridges, churches and a pilgrim hospital.

In the end, Escohotado decided Domingo was a man ahead of his time and thus viewed with suspicion and malice both by the monasteries where he requested entry and by the local population. At every turn he met with difficulties. His efforts to clear forests were opposed. He was denied trees, labour and land for his building projects. Because of political and ecclesiastical tensions, funds

---

[5] In medieval Europe Cluny was an important monastery and is mentioned several times in this book. I expand upon Cluny's significance in Chapters 4 and 6.

were difficult to raise. As James before him had had to be promoted by the telling of tales, tantalizing stories were now told of Domingo in order to neutralize the people's hostility. He, too, was said to have tamed bulls, the sickle he used for clearing the forests was proclaimed magical and it was alleged he kept locusts at bay. His greatest miracle, however, was his supra-natural rescue of life and the resurrection of a partly cooked rooster and hen.

Escohotado concludes his analysis by claiming the rivalry generated between the two saints had been deliberate. Where James as Moor-Slayer had been successful in consolidating the Christian armies in the north, the lesser saint, Saint Domingo de la Calzada, managed the much smaller task of providing la Rioja with a sense of ongoing autonomy. Even though Alfonso brought this district under the umbrella of Castile, Domingo's miracle story had singled out the region because the tales told about this saint more readily caught the imagination of the populace. James' miracle now seemed staid and conservative.

To this day la Rioja cultivates and promotes itself through its saint, keeping live chickens in the cathedral to commemorate Domingo's success. The birds are even claimed to be descendants of the original strain. Pilgrims visiting the small town of Santa Domingo de la Calzada in la Rioja are either intrigued by the caged birds or else, like Terence and me, appalled at this cruelty. Domingo's very elaborate tomb can also be seen in the cathedral crypt where it is protected by a very stout and overly ornate grill.

Most people as they walk the Camino are oblivious of the early political significance of James and Domingo. In days of old pilgrims journeyed to the Santiago shrine in the hopes of healing a malady or gaining a boon. Today many people are still hopeful they may gain from visiting the shrine. Terence and I were no different. When we got lost on a mountain-side, Terence thought it a good idea to appeal to James for help. At this point we were centred in Puerte la Reine and had walked to the strange octagonal church at Eunate associated with the Knights Templar, dedicated to Mary and believed to have once served as a funeral chapel. On this particular day, standing alone in a sun-drenched green field, the little basilica seemed magical. While we were there a bus-load of middle-age German women arrived, pilgrims of another kind. They assembled in the church and sang a hymn to the Virgin. It was hauntingly beautiful. Then, as we were about to walk away, we noticed a signpost directing us to a chapel, apparently at the top of a fairly steep hill. We decided to visit.

The day was mild and we enjoyed the climb, but, when it seemed to go on for too long, it occurred to me that the motley collection of stones we had seen along the way may have been the chapel now in ruins. I advised returning. Terence, however, can be stubborn and does not like retreating. When I insisted he decided, rather than turn back, we would take a short cut by simply leaving the path, climbing down the hill and so arriving at the main road below. The route would be direct—from the top straight to the bottom. All went well until the scrub through which we were beating a path gave way to growth so thick we could hardly move. Eventually we were wedged, unable to go either up or down. Terence decided it would be best to tunnel through and, dropping to his stomach, inched forward only to become firmly caught in bramble thorns. At this point I was not far from panic, but Terence, still prostrate, decided to address the saint. Exasperated and furious, I stepped over him only to discover within inches of where I stood a narrow, ill-defined track leading to the foot of the hill. Terence laughed, claiming he always knew the saints were alive and still functional, but I was disconcerted. After the names and dire threats my husband had used against him, how could James possibly have helped us?

In Europe the saints made an early appearance, inadvertently inaugurated by the Romans as they tortured Christians, making them martyrs by way of torture: stoning, crucifixion, burning at the stake or feeding them to wild animals. Though some twentieth century scholars reject these historical allegations, the stories told of this cruelty, and the pleasure it afforded the Romans, was at that time not only accepted, but also understood as the work of the Devil, a mighty being wielding malevolent powers. Supposedly taken straight to the bosom of God, the martyrs were seen as having conquered this evil and so were now able to share a profound intimacy with their Maker.

Martyrdom was thus acknowledged as a triumph and associated with baptism. As a person could be cleansed of sin by way of water, the martyrs were totally purified by the supposed spilling of their blood. As a consequence, the early Christians venerated saints, believing them capable of powerful intercession. Welcomed in heaven by God and his saints they would there plead for the living on earth. It was as though a two-way communication system had been established linking the two realms. In late antiquity and in the early medieval era this understanding resulted in a profound shift in the general Western understanding of how the world worked, and how humanity stood in relation to its gods. Peter Brown explains this by resorting to an old, overarching understanding belonging to Western classicism.

Brown tells how the classical world believed that there had always been an important, inviolable division in the universe: an invisible barrier which completely separated heaven from earth. The divine quality of the universe could be observed in the skies above in the unsullied splendour of the unreachable stars. Below there was no more than a swamp of dregs. For the early medieval Christians death was the only way this divide could be breached, the point at which the soul was finally able to vacate its dank, bodily prison. If worthy, its place in the heavens was established in an instant. It was a one-way upward movement. Until this moment, heaven and the divine were out of bounds, forbidden alike to Christians, Jews and the ancients. While the classical gods did sometimes dally with humans, once the human was tarnished by death, the boundary between the god and the human was almost always firmly reasserted.

In the first centuries of the first millennium the Roman persecution of the infant Christian church and the inauguration of martyrs as saints sundered this once securely fixed boundary. This rupture now allowed the faithful on earth access to a measure of God's power and mercy. Miraculously, humanity no longer felt exiled from God's goodness. The saints who had precipitated this benevolent paradigm shift were therefore honoured and revered.

When reading of the cult I found it eminently reasonable that non-Christian people of late antiquity and early medieval times, still trying to maintain a classical lifestyle, should be appalled by the Christian preoccupation with the digging up, dismembering and moving about of bones. Not only did the practice violate human sensibilities, but it also upset one of the dicta upon which Roman cities had been founded. This was the insistence that the living be kept separate from the contaminating dead. Like the pagan gods, Roman citizens regarded death as taboo and shunned this reality. The Christians' reverent touching and kissing of long buried but now unearthed bones generated repulsion as well as religious anger. Capable of imagining the smell of musty earth and rotting flesh, and able to envisage possible fungus and worms, I find this attitude understandable and am amazed that the cult persisted, followed as it eventually was by peasants and those high-born, males and females, laymen and clerics. This was possibly because at the end of antiquity the West had been destabilized by changing power structures and floundering ideologies. Existential insecurity usually drives people to search for alternative ways, and in its questing medieval Europe found the saints. Understood as the main channel through which God's supposed benevolence could be reached and pain alleviated, people accepted the saints and the abhorrence of old bones eventually subsided. Relics became the most important phenomenon in both secular and religious life.

By the turn of the first millennium every church and monastery had at least one relic, sometimes a great number. As early as 787 it had been decreed that a relic be secreted into every altar in every European church. By lifting as many altar cloths as he could, Terence attempted to prove that in Spain this was indeed so. Because he always found evidence of a relic, or a relic niche sunk into the wood or marble surface, he was not disappointed.

Kings also relied on saints' bones, concealing them in their crowns, sinking them into the hilts of their swords or wearing them openly round their necks. The historian, Sir Richard Southern, has suggested that in the early medieval era (700 – 1050), the safety of some European kingdoms was entirely dependent upon the apparent potency of the King's relic collection. Relics were given as royal gifts and paraded through the land on lucrative fund-raising tours. They were carried into battle and brought out to authenticate the work of justice, validating vows and promises. Legal documents were signed in the presence of a bone. As well as instruments of state, bones were also used for personal well-being. At this time many people, recognising their powerlessness, felt they could only survive through a dependence on the supernatural which they believed they accessed through the saints.

As I read this I was both envious and sceptical, envious because it seemed such a simple way to become empowered, and sceptical because I doubted that a mere bone could actually alter a person's political or social standing. My response, however, was shallow, the phenomenon of the saints at this time being much more profound than mere wishful thinking.

Ernest Brehaut, fascinated by the astonishing energy generated by the saints in the ninth century, attempted to understand the practice. He realized the bones were usually experienced as uncanny phenomena; a mystery emanating from another realm. For medievals, caught up in what was for them, a destabilizing clash of two separate realities, that of earth and that of heaven, it was as though the relics had been possessed by the mysterious power of the spirits but, unable to access that spiritual reality, or hold on to the supernatural moment, they projected the power, transmitting it to the saint, his or her burial place or the material bones. Though the uncanny could not be sustained, the one who had experienced the uncanny moment was not totally bereft of the seeming holiness, contained as it now was in the relic. Thus saints were regarded as sacred and their bones accepted as animated and potent. When I stood in the royal monastery in Madrid I was without this knowledge, but even so, I am certain that I could feel the animation still clinging to that bizarre collection. To me they seemed more than mere bones.

Peter Brown also addresses the meeting of the human and that which is seemingly 'other', articulating the moment as a 'strange flash that occurs when the contrasted poles of heaven and earth meet'. He claims medieval Christians concentrated obsessively on this flash that occurred when the once distinct categories were suddenly made to collide in the minds of men. Though disconcerting, it was a moment of profound importance. In a world deemed fallen and ravaged by sin, God's benevolence had at last arrived by means of a bone. Seemingly delivered to the people by Heaven, relics were indicative of divine mercy and spoke of amnesty. At last God had made manifest his approval. At this point what was really significant was God's invisible gesture of forgiveness and not the actual bone. It must have been a wonderful moment, but to experience it one has to have a firm belief in the Christian God, his benevolence and his Heaven up on high.

Patrick Geary has another insight. He understands the saints' bones as symbols, but unusual ones. Where normally a symbol has an established, easily recognized meaning, bones in themselves denote nothing special. As relics, however, they have meaning imposed upon them. It is as though they become repositories for a particular narrative. It was how this story served the community that really mattered. Should the story and its purpose be lost because the relic was stolen, relocated or forgotten, the bones became meaningless. Without their stories and the purpose for their acquisition they are either strange anatomical curiosities, or else they fill the beholder with sadness or disgust. Remembering that one solitary bone on the chancel wall in the Irache Monastery now bereft of its meaning, I agree with Geary.

Because of their perceived profundity, medieval ceremonies that incorporated relics were afforded the highest importance, the most significant being the removal, or translation, of a relic from one locality to another. This was usually to a place of higher status or to a church or cathedral where the relic would be installed in a shrine where, it was hoped, it would act as a guardian and benefactor, or perform healing miracles for visiting pilgrims. Of course they would also boost the cathedral coffers. The selection of the bone or bones was often a hit and miss affair, the saint to be moved often having been dead for centuries and the gravestone either unmarked or lost. In such cases the saint's whereabouts could be revealed by way of a sign or by the consensual agreement of the clergy who seemingly had an inexplicable but unchallenged knowing.

Again I felt qualms. Was the simple appropriation of someone else's bones morally apposite? What if the newly moved skeleton had belonged to a criminal or, even worse for a medieval, a heretic? This did not concern Geary. He accepts that the supposed saint, and his or her capacity to generate miracles, may well be the result of devout supposition and wishful thinking, but he also claims that the sceptics who dismiss these miracle stories as flamboyant nonsense, or who insist the bones must be inauthentic, miss the point. Rather than simply provide facts, the tales are recognized by both historians and theologians as reflecting the human needs of the time. If we wish to understand the significance the bones once held, it is a mistake to read the stories literally or insist on the bones' authenticity.

The removal of saintly bones was a formal occasion, accompanied by fasting, vigils and festive processions. The day on which the relic was moved became the saint's feast day, a day that had to be remembered and commemorated if the community wished to stay on-side with its saint. (In Spain Saint Zoilus, martyred by the invading Romans in 304, is reputed to have been particularly vengeful if he noticed harvesters and blacksmiths working on his particular day.) The whole community was involved in the translation, resulting in a temporary breakdown of class barriers and the spreading of general concord. This in itself can now be viewed as a sort of miracle. Because of the tensions generated by the crumbling Roman Empire, the heightened occasion reminded the community of God's capacity to include, forgive and restore. If the relic failed to provide relief, the community usually blamed itself and humanity's enduring sinfulness. However, when circumstances were really dire, a failing saint could be humiliated, thrown out and totally abandoned.

In León, and visiting the Basilica of Saint Isidore, Terence and I read of a splendid saintly translation. The story tells how, in the eleventh century, Princess Sancha, later Queen of León, requested of her husband, Ferdinand, later King Ferdinand I, that the poorly built Léonese monastery be completely renovated and the portico of the new church prepared as a royal burial vault. She then asked her husband to arrange that both their bodies in due time be interred there. Ferdinand was agreeable and to honour and support them in death, he organized the translation of a saint. In this endeavour a bargain had to be made with the Moorish king of Seville and Ferdinand was granted the bones of the little known Santa Justa.

In December 1063 the bishops of León and Astorga were sent to fetch the prize, but when they arrived in Seville, the relic was nowhere to be found. However, Saint Isidore obligingly appeared to the Leonese bishop in a vision and offered himself as an alternative. He even revealed his hiding place in death, but warned that once his bones were unearthed, the bishop would die. The good ecclesiastic, wishing to honour his king, went ahead with the translation and, as prophesied, was dead seven days later. Because she felt the prophecy and the death of the bishop authenticated the bones, Queen Sancha was unperturbed by both the unfortunate demise and the change of saint and celebrated the occasion by donating to the church exquisite jewels and beautiful liturgical ornaments. Many of these are now displayed in the church museum, wonderfully off-set by the splendidly preserved medieval rooms in which they are housed. Terence and I gazed upon the magnificence of both architecture and treasure with a profound sense of awe.

Isidore of Seville (560-636) was considered one of the great Latin Church Fathers and the most learned man of his age. His writing included theological and mystical treatises, histories and an ambitious work in which he attempted to record all universal knowledge. This work became the favourite encyclopaedia of the Middle Ages, was published many times and endlessly perused for information on history, medicine, mathematics and grammar.

As archbishop Isidore attempted to eliminate heresies by the strengthening of religious discipline. Conservative and highly orthodox, he is looked upon as Spain's one great ecclesiastical Father. It was therefore apposite for Ferdinand and his lady to lie near Isidore in death. Extolled as an 'exceedingly strong emperor', Ferdinand, too, was called 'The Great' because he was the first to have himself crowned Emperor of All Spain. Strolling through the peaceful streets of León in springtime, admiring the cathedral, the old Roman wall and the quaint medieval streets and imbibing the wonderful Spanish wine, it was difficult for Terence and me to fully appreciate the totality of the political power and spiritual commitment that fuelled these devout medieval endeavours.

Medieval sources used to glean information on saints such as James, Isidore and Domingo refer mostly to the elite classes, all the primary documents written in Latin by clerics or members of the aristocracy. In Europe generally knowledge of how the masses responded to the saints is almost entirely lacking or, as Patrick Geary suggests, contemporary authors simply present what they wish to find. This was not entirely the case in Spain. Between the years 1575 and 1580 King Philip II sent a printed questionnaire to all towns and villages in New Castile to find out the religious beliefs and practices of the ordinary people. The royal chroniclers drew up fifty-seven questions which they claimed would provide them with a history of each town. The information was duly collected, though it is not known what use Philip made of it.

William A. Christian has perused the king's questionnaire and the village responses and has recorded his findings. He claims that in the country supplications to the saints were rarely orthodox. When disaster struck and the local cleric was unable to ward off the danger, the villagers would often call in one of the many unscrupulous lay professionals circulating through the Castilian countryside at that time selling dubious magical methods to supposedly protect the people. Or else the people would take matters into their own hands. One common tactic was to avoid the clerics and to negotiate privately and directly with a saint by way of a solemn vow. If the need was great the whole village might promise to build and maintain a shrine, or more diligently venerate that particular saint. Private vows for individual help might offer chastity, the taking up of holy orders, fasting or the making of a pilgrimage. Once made, the vow was binding and had to be fulfilled under penalty of falling into mortal sin, a potentially disastrous calamity as unconfessed mortal sins disallowed the sinner entry into heaven. When a vow could not be accomplished a priest was called in, either to absolve the one who had undertaken the vow or to pardon the penitent.

Devastating hail storms, plague, drought or locust infestations were all seen as necessitating saintly intervention. There were several methods for choosing this holy personage. The saint on whose feast day the disaster had struck might be called upon, the villagers believing they had in some way offended him or her. Alternatively a specialist saint could be used. Saint Sebastian was reputed to be efficacious in countering epidemics, probably because in life he had been considered a hardy being. Condemned to death by the Roman authorities, he was tied to a stake and shot with arrows until he was believed dead. When his body was retrieved for burial it was found that he had miraculously survived the attack and was once more restored to health, only to be slain again. Thus in times of sickness Sebastian's touch could be advantageous. When insects attacked the grape vines, villagers preferred Saint Pantaleon, possibly because of his generosity and great heart. Another robust saint almost impossible to kill, Pantaleon prayed that all his Roman murderers be forgiven of their sins.

When the choice of a saint was not obvious because the needed attributes were lacking or there had been no illuminating natural sign, villages organized a lottery, the name of the saint being drawn from many and the holy intermediary thus chosen by chance. In medieval times, so William Christian reports, this was quite orthodox and, if done reverently, considered a legitimate way to know the will of God. If only things could be so easily decided now!

It was interesting that in Christian's research into local religion in medieval Spain he found no existing reports of villagers calling upon James. This might be because James, as a great warrior saint, dealt with crises of state, the survival problems of the common Spanish people more readily handled by the lesser saints. However, medieval pilgrims travelling to Santiago from foreign countries were extremely enthusiastic in their veneration of James. These travellers from times long gone stood in marked contrast to the well-behaved and conservative pilgrims I observed in the Santiago Cathedral. There might have been two reasons for this reticence. I had arrived in Santiago in a Jubilee Year together with a horde of tourists who had not undertaken a long hard walk but had arrived at a tourist destination fresh off an aeroplane and were not taking James seriously. Or else, like me, they found the Moorslayer and his mighty sword unattractive. Where once James had been a powerful and necessary force, it would appear he is now inappropriate for the troubles of the twenty-first century.

Works cited in this chapter

Attwater, Donald. *The Penguin Dictionary of the Saints*. England: Penguin Books. 1980.

Bower, Scot. *Saints*. Oxford, UK: Lion Hudson plc. 2009.

Brown, Peter. *The Cult of the Saints: Its Rise and Function in Latin Christianity*. Chicago, Ill: Chicago University Press. 1982.

Coffey, Thomas F, Linda Kay Davidson & Maryjane Dunn, trans. & eds. 'The Miracles of Saint James', *The Liber Sancti Jacobi*. New York, NY: Italica Press. 1996.

Christian, William A. *Apparitions in Late Medieval and Renaissance Spain*. Princeton, NJ: Princeton University Press. 1989.

_____ .*Local Religion in Sixteenth-Century Spain*. Princeton, NJ: Princeton University Press. 1989.

Dunn, Maryjane & Linda Kay Davidson, eds. *The Pilgrimage to Compostela in the Middle Ages*. London & New York: Routledge. 2000.

Escohotado, Javier Pérez, trans. Jennifer Brooke Hoge. *St. Domingo de la Calzada: Engineer of the Land*. Logroňo, Rioja: Ediciones. 2009.

Frey, Nancy Louise. *Pilgrim Stories on and off the Road to Santiago*. Los Angeles, Cal: University of California. 1998.

Geary, Patrrick J. *Furta Sacra: Thefts of Relics in the Middle Ages*. Princeton N.J.: Princeton University Press. 1990.

_____ . *Living with the Dead in the Middle Ages*. Ithaca, N.Y.: Cornell University Press. 1994.

Gregory, Bishop of Tours, trans. Ernest Brehaut. *History of the Franks*. New York, NY: Octagon Books. 1965.

Mullen, Robert. *Call of the Camino: Myths, Legends and Pilgrim Stories on the Way to Santiago de Compostela*. Scotland: Findhorn Press. 2010.

Rabe, Cordula. *Camino de Santiago: Way of Saint James from the Pyrenees to Santiago*. Munich: Rother. 2007.

Sumption, Jonathan. *Pilgrimage: An Image of Medieval Religion*. London: faber & faber. 2002.

Southern, Sir Richard. *Western Society and the Church in the Middle Ages*. Middlesex, Eng: Penguin Books. 1976.

Williams, John & Alison Stones, eds. *The* Codex Calixtinus *and the Shrine of St. James*. Tübingen, Germany: Gunter Narr Verlag. 1992.

Whitehill, Walter Muir. *Spanish Romanesque Architecture of the Eleventh Century*. London: Oxford University Press. 1968.

2

To be a Pilgrim

And the pilgrims who make the journey to visit James and his holy bones: what manner of people embark upon such an endeavour?

In medieval times pilgrimage was undertaken in order that one might be absolved of sin, or receive healing or similar boons. The Western world today being mostly secular, many 'pilgrims' are unsure of why they stride forth, but nevertheless they walk out in droves. The Oxford English Dictionary seeks to sum up their status by defining a pilgrim as a wanderer going from place to place; or as a sojourner on a journey, the destination being a sacred location. The present day Camino crossing Northern Spain confirms this second dictionary definition, the walk progressing through a long series of delightful medieval villages and towns before terminating in Santiago.

The walk is long and most pilgrims avail themselves of the many refuges found along the way. For those who prefer more privacy, hostelries and inns are plentiful. Well-placed way-markers ensure the alert are never lost. Those who walk the entire eight hundred kilometres usually arrive weary and foot-sore, often suffering from blisters and other minor complaints, but on the whole little worse than that. However, when travelling to Santiago in medieval times the risks were extreme and to undertake this journey was to jeopardize life. Nevertheless, obsessed by sin and fearing damnation, the medievals took to the road.

The preoccupation with sin was exacerbated by a belief in the reality of the Devil, an absolute that was mostly encountered in the dark and during such phenomena as howling wind or thunderstorms. A lightning flash or an eclipse could create havoc. Satan was also manifest in the shape of wild animals. Peter the Venerable, a significant twelfth century abbot attached to the Cluny monastery in France, collected together a large volume of stories illustrating the various forms through which the Devil could strike: a vulture in the sky, a black bear in the woods, a black pig fossicking in the Norwich chapter-house, a spider, wild dogs and so forth.

While educated men could well have been sceptical about such tellings, many others endorsed the Devil's authenticity, notably the English Venerable Bede, Gregory the Great and Saint Isidore of Spain. This constant presence of a malignant force and the sense of imminent death because of war, disease or famine heightened the medieval sense of powerlessness. The only remedy was prayer and the performance of pious acts, of which pilgrimage was the pinnacle. Particularly from the ninth to the eleventh century royalty, aristocrats, clergy, scholars, diplomats and tax collectors, leather and cloth merchants, vintners and brewers, craftsmen and their apprentices, pedlars, tinkers and peasants would all undertake this arduous journey.

A medieval pilgrimage was costly. Boons were expected.[6] These had to be paid for by way of offerings, both at the shrine of one's destination as well as at other

---

[6] A boon is something that is helpful or beneficial, bestowed in response to a request and considered a timely blessing. In medieval times it was believed the saints could award boons to those who were worthy.

lesser tombs along the way. Monasteries, too, expected donations. Royalty and nobility, anticipating these on-going costs, travelled with such items as wax, jewellery, exotic fabric or valuable works of art to donate along with coin, though the Cathedral authorities at Santiago accepted only jewellery or coinage. For wealthier pilgrims the risk of robbery was great and meant one's entourage had to include an armed guard. For accommodation paupers could rely on ecclesiastical charity, but ordinary citizens not only had to forego profitable employment during the long absence from home, but had also to pay for their beds in inns or at monastery guest-houses. In return for the pilgrims' commitment and generosity and the risks that had to be borne, considerable benefits could be gleaned, the least being the possibility of a miraculous intervention by the saint whose shrine they had come to venerate. However, the boon of greater value was the acquisition of an indulgence.

From a secular and modern viewpoint the medieval concept of the indulgence and its association with sin and redemption is difficult to comprehend. Granted by the church, indulgences were entirely ecclesiastical and always predicated on two beliefs, the first being that humanity was sinful and had to be redeemed. The second, promulgated after the onset of the twelfth century, was that penance, confession and absolution were not sufficient for the soul to gain entry into heaven. Punishment had first to be endured, the amount depending on the seriousness of one's past sins. The penitentiary where this suffering was managed was Purgatory, a nebulous place found in the next life.[7] Here one could cancel the accumulated sinful debt. If, however, one was

---

[7] The concept of Purgatory will be expanded in Chapter 7.

granted a formal indulgence, this temporal punishment could be remitted and one's time in Purgatory reduced.

Indulgences were not therefore forgiveness of sin or release from eternal punishment, but a full or partial remission of the necessary transitory time one spent in Purgatory before the soul could experience the eternal joys of Heaven. Medieval theologians believed this subsidy was possible because Christ, by his sacrifice on the cross, had accumulated in heaven a 'treasury of superfluous merit'. The virtues and penances of the various saints also helped swell this ethereal coffer. The church was now able to dip into this 'treasure' and distribute it to eligible Christians in the form of an indulgence. Naturally there had to be an exchange of prayers, rich offerings and good works. Even those of high office, or beings who lived exemplary lives were not exempt, everyone having initially been stained by Eve's original sin! Indulgences were therefore sought after by all, no matter their station. Pilgrimage, possibly because it was lucrative to the church, was a prime way to elicit one.

The value of an indulgence procured by way of pilgrimage depended on the distance the pilgrim had to travel. For those who journeyed to Santiago from a European starting point, the standard indulgence was the remittance of one-half of all confessed sins, with an additional forty days for attendance at each celebration of the sacrament while in the holy city. On feast days this was raised to three hundred days and six hundred on James' own particular day in July. In Jubilee years, the year James' feast day fell on a Sunday, a plenary indulgence was granted and was available for the whole year. This meant that the penitent fortunate enough to be in Santiago at this time was totally absolved and so would spend no time at all in Purgatory, at least until he or she sinned again in this life. In such years the crush in the city must have been almost unendurable.

To me all this is not only incredible, but I wonder, too, how the ecclesiastical authorities of the time could have had this extensive knowledge of God's divine beneficence. The length of time many expected to suffer also suggests that God was understood as a hard and vengeful task-master. However, this was the age of belief and the reciprocal rights and obligations of medieval pilgrimage not only went unquestioned but seemed quite reasonable, and the purchasing of spiritual security was thought worth the physical and monetary sacrifice.

In this atmosphere of spiritual zeal it was advantageous for the church to show up the smallness of mere pilgrims who stood in stark contrast to the glories of God. The physical hardships the pilgrims had to endure in order to reach the shrines were, in all probability, not only regarded as essential and appropriate, but also seemed to satisfy these early travellers, opening them up to the prospect of a 'second baptism'. Because the Latin liturgy was incomprehensible and ecclesiastical doctrine obscure and beyond the reach of all but the church-educated, many found little solace in the practice of their religion. An arduous journey to a place associated with a saint who supposedly had direct access to heaven provided tangible experience of the faith deemed so necessary for the saving of their souls.

My objective in Northern Spain had not been a desire to gain Christian redemption. I also have no fear of spending time in a spiritual penitentiary since I do not believe one exists. However, I am intrigued by the thought of those who were so committed they would risk their lives in order to gain this remission of afterlife punishment.

Fascination with medieval wayfarers began on the first night of my Camino journey. I was in Roncesvalles, a remote religious community nestled into the Pyrenean foothills and still following the rule of Saint Augustine. The abbey canons had been offering refuge and hospitality to pilgrims since the tenth century. Starting at St-Jean-Pied-de-Port in France, I had just completed the first leg of my journey. The crossing had been long and arduous and I was walking in summer, one that was hotter than usual. The early dawn walk through pretty pocket-sized French farms, the air redolent with barn-yard smells, had been idyllic. Quaint bridges spanned sparkling streams and welcoming dogs rushed out to greet me, but as I climbed the charm evaporated. Farmland gave way to sweeping vistas and then thick, dark forest. I wondered how pilgrims had fared in medieval times when wolves were plentiful, brigands at large and before technology had made possible the taming of these remote mountains.

The climb had taken a long time and it was late when I arrived. Because I had expected Roncesvalles to be a village, I was surprised to find nothing more than a conglomeration of austere zinc-roofed buildings, only two of which were not in some way ecclesiastical. These were hostelries, one serving beer to a fairly rowdy throng. Pilgrims were plentiful, but I spotted no-one who looked in any way clerical. The pilgrim refuge was a huge, grey, windowless edifice patrolled by several male guardians. Inside the walls were lined with two long rows of bunks, a third row filling the space in-between. As I am a private person I was appalled by the vast number of people with whom I was obliged to share this space. I was told to find an unclaimed bunk and then obtain a shower. Dog-tired and only moderately clean—the shower water had been cold and the waiting queue still long—I made my way to dinner.

In the larger of the two hostelries pilgrims were served a communal meal. On my table no-one spoke English. I did not mind. I was in no mood for conversation. The food was simple: bland pasta, not quite *al dente*, followed by a whole trout large enough for its scaly head and tail to extend beyond the rim of the plate. There were no vegetables, just dead fish seemingly everywhere I looked. Later the warders firmly and unceremoniously locked us into the dormitory. I felt claustrophobic. At this point only a few pilgrims knew how to manage their gear so I was hemmed in by a litter of back-packs, boots, spare clothes and walking equipment. Rather than sanctuary this refuge seemed chaotic.

Staring into the tall, vaulted ceiling and looking at the unyielding grey-stone walls, I suddenly realized this building bore no relation to anything in my own safe, sanitized home where I was always protected and safe from disease. Overwrought, my imagination jumped backwards, focussing on the pilgrims who may have lain here in times long gone. On what beds had they slept? What kind of meals had they been provided? Even though I knew this gaunt building had, over the years, undergone renovations, I was still able to sense fetid straw and festering feet. Plague and scurvy rose to mind, as did pilgrim groans and the soft swish of a monk's robe.

Imagination is an inappropriate way to gain accurate information and, home once again, I turned to books. I began by reading Jonathan Sumption's text, *Pilgrimage*. The general time-frame for his work is 1050 to 1250. By medieval standards these two centuries following the millennium were relatively peaceful, allowing for a mood of optimism and spiritual intensity. At this time the Benedictine abbey in Cluny was at the pinnacle of its power. Not only had this religious house organized the pilgrimages to the Holy Land, but it also promoted the

Way to Santiago. During the reign of Alfonso VI of Léon and Castile (1065-1109), Cluny obtained a firm grip on the church in north-west Spain, organizing and helping the financing of roads and bridges and establishing and patronising new monasteries and hospices.

Sumption begins his book with a general insight into the world the pilgrim would have left behind before setting out. Except for a small number of towns most Europeans lived a rural existence, the villagers confident that God was real, judgemental and that eternal damnation was a continual hovering presence. No doubt village life was oppressive. No-one was allowed leave without permission and no stranger permitted to enter. Each village was dominated by a parish priest and the villagers obliged to attend the parish church and confess their sins at least once a year to that specific cleric. Confession was a public affair. Small venial sins, or those easy to conceal, would be observed by the congregation, but the confession was audible only to the priest. Grave offences, however, were another matter. Not only was the transgression heard by all and the penitent duly humiliated, but often an arduous long-haul pilgrimage to Jerusalem, Rome or Santiago was prescribed if the penitent wished to gain pardon.

The most common crimes to elicit a pilgrimage were murder, incest, sacrilege, arson and heresy. Of these heresy was deemed the most heinous, the heretic not only tried by the early medieval Inquisition, but also committed to perpetual punishment.[8] Accordingly, before

---

[8] The medieval Inquisition operated in Europe under papal control, but in Spain it had little effect. In 1478 the Spanish Inquisition was inaugurated by the monarchs, Isabella I and Ferdinand II. Its purpose was not only to combat heresy, but to unite Spain as a Christian country by either converting the Jews and Muslims to the Christian tradition or exiling them as heretics. The Spanish Inquisition operated under the auspices of the crown and was independent of the papacy.

setting forth the disgraced felon, who had had the audacity to blaspheme against the Lord, was compelled to stitch onto the front and rear of all outer garments a saffron-coloured cross. These were never to be removed and had to be replaced when worn out. The general public were then encouraged to humiliate those they saw wearing this emblem. On the pilgrim road saffron cross-bearers were excluded from inns and hospices. Such stigmatization was catastrophic as all social interaction ceased for the heretic: business deals were made void and young women, whether the wearer of a cross or the daughter of a denounced parent, could not marry. Derision and prohibition continued to the end of their days. One had to suppose that Christ forbade his 'treasure trove' of indulgences to be extended to such as these.

Where a criminal court was responsible for the conviction, the accused was excluded from both the life of the church and village and often sent off in chains, the fetters attached either to arms or feet. Some walked with iron collars. In the case of murderers, the murder weapon would be fastened to the pilgrim to advertise the crime and invite further humiliation. Not everyone survived the journey, particularly those sent to remote shrines. However, for the criminal who did arrive, there are records relating the miraculous and spontaneous sundering of the chains, James apparently releasing the bonds because he knew God had forgiven that particular wrong-doer. Upon returning home these pilgrims could seek re-admittance to their villages providing they promised to live exemplary lives. Recidivists, however, were once again banished and, like those convicted by the Inquisition, condemned to perpetual exile. As late as the thirteenth century Thomas Aquinas still regarded pilgrimage as the obvious, most suitable punishment for a grave breach of public order.

In the twentieth century a few wrong-doers were still sent off on a penitential pilgrimage. Since 1982 the Dutch and Belgian juvenile penal courts have used the Camino as a path to rehabilitate young social reprobates. Supervised, but without chains or saffron crosses, they walk out into nature where it is hoped that they will mature and become sufficiently reflective to be reintegrated into society through physical activity and the learning of self-reliance. Supported and anonymous, they experienced no humiliation. I have been told the system is effective.

Medieval penitents frequently made attempts to evade either their shame or the actual pilgrimage journey by tearing off the saffron cross or hiding out in the forests and then returning home at a later date. These miscreants were hunted down and, if caught, severely punished, sometimes by decapitation. In 1122 Pope Calixtus II proposed Santiago issue the 'compostela': a document to be carried home and presented to the parish priest as authentication that the pilgrimage had been undertaken. The original certificates were hand-written, stamped and specifically sealed and so were difficult to forge.

Pilgrims arriving in Santiago today are still granted a 'compostela'. Like the medievals they, too, are obliged to fulfil certain conditions before they can access this document: sins must be confessed, mass attended, prayers for the intentions of the pope said and charitable work undertaken. Both now and then the preferable 'charitable work' was a donation to the cathedral. When I got to Santiago I decided the state of my boots was sufficient verification and I did not bother with the compostela. Maybe this was foolish. A notice pinned up in the pilgrim office in 2006 stated that plenary indulgences were still available and, I am told by those who did go to the trouble of obtaining the document, the current authorities are remarkably lax in their insistence that pilgrims meet the necessary requirements.

Pilgrimage was not always occasioned by crime. Many set off voluntarily because they were unable to endure the fear of damnation, or the thought of a lengthy stay in Purgatory. Sumption suggests some may have ventured forth to avoid the priest who had such a complete monopoly on their spiritual well-being. Records reveal that some even walked at the behest of a dream, provoked maybe by the gradual awakening of the idea that there might be more than the confines of feudalism in the supposedly dark unknown world beyond their particular village. Whatever the reason, and in spite of the dangers to be met along the road, there were many who sought a break from monotony, were keen for adventure and prepared to abandon the security of village life and brave the wilds. One might suppose for these a shorter pilgrimage to a near-by shrine could well suffice, but this was not often the case, especially for those who could afford the monetary outlay.

To travel to medieval Santiago or, for that matter to any shrine, there were certain obligatory preparations. A will had to be made. A person of substance had to pay his or her debts and make satisfactory arrangements for the safe-keeping of house and chattels. The poor were instructed to make amends with any they had offended, and then ask their spouse, the parish priest and anyone else to whom they owed obligations, for permission to travel. Before setting forth would-be pilgrims had also to negotiate their departure with the feudal lord, obtain a document to authenticate identity and the motive for travelling and then confess all their sins to the priest and afterwards receive mass. It was generally understood that if a penitent left without having made a confession, did not obtain the approval of those in authority or went without the blessing of those who had been wronged, the pilgrimage would be void. This meant the indulgences, though granted at the shrine, would not work after death.

The official dress had then to be procured: a sturdy staff for protection, a long coarse tunic known as a sclavein and reputed to repel the rain, a leather scrip or pouch to hold food, a mess-can and whatever money was available. In time this uniform became symbolically significant. The staff with which wolves could be kept at bay represented the snares that the Devil was bound to set, the wood a reminder of the redeeming cross. The tunic stood for the humanity of Christ and the pouch, because it was small and could carry very little, was to remind the pilgrim of almsgiving and his need to receive, as well as give, charity. While I did not realize it at the time I, too, had purchased a pilgrim uniform before setting out to walk: stout boots, easy-to-dry trekking trousers and T-shirts and a strong but lightweight back-pack.

On the train to Saint-Jean-Pied-de-Port it was easy to pick those who were pilgrims as each one had purchased nearly identical items. When Terence and I were travelling on our own in Spain the pilgrims stood out. Even in the larger cities their singular attire identified them.

On the first morning of my pilgrimage I stepped out with others onto a specific trail identified by carefully placed way-makers. Medieval wayfarers were never so fortunate. They had to fight their way through forests, ford fast-flowing rivers, often in spate and navigate ill-marked and unpopulated tracks. The fifth book of the five-volume medieval text, *Liber Sancti Jacobi*, is a guide for pilgrims of that time. As well as offering information about towns and appropriate hospices along the way, it provided travellers with the full range of possible catastrophes. The dangers were predictable: wolves, grim weather and deep forests thick with mosquitoes. Also listed were the marshes where pilgrims straying off the road would be likely to sink to their knees in mud. Where travellers had to be ferried over rivers on tree trunks horses often drowned. Other rivers were undrinkable, like the salt stream at Lorca where the author of the *Jacobi* guide had found two Basques making their living by skinning horses that had died from imbibing this water. The author clearly had a poor opinion of the Basque people, generally finding them corrupt and devious. On certain parts of the track medieval readers were warned that there would be a constant struggle to procure edible food and fodder. All Spanish meat was to be avoided unless the diner was used to eating it. A hardy constitution was even necessary to digest the fish on the Camino trail. It seems most food was intolerable.

There were also strident warnings against the many unscrupulous inn-keepers and banditry on the road was dire, even though, in theory, the church offered protection by imposing severe penalties on those who molested travellers. William Manchester writes of brigands standing by the side of the road disguised as beggars or pilgrims, knives at the ready, waiting to ambush those on their way to Santiago. He claims, '[h]onest travellers carried well-honed daggers, knowing they might have to kill and hoping they would have the stomach for it'.

For all pilgrims, those sent by the law courts, the Inquisition, as well as voluntary travellers, there were other terrors too, terrors possibly formulated by imagination but projected out into the misty mountains in the form of the *bruja*. This was the intimidating Spanish witch. Spain has always been associated with witchcraft and particularly in medieval Navarra the practice was especially rife. Ian Frewer maintains that even in the twenty-first century white witches, still allied with the owl, are alive and flourishing but, because of Spain's formal dedication to Roman Catholicism, witchcraft can never be publicly discussed.

Whether we accept white witches as real or figments of the imagination, the general response to witchcraft nowadays in the West is mostly benign and the thought of the *bruja* does not disconcert the average twenty-first century traveller. The medieval pilgrim, however, could not be so casual, witches at that time not only being accepted as authentic entities, but also taking on a variety of interesting (to me at least) guises, many of them malevolent. For instance, entering the Soringaritzaga or White Oak Forest surrounding the Augustine Abbey of Roncesvalles, pilgrims would have to look out for the Basa-Juan and his wife, Basa Andere.

An encounter with Basa-Juan would have been daunting because of his immense height, long locks and a satyr-like body. Descriptions of Basa-Andere are hazier because of her ability to shape-shift, sometimes manifesting as a nasty sorceress, at other times as some kind of beautiful 'land-mermaid' sitting in a remote cave and combing her locks with a comb of gold. Keeper of the forests, meadows and waterways, Basa-Juan is normally a placid being but should a pilgrim fell a tree or soil the waterways, this liminal being became extremely hostile. Because of his hairy body, some associated Basa-Juan with the goat, an animal then linked to the Devil, and for this reason these enchanted folk always inspired a sense of terror.

Also to be avoided in the Basque forests were the Laminak and the Tartaro. The Laminak were little people similar to Celtic fairies. Initially they were not averse to helping humans, but after being frequently cheated of their dues, they became hostile and unpredictable. It was believed they inhabited the waterways which could have made the crossing of rivers and streams hazardous. The Tartaro was a one-eyed giant similar to the Cyclops and, like the Cyclops, short on grey matter. As he was reputed to have a taste for human flesh, travellers to Santiago had always to remain alert.

Today such myths are known to only a few and are of little consequence, but the stories told of the *bruja* are a different matter. In early medieval times it was believed many human witches roamed the Basque forests. Initially they wandered unmolested. However, with the advent of the reformation they were not only accepted as real but were now understood as a threat to Christianity and thus presented a challenge for the Spanish Inquisition. Possibly at this time the witch problem arose from the fact that little was known of the Basque people. Even now Basque country, covering the remote Pyrenean Mountains, is isolated and wild.

The Basques are an ancient and mysterious race who value their unique culture and keep it to themselves. Not able to understand their unusual language in either south-west France or in Navarre, it was not surprising that the conservative Inquisition of the sixteenth century would be suspicious of these folk. When, in approximately 1600, outrageous and heathenish rumours began to circulate, the Inquisition were alerted and it was decided to investigate Basque women. A list of suitable questions were formulated and inquisitors were sent to the mountains to interrogate the supposed witches. What resulted was exactly what the Inquisition wanted to hear.

Much of the archival material in Logroño was destroyed during the French invasion of 1808 but from what was saved we know that the inquisitors travelling in

Basque country had been regaled with wild and wonderful stories concerning women who met with the Devil in Bacchanalian-like frenzies. They were told that Sabbats were held in a place known as the 'Field of the He-Goat' just outside a remote village called Zugarramurdi. It was claimed that at the end of this field was a sheer cliff. At a certain point in the rock-face a large cave could be found. This cavern was supposedly used by the witches as a temple. A river known as The Stream of Hell ran through it and on a ledge above the water stood the Devil's throne. At certain phases of the moon, so it was said, the witches ran riot here, kissing the Devil's anus and allowing him to penetrate them with his 'slim, cold, black penis'.

The Inquisitors found this cave and made it their business to expose and depose these wicked disturbers of the faith. Many women, mostly midwives and herbalists, were hauled off to Logroño where the Inquisition had their headquarters. Here they were tried as heretics. It seems the witches' fervour, or maybe the Devil himself, contaminated the Inquisition because the inquisitors too became completely irrational, extracting confessions by torture, believing the most implausible stories and imposing the cruellest punishments.

Because of the scanty archival reports it is unclear exactly how many women were convicted. One outrageous account claimed forty thousand witches had been exposed, another said one thousand five hundred and fifty-six. More reliable sources assert seven thousand were accused, but many of these were children who were warned, excused and then freed. Another source stated two thousand adult females confessed to their supposed crime. Of these twelve were burned at the stake and another twelve died by other means. Many more languished in prison where they also later perished.[9] When Terence and I were in Pamplona there was no way we could find out the truth of this story, but I discovered the cave and village did indeed exist. I was determined to find both.

The caverns are now a tourist attraction. Because they are remotely located there is no available bus service. I asked a taxi-driver to take us, but he refused. Terence appealed to our pension proprietor, a delightful man who obligingly organized one of his friends to drive us there in her car. Her fee was high but we paid. The trip there not only explained the cost, but also demonstrated why the bus companies did not serve this area. It was indeed remote and the mountain road proved hazardous. The day was damp, a thick mist wafting down from the peaks often covering the entire road. Undeterred, our driver negotiated the hair-pin bends at speed and without fear. Twice we got lost and had to ask for directions, but we got little decisive information. It was further away than we had anticipated, but eventually we did arrive in Zugarramurdi.

Disappointingly there was no discernible 'field' for the 'He-Goat', just a car-park and a path leading not to a 'sheer cliff' but to a rounded but sizable hill. Four other visitors were there and a guide led us down a wet, slippery path into the cave. It was indeed large enough for a Bacchanalian-like frenzy. The back of the cave petered out, becoming a labyrinthine tunnel through which a small river did run, its watery tinkling eerily bouncing off the damp rock. This musicality and the coldness in the cave countered its reputation as a 'Stream of Hell'. I saw no evidence of the Devil's throne or a likely place where it

---

[9] These witch hunts have sparked popular imagination and there are many unofficial accounts, the number of victim and the tortures endured varying in each telling.

could have reposed. The stalagmites and stalactites were not unlike others we have seen on past travels. However, there was an uncanny attractiveness about these caves not explained by mere geology. Serpentine tree roots intruded, some merely hanging, others creeping their way down the stalactites. These roots seemed strangely animated. The colouring in the rock formation was also beautiful.

At the end of the tour I remained behind in the large outer cavern, hoping to glean some lingering witchy presence. All I got was the sound of watery music and a deep sense of tranquillity. Maybe this was on account of the *Cruz Blanca*, or the White Cross, which, following the trials, had been erected in the forest by church authorities to keep pilgrims safe from witches and other fairy folk when they navigated their way through Basque country.

All through that day Terence had barely spoken. I had not really expected him to be enthusiastic about this visit because he is a sensible realist and sceptical about such phenomena as witches. I was even surprised he had volunteered to accompany me. However, back in our pension I had anticipated some comment. When it comes to driving Terence likes to be at the wheel and so usually makes an extremely anxious passenger, so I thought he would have a great deal to say about the horrendous mountain journey. But no, wise as well as sensible, Terence said he had kept his eyes closed for almost the whole day and returned to the hotel with his nerves quite unscathed. Mine, however, were in poor shape and needed a stiff, steadying drink.

For medieval pilgrims on the road the prospect of meeting a witch could well have been more problematic, more so than for us. However, before taking to the road there was another difficulty, particularly for voluntary walkers. Of all Europe's shrines which would have been the most appropriate? Mostly the choice depended on the miracle desired and the reputation of the saint who was to deliver this miracle. Usually the clergy attending to the various European sanctuaries had no need to promote their particular saint, or the feats they were supposedly able to accomplish, news of miraculous happenings spreading without the need of their assistance. Sumption provides the example of a blind man from the French town, Saintes. Records claim that, his eyes restored to sight by Saint Eutrope, the healed man sat by the side of the road in 'a deafening clamour' raised from the folk from the nearby villages. Observing the miracle, people rushed up to the man clapping in delight. The whole city throbbed with excitement and everyone was 'increased by love of Christ'.

Another pilgrim, visiting the same saint, is reported to have gone home and invited all his neighbours to return with him so they too could benefit. Sumption claims that if the miracles performed were of a superior quality, the saint's fame was easily spread. Some clerics, however, did keep catalogues of the various wonders performed at their particular shrine and in time these became valuable sources of social medieval history.

With James' shrine things were somewhat different in that the tenth century bishop looking after his relics, Diego Gelmirez (1100-1140), went to considerable lengths to support James' efficacy. As an admirable administrator and a politically astute man he initially managed to put Santiago on the map for Spain's elite by persuading Alfonso VII (1105-1157) to be crowned king in his cathedral. He then set about wholeheartedly endorsing the monastic reforms emanating from the abbey of Cluny and so coaxing the Cluniac Pope Callixtus II into granting the cathedral remarkable privileges. Diego also

67

coerced Callixtus into making him a papal Legate. In due course Diego became a law unto himself. His promotion of James not only increased the saint's popularity, but also made the cathedral extremely rich, so much so that Alfonso demanded a share of the shrine's riches.

Notwithstanding Diego's promotion of James' miraculous power and the political machinations associated with this, a strong reason for the general public to undertake a Santiago pilgrimage was illness and the hope of gaining a cure. Medievals, even in the absence of epidemics and famine, were always physically vulnerable. Grain for making bread, almost the only carbohydrate available and chief source of vitamin B, was difficult to store and transport. In winter the grain got wet and became fetid. The scarcity of fresh vegetable and fruit lead to scurvy and malnutrition. Because they were not understood, dietary disorders were always recognized as the consequence of sin. Most skin conditions were diagnosed as leprosy and this disease was believed to be the result of fornication; barrenness was seen as a sign of God's displeasure. Kidney and bladder stones were wide-spread and attributed to a close proximity with the Devil.

Pilgrims to Santiago who experienced a healthier diet and the warmer Spanish climes were often 'miraculously cured', particularly northern travellers from those countries reliant on rye and subject to 'Saint Anthony's Fire', a disease we now know to result from damp ergot-infected grain. The prolonged ingestion of this fungus causes convulsive symptoms or dry gangrene. Those medievals suffering this disorder were understood as possessed by the Devil. Fed with Spanish bread made from good-quality wheat, they were released from the madness of Satan's clutches, a recovery which could be understood, even today, as miraculous.

When I returned to Spain with Terence we viewed these wheat fields from a sombre castle strategically placed on top of a small mountain. I had brought Terence to Castrojeriz, a medieval village more or less halfway along the trail. It was just as I remembered it: long, sleepy and crouched round the foot of the mountain, the castle brooding above. The vista from this ruin was wonderful: acres of unimpeded wheat billowing in a stiff, spring breeze and extending past the distant horizon. The next day, in spite of a lowering grey sky, we went walking through the fields and even Terence was enchanted by the verdant, green growth and bright-red poppies.

Our walk took us to the ancient ruins of San Anton, a monastery and hospice once affiliated to the Antonine Order founded in France in the eleventh century. The community was associated with Saint Anthony of Egypt, a third century ascetic opting for a solitary desert lifestyle in order to better serve his God. His sacred symbol was a 'T'-shaped cross known as the Tau. Terence's sharp eyes found this emblem carved into the crumbling walls of the old hospice, and in the intricate stone tracery of the rose window in the west wall of the now ruined church. The monastery, well placed in wheat fields, was known for its ability to cure Saint Anthony's Fire. In this instance, rather than good, wholesome wheat, the monks were believed to have performed their miracles through love and the use of the Tau. We passed under San Anton's archway in a soft, misty drizzle that impeded visibility and made possible the evocation of those big-hearted, long-gone monks. Because their presence seemed so palpable I found these ruins among the most profound we came across.

Unless one can attribute them to improved health, it is difficult to know what to make of many of the medieval miracles, particularly those related in the second book of the *Liber Sancti Jacob*. This one for instance, supposedly narrated by the Venerable Bede, reports how James intervened on a sinner's behalf, on this occasion an Italian whose sin was so severe his bishop refused to absolve him, sending him instead to Santiago. With him the pilgrim carried a letter providing the details of his grave crime which he was to show to his new Santiago confessor. When the Italian eventually presented this document, the priest found the paper had been wiped clean, because, claimed the author, James knew the sinner had arrived with a penitent heart. Today there are many who would suggest the pilgrim destroyed the bishop's letter and substituted the blank page. However, it seems Bede, was not a sceptic. He accepted that a miracle had taken place and claimed the Italian went home forgiven and blessed.

Another improbable story was allegedly recorded by His Excellency, Pope Calixtus II, who tells of a great war that arose in France between the count of Forcalquier and a soldier named William. Each raising an army, they rode forth to battle. Unfortunately William's troops were weak and few. In the fray all turned tail and fled except William. The irate count ordered that this renegade be beheaded, but William called upon James who listened to his plea. Three times the slayer's blade glanced off his neck. When he saw he could not harm the soldier, the executioner directed the point of his sword at his stomach so that he might run him through. James dulled the sword and again no harm came to William. Exasperated, the count ordered his enemy to be bound and locked away in his castle.

The following morning James once more heeded the call of a weeping William, appearing in 'a cloud of the most serene light'. A fragrance of 'such sweetness filled the air' that all who watched thought they had been transported to the 'delights of paradise'. In this gleam

William was miraculously released from his bonds and, holding the hand of James, was led to the outermost castle gate. Everyone looked on except the guards who were, at this point, inexplicably blinded. For one mile more William and James walked together. James then vanished and William, burning with love for the apostle, journeyed on to Santiago where he told this story.

For us today tales such as these are problematic, especially those narrated by onlookers who claimed to have been present at the time. Some theorists accept the stories as fraudulent, merely the consequences of hysteria provoked by superstition and suggestion. In the case of sundered chains a probable explanation is that the chains had been voluntarily donned and then removed by the pilgrim upon arrival at the shrine. If this was because the penitent believed he had been pardoned, Sumption generously suggests we accept the relief from feelings of guilt as the real miracle.

Many view such tales as fabrications conjured up by clergy and promulgated to serve missionary ends. It has also been suggested that being the subject of a miracle was a sign of God's favour and in such instances many of the stories told could have been no more than wishful thinking and gross exaggeration on the part of those who wished the world to know they were esteemed by God. Assumptions such as these do little more than reveal the attitudes and prejudices of those who make the judgement.

Jean Leclercq provides deeper insights. Tales that record the lives and miracles of the saints are known as hagiography and these accounts are often mistakenly understood as history or biography. Leclercq claims that the intent behind these stories was never to provide the actual truth of that life, but simply to praise and glorify

God and his saints. Because of the fervour of the writer, his tale was bound to be conducive to gross exaggeration. Hagiography was also didactic, written to advance a moral, the facts of the life being of no importance. It was the sense of sanctity that could be generated through the telling that really mattered. Such literature would also provide appropriate reading in the refectory as the monks dined, as well as for their private reflection. The stories thus also served devotional purposes. There were also lesser motives. Sometimes the tale was directed to the pope to lay the groundwork for a possible canonization, or a writer might have been anxious to attract the attention of a bishop so as to promote a particular shrine and establish a profitable cult following. If one reads these accounts from such medieval view-points the stories become creative ways to articulate the universal ideals of the time and no longer seem like ridiculous and improbable hyperbole.

It is Peter Brown's contention that, because we will never really know what underpinned the miracle stories, or if any of the hagiographic accounts actually occurred, we should give up trying to fathom what really went on. Instead he recommends we simply accept the vigil at the saint's shrine as a 'heady elixir', the consequence of a glorious abandonment of known social structures and the alleviation of boredom. In this way the medieval shrine, and the stories attached to it, became a point where people, no matter their station, came together as a wondrous whole. Because of the overall physical and occasional political violence of those times, this release of spontaneous fellow feeling and comradeship can be considered the real 'miracle', becoming one of the ongoing and enduring appeals of pilgrimage, in medieval times as well as now.

Pilgrims in the Middle Ages, as well as those of today, all want to negotiate the road safely and arrive in Santiago. When I eventually reached this city as a tired but satisfied pilgrim I was also somewhat disappointed. It was high summer, the strong sun unmercifully revealing the antiquity of the cathedral. Centuries of rough Galician winds and harsh weather had worn the stone to a dull, dirty black. Lichen encrusted the walls. The architectural style is predominantly Romanesque and I found this solid, dark heaviness daunting. When I arrived with Terence two years later it was spring and rain was falling. The sky was dove-grey and the wet flagstones of the various cathedral squares shone, reflecting back to me a softness I had not experienced the first time round. Without the relentless sun, the cathedral was mellower, though I still found its line formal and its extravagant façade too authoritative. I suppose I could hardly have expected less, the cathedral built at a time when Christianity in Europe reigned supreme.

On this second visit I was also impervious to the shock afforded by the high altar. Initially I found the flamboyant extravagance of the Baroque chancel not only claustrophobic but also much too garish for my taste. An attractively painted large stone statue of James is seated under a ridiculously elaborate canopy held aloft by enormous gilt angels. I thought it, and the rest of the chancel ornamentation, too over-done to be beautiful and too great a contrast with the rest of the cathedral which, on my first visit, I thought stark and cavernous, possibly because no choir fills the nave. However, when I was with Terence I was more generous, realizing that when those from 'the Age of Faith' sought to glorify God through one of His most powerful saints, the outcome was bound to be overstated. At this point I was saddened, realizing there was nothing in my life that demanded such an exaggerated out-pouring of heart.

While Terence perambulated the chancel marvelling at this medieval and Renaissance grandiosity, I paid attention to the other earlier Romanesque particulars: the beautiful carved capitals, the elegant doorways, the geometric regularity of arches and ceiling and the gracefully engraved stairway leading up to the pulpit. This time I also gave due regard to the exquisite Glory Portico, an early twelfth century triple arch allowing entry to the cathedral. Because it is fragile a porch was eventually built and doors fitted to protect the portico, somewhat hiding its splendour. As a pilgrim I had neglected to observe its exceptional beauty. I now visited the doorway at least twice a day taking Terence with me, his sharp eyes spotting things I had failed to see and expanding the story revealed in this exquisite sculpture.

Of course in Santiago the *piece de résistance* is the crypt. It is a pity that the medievals for whom this reliquary meant so much could not see it the way we do in contemporary times; spotlighted in brilliant electric light, the silver of the casket made to radiate breath-taking luminosity. Maybe the blaze would have been just too much, these pilgrims already over-stimulated by the 'raucous tumult' that greeted new arrivals in Santiago. Sumption envisaged the city as a buzzing place alive with rowdy hawkers and souvenir-sellers, jugglers, conjurers, pick-pockets and buskers playing horns, zithers, and tambourines. It is easy to imagine overflowing taverns and rickety food stalls all plying a brisk trade. It seems that such noise and vulgarity infested all the major European pilgrimage sites.

On many of the feast days a fair held in the cathedral precincts increased the excitement as well as the pollution. At various medieval synods strident complaints were lodged but, because the clergy gained considerable revenue from the trade generated at these festivals, the objections were largely ignored. With Santiago's lack of efficient sanitation, poor water supply and the constant threat of fire, one wonders how the civic authorities coped. These were the *Santa Hermandad*, voluntary peace-keepers whose efficacy was rather dubious.

Terence, observing the constant stream of contemporary pilgrims mounting the stairs at the back of the high altar in order to hug the statue of James sitting resplendent on his throne, and then dismount on the other side, was appalled that this practice was allowed to continue during high mass, even as the host was being elevated. A good many of today's pilgrims are in northern Spain intent on adventure and relaxation. Others are secular or agnostic. Many arrive in Santiago by plane as tourists and are not at all concerned with James so possibly this lack of respect can be dismissed and my husband's complaint understood as super-sensitive.

However, the manner in which the medievals conducted themselves in the cathedral was quite another matter. On the eve of a feast day, in particular the Feast of Saint James, so passionate was their veneration that the clergy were quite unable to contain the crowd, especially when the sick, who had been carried in on litters, were miraculously cured. The shrieks and moans of the newly healed, the praise of those who watched or the lamentations of those still afflicted was deafening, the cacophony reverberating in a multiplicity of European languages. Many pilgrims also came into the cathedral with musical instruments to further express their euphoria. Sumption articulates the scene as 'discordant and barbaric'. Where a silent line of pilgrims behind the altar can now be seen to disturb the mass for the few devout, in medieval times the entire liturgy was not only unheeded but totally unheard.

Records claim that at these times accidents were frequent as enthusiastic pilgrims struggled to get closer to the relics, anticipating a miracle or an instant cure. Women in the crowd were particularly vulnerable and, to avoid being crushed, many females had to be lifted over the throng by strong and kindly men. Often an unfortunate was trampled to death. This would necessitate the re-consecration of the cathedral. And then there was also the stench, something not mentioned by Sumption but suggested by the cathedral guide. While hospices were plentiful in Santiago, there were still large numbers of pilgrims who could not find a bed. Such were allowed to doss down in the cathedral, sleeping in the triforium. Usually this is a high arcaded passage built high above the aisles on either side of the nave and looking into the church. In Santiago, however, this is no passage but a wide balcony which could sleep hundreds of pilgrims each night. As medieval penitents were not renowned for their hygiene and most possessed only the clothes they wore when leaving home, they would not have smelt sweet, the only water to have touched either body or garments coming from the rivers they had had to ford.

The way the ecclesiastical officials sought to combat the odour was to install the *botafumeiro*, the largest thurible in all Christendom. Hanging from a pulley in the transept it needed six red-robed acolytes to get it going. The incense burnt within swung the length of the crossing and was used as a deodorant rather than a fragrant smoke meant to waft prayers heavenwards. A ritual burning of clothes was also instituted to cope with body vermin. The pilgrims were told that the new clothes provided for them by the church were symbolic of a new spiritual beginning wrought for them by the greatness and generosity of Saint James, martyr for the Lord Jesus Christ.

To most contemporary minds the hysteria generated at these shrines is incomprehensible unless one remembers that most medievals lived frugal lives and endured grave hardships, in particular drought, locusts and famine, disease and epidemics such as plague. With no means to overcome the horrendous hazards they put their hope in Heaven, their eventual arrival at this nebulous place their only consolation.

While today living conditions for most Westerners are no longer so dire, there are contemporaries who still walk with commitment. For a short while I accompanied an elderly Austrian couple who told me that in recent years they had been to the Holy Land, had walked to Rome and were now intent on completing the Camino. 'When we return home', they said, 'we will be ready to die'. As they were still spritely and energetic I thought this lack of ambition unfortunate. A young New Zealand student told me she had come to Spain to ponder 'life's great questions'. In particular she wanted to know if there was a God or if there was only nothingness? I am not sure if she was serious, but all the same I wished her luck. I also spoke to two middle-aged American teachers who explained that together they walked the Camino every second year because the walking granted them 'equilibrium' and kept them focussed on a profession that was becoming increasingly difficult for them to cope with.

I saw one pilgrim hauling a gigantic wooden cross mounted on a wheel, the cross brace borne on his shoulder. Because of the way he was walking I knew it was a heavy load. Initially I considered his effort ostentatious, but then decided he may have committed some serious wrong-doing so did not speak with him, but later I met someone who had. I was told that for this penitent life had been over-abundant. He had a wife who loved him, exemplary children and a satisfying job. Rather than wait for fate to demand payment for his good fortune he decided he would pay in advance. It seems that for some suffering is still a necessity.

Pilgrims today still debate the necessity for suffering while they walk. Some castigate those who fast-forward through Spain on a bicycle, sleep in comfortable pensions or avail themselves of transport services to carry their packs from point to point. Others suggest that the blisters, the long-haul suffering and interrupted communal sleeping interfere with their ability to be reflective. On the Camino trail I always shunned this discussion, deciding each pilgrim had to opt for the experience that most suited his or her needs, but when I returned home I did ask Terence for an opinion. He refused to commit himself. A solitary man, overly fond of his books and music room, he dislikes walking and is usually reluctant to leave his study. While he never articulated it, I strongly suspect he thought my tramping eight hundred kilometres under an open Spanish sky a ludicrous undertaking. When I suggested the Camino walk might in some way be redemptive, he snorted and told me he had years ago overcome the religiosity of his formidable Roman Catholic grandmother and was now not prepared to engage with such notions. I was not convinced by this casual brush-off.

Works cited in this chapter

Bell, Adrian R. & Richard S. Dale. 'The Medieval Pilgrimage Business'. *Oxford Journals Humanities & Social Sciences, Enterprise & Society*. (2011) Vol 12 Issue 3. Pp. 601-627.

Brown, Peter. *The Cult of the Saints: Its Rise and Function in Latin Christianity*. Chicago, Ill.: Chicago University Press. 1982.

Coffey, Thomas F., Linda Kay Davidson & Maryjane Dunn, trans. & eds. 'The Miracles of Saint James', *The Liber Sancti Jacobi*. New York, NY: Italica Press. 1996.

Edwards, John. *The Inquisitors: The Story of the Grand Inquisitors of the Spanish Inquisition*. Stroud, UK: Tempus Publishing. 2007.

Frey, Nancy Louise. *Pilgrim Stories on and off the Road to Santiago*. Los Angeles, Cal.: University of California. 1998.

Frewer, Ian. 'Weird and Wonderful: Witchcraft in Spain'. *Expatia*. March. 2005.

Knox, Tom. 'Marks of Cain: The Witches of Navarre', cited in the Fortean Times. 2008.

Leclercq, Jean, trans. Catherine Misrahi. *The Love of Learning and the Desire for God: A Study of Monastic Culture*. New York, NY: Fordham University Press. 1998.

Melczer, William. *The Pilgrim's Guide: To Santiago de Compostela*. New York, NY: Italica Press.1993.

Nardo, Don. *Life on a Medieval Pilgrimage*. San Diego, Cal.: Lucent Books. 1996.

Rabe, Cordula, trans. Gill Round. *Camino de Santiago: Way of Saint James from the Pyrenees to Santiago*. Munich: Rother. 2007.

Sumption, Jonathan. *Pilgrimage: An Image of Medieval Religion*. London: faber & faber. 2002.

Wentworth, Webster. *Basque Legends*. London: Griffith & Farran. 1877.

3

Give all Thou Canst

Even though a pilgrim might choose to walk alone, a pilgrimage is never a solitary undertaking, many people having to provide for the needs of those who venture out. Once on the road, a modern pilgrim's main concern is usually to find a bed for the night. When I made my pilgrimage I chose to stay in the many pilgrim refuges to be found along the trail. It is always dormitory accommodation and always cheap.

To gain a bed in one of these refuges one had to present a pilgrim 'passport'. This was a document issued at the start of the walk, not only authenticating one as a *bone fide* walker, but also entitling the pilgrim to the right of hospitality and the promise of safe passage. Each night it was stamped by the refuge hospitaller and, at the end of one's journey, it provided a record of one's travels. While the refuges were usually stark, they were clean and I always found the company of my fellow travellers stimulating, the rich evening conversation compensating for the austerity and communal sleeping.

After a short time I learnt that the privately owned refuges or those run by various Saint James confraternities provided better accommodation. Here pilgrims were always warmly greeted and provided with dinner and breakfast. The colourfully tiled home in the well-preserved hill-top village of Cirauqui was a delightful private stay. It was run by a gracious lady who was more a hostess than hospitaller. Her family had been vignerons and she served a wonderful pilgrim dinner in the family's renovated wine cellars. The Dutch evangelists in Villamayor de Monjardin were also great hosts. Their breakfast was the best I had on my Camino.

I also favoured refuges run by the various monastic orders. Here no meals were provided, but sometimes the houses were of particular interest. Pilgrims stopping over with the Santa Clara nuns in Carrión de los Condes are housed in the original thirteenth century guest-house, accessed through a delightful courtyard. I found the small rooms, low ceilings and thick walls appealing. That Francis of Assisi allegedly stayed here too added to the mysterious ambiance. For some reason I was prompted to listen to the Santa Clara nuns as they sang Vespers in the monastery church, the nuns occupying a back choir separated from the nave by a stout iron-work grille. The choir was lit and from the nave I surreptitiously watched eighteen nuns file in. They were dressed alike in the full habit of a bygone age: black robe, veil and scapular (a length of cloth suspended both front and back from the shoulder and reaching the knees. It served as an apron). The wimple (a garment worn around the neck and chin and covering the head) and guimpe (a deep heavily starched linen collar covering the shoulders and chest of the wearer) were in stark white. Their anonymity was disconcerting but they sang vespers very sweetly.

The atmosphere of the Benedictine monastery of Santa Maria de Carbajalas in León stood in stark contrast. When I stayed a water pipe had burst and the floor of my cavernous dormitory was flooded. The building was partly underground, poorly lit and everyone, even the nuns, in a state of chaos. I spent a very claustrophobic night here.

I tried to avoid refuges run by municipal authorities as they tended to attract younger and noisier travellers. Sometimes the staff in these houses also tended to be bad tempered, one in Frómista flicking me with a dish-cloth in an effort to hurry me along as I ate breakfast, another in Estella flatly refusing to grant me another bunk, a slat in the one allocated to me having broken. At the conclusion of my day's walk and hunting for that night's refuge I was always glad Terence was not with me. Had his knees been good it is just possible he may have enjoyed the walking and the company at the end of each day, but he would never have coped with the communal sleeping. Later when travelling together in Spain but not as pilgrims, we stayed in pensions or in small boutique hotels.

Because I had taken Spanish lessons before leaving home Terence deemed me an expert in this language and made me responsible for procuring accommodation. I tried to live up to my reputation and managed to book many delightful places, but I usually had to augment my supposed fluency with a good deal of mime. Terence chose not to notice this except on one occasion. We were in Burgos and my husband wanted a hat, the cap he had brought to Spain failing to protect his ears from the strong Spanish sun. When they were thoroughly burnt he asked me to find out from the hotel proprietor where he could purchase proper head protection. I gathered together what I thought the necessary vocabulary and fronted up to the desk. Unfortunately the helpful proprietor from the previous evening had been replaced by an unaccommodating older woman with a demeanour that matched her severe, iron-grey hair. Clearly my Spanish was inadequate. I resorted to mime. Her gaze was stoic. Anxious to make this purchase, Terence rallied and drew a picture of a hat, a man walking and an arrow pointing to the word *tienda*, my contribution. She did not blink an eyelid.

I am not sure where this would have ended if the kindly proprietor had not at that point appeared, apologized, laughed and directed Terence to the most delightful hatter in Burgos: a dapper, moustachioed and elegantly dressed gentleman, his old-fashioned refinement reflected in his wood-panelled shop, beautifully bevelled mirrors and the hat-sized cupboards and boxes in which he tidily stored his merchandise. As an enthusiast of Victoriana, Terence was charmed and spent a great deal more on his new hat than he would normally have done.

When searching for a pension I usually looked for old homes that had been restored as guest-houses. The Bidean in Puente la Reina was a prime example. Centrally placed in the village, this delightful old stone residence had witnessed the passing of pilgrims since early medieval times. This guest-house served meals in a dining room that had once been the main kitchen, the old indoor well still intact but now securely covered with plate-glass and maintained as a central feature. This kitchen served the best paella.

In Villafranca we found La Puerta del Perdón, so named because it is close to one of the few Camino churches with a specially consecrated door. Should a floundering medieval pilgrim pass over its threshold, his or her poor health or weakness would be pardoned, the truncated pilgrimage deemed complete and the promised indulgence still available. The adjacent guest-house overlooked a restored fifteenth century castle, two distinctive turrets dominating the view. The lady of the establishment went out of her way to welcome us and her extraordinarily handsome husband played classical music at breakfast and served our meals at a window table overlooking a rose garden, at that point in full flourish.

In Hospital de Orbigo we were also enthusiastically welcomed, this time with a generous amount of wine and tapas. This house was a highlight for Terence not only because of the refreshments but because he found in the back garden two large and particularly friendly cats.

In Rabanal the high point was music. We were staying in the rustic Hosteria el Refugio, an attractively converted old barn attached to a twelfth century church built by the Knights Templar, tastefully restored and now utilized by a small number of Benedictine monks recently arrived from Bavaria. Each evening the brothers sang evensong in Gregorian chant. We were invited to attend. Maybe it was the poorly lit church and the indeterminate light of dusk that made this service a memorable experience.

In the twenty-first century travellers like Terence and I will mostly have pleasurable experiences in northern Spain. The bus service is good and accommodation satisfactory. We found few hazards. However, this was not so for the medieval traveller looking for overnight lodging. A sixteenth century memoir written by the French Baroness d'Aulnoy tells the tale of a more challenging Iberian experience.

In her text the Baroness claimed that all the taverns in Northern Spain at that time were appalling, not only because they were ill-provisioned and unhygienic, but because nowhere could she find accommodation like she had found in France and Italy where the guest was offered both board and lodging. Instead she had to provide the innkeeper with all her necessities, even procuring the meat she would eat for her evening meal. Sometimes she was lucky and met hunters on the road who would sell her a partridge or a rabbit. To prevent being swindled the

Baroness advised other travellers to carry all their purchases in their personal saddle bags. Once at the inn the host could only offer wine and a bed so infested with fleas and bedbugs she said it would have been better for her to sleep on the floor with the servants who had simply been provided with straw. She declared all Spanish inns were 'filthy', the kitchen fires unflued and 'belching black smoke'. A visit to one had made her feel like 'a fox being smoked out of its den'. The innkeepers not only looked like 'wretched vagabonds' but were unscrupulous. She suggested that at the conclusion of each visit one went through all one's bags because there were bound to have been thefts. And, to add insult to injury, the northern innkeepers served the wine out of goat or pig skins rather than the barrels used in the south. As a consequence, rather than fortify, this beverage did no more than taste and stink of hide. The dining hall was communal and the servants and muleteers dined with their masters. This, too, she took as an affront. It seems her only consolation was to be found in the cheapness of her travel.[10]

The Baroness' assertions are verified by Domenico Laffi's seventeenth century pilgrim diary. He tells of another sorry inn incident. He and his companion were in Logroño and, arriving at their rooms late one evening, he wrote,

'...we returned to our lodging, buying bread and wine and everything else we needed. This was not to be wondered at because an inn in Spain provides nothing but sleeping accommodation. You have to buy everything else going here and there through the city, because he who sells one thing may not sell something else you need'. (Laffi. p. 127)

---

[10] The editor claims this account to be ersatz, the baroness relying heavily on the information provided by three earlier Spanish travelogues.

The social elite, the upper echelons of the aristocracy, highly placed clerics and freemen engaged in lucrative commerce, were also wary of Spanish hospitality. Travelling on horseback they would take with them a large entourage to carry the domestic comforts deemed necessary to their station. If there was no appropriate monastery guest-house in the vicinity, an equerry was sent ahead to secure suitable accommodation. Depending on the status of the master, this would often require taking over a whole inn and, for that night, replacing all the staff.

Wealthy travellers in Spain now have a much easier time. Where once inns and taverns may have been commandeered, the present Spanish government has appropriated a goodly number of ancient castles, redundant monasteries, fortresses and palaces and tastefully converted them into paradors. These are hotels providing luxurious accommodation and, at the same time, preserving much of Spain's medieval heritage. While Terence and I frequented the humbler guest-houses, we did visit two paradors, one where we treated ourselves to a splendid meal, the other because it had been the motherhouse of the Knights of Santiago, a military order in part responsible for the care of pilgrims.[11]

While the rich, whether medieval or contemporary, are usually able to take responsibility for themselves, the poor are another matter. In the early medieval era impecunious or infirm pilgrims who were forced to take a pilgrimage had to depend on charity in order to obtain a bed for the night. This was always provided by religious institutions. Late-comers not able to secure a bed would be provided with straw and floor space. In the early medieval age the patristic fathers assigned the task of

---

[11] I will discuss the help provided by the Knight of Santiago in the next chapter.

87

hospitality to the bishops and as a consequence they became known as 'Lovers of the Poor'. The fifth century writings of Saint John Chrysostom, Saint Basil the Great, Saint Jerome and Saint Augustine of Hippo not only promote the notion of ecclesiastical charity but also reveal contempt for wealth and those who own it. These writers assert too that God would only consider rich individuals worthy if they renounced the material world, sold their excess goods and donated the proceeds to the poor.

In an ecumenical council in the mid-400s Pope Leo I warned wealthy Christians of the dire repercussion awaiting those who were parsimonious in their giving. Bishops, too, were told to set aside one quarter of their personal income which was, ironically, quite considerable, and use it to cater for needy travellers. Isidore of Spain (560-636) recommended the poor received a third of all monastery resources. Through the medieval years the mandate to provide charity was repeated time and time again, various church councils even prohibiting clergy from charging the poor baptismal fees or demanding that those who took what was intended for the downcast and destitute be excommunicated. In the tenth century Jerome's injunction was again repeated at the Council of Aachan, this time reading, 'A layman who receives one of two paupers fulfils his obligation of hospitality; a bishop who does not take in all of them is inhuman'. Pope Gregory claimed that a bishop who did not practice charity was unworthy of his title.

Today we tend to understand charity as an organization that collects money and other voluntary contributions to help people in need. Rarely are givers inconvenienced, instead they are either relieved of extraneous goods or compensated with tax-deductions. Charity can also be understood as willingness to judge people in a favourable way. However, in early Christian usage the term was more closely associated with the term *caritas*, a Latin word related to that which is precious, dear, highly esteemed or deeply cherished. It came to denote an affection that was non-physical and directed not to humanity but specifically to God. If genuine this love for the divine Father would swell and flow from the one who loved to other human beings—firstly to oneself, then to one's family, neighbours, strangers and even enemies. It was a practical love, initially taking the form of a meal. Only gradually did charity also come to designate the distribution of alms.

Benedict of Nursia (480-547) was one of the first to wholeheartedly embrace the concept of charitable hospitality, and he provided directives for its organization. In chapter 53 of his Rule Benedictine monks were specifically charged to receive guests as though they were Christ himself at their door. No matter their wealth, creed or gender, all who arrived at a Benedictine monastery were to be admitted. Given that these monks had retreated from the world, it could be seen that welcoming in outsiders was incompatible with Benedict's philosophy, but caring for visitors was a Biblical directive, Christ having declared, 'Inasmuch as ye have done it unto one of the least of these my brethren, ye have done it unto me' (Matt 25: 35-40) As a consequence catering for guests was not only taken seriously but considered one's bounden duty. If shirked, the eventual outcome would be calamitous.

Upon arrival the monastery superior, or a delegated monk, would greet the visitor and first pray with him, an act believed to foil the deceits of the Devil. Then the kiss of peace would be exchanged. The guest was then admitted to quarters appropriate to his or her station, distant from the cloister and provided for from a kitchen apart from the one catering for the community. Guests were attended only by the guest-master and the cellarer, the monk who had been assigned the tasks of organizing provisions for the monastery. If the guest was ill the infirmarer, the monk who attended to the sick, would also be called. Having been welcomed, the visitor was then expected to take part in the prayer life of the community, participating in some of the offices said throughout the day.

As well as guest-houses attached to the large monasteries, independent hospices for pilgrims and travellers were also established in the eleventh century. In modern usage the words 'hospice', 'hostel' and 'hospital' have each acquired a specific and distinctive meaning, but in medieval times these terms were interchangeable. Because 'hospice' and 'hospital' are both derived from the Latin terms *hospes* meaning host as well as guest, and *hospitium* which translates as guest-house, a pilgrim arriving at an autonomous house would always expect hospitality. That he or she might also receive medical care was an added bonus. These establishments sometimes operated under the auspices of a large monastic house or the Hospitallers of Saint John or, particular to Spain, the Knights of Santiago or those in the order of Calatrava. In the early Middle Ages the cleric, monk or hospitaller in charge would receive all who came to the door whether they were rich, homeless or sick.

The Hospital del Rey (Hospital of the King) in Burgos was a prime example of a prestigious medieval hospital. Founded and endowed in 1195 by Alfonso VIII, it was entrusted to the Knights of Calatrava but dependent on the Cistercian Monastery of Santa Maria la Real de las Huelgas, a notable monastic house for royal women a short distance away.[12] The conditions of its inauguration

---

[12] The significance of this house will be discussed in Chapter 7.

were specific. The hospital was to be headed by a prior assisted by a large staff: twelve men who had to be well-born and over the age of thirty, eight nuns of at least thirty-five years, a sacristan, an organist, presbyters, two physicians, a surgeon, a bonesetter and some interpreters. Later Alfonso X legislated for the hospital's hospitality, stating:

"All pilgrims who pass by on the French road and other roads, whatever their origin, no one shall be refused there, and all shall be received; and they shall have every necessary thing there to provide them with food, drink, and lodging, at all hours of the day and night, whenever they arrive. And all who wish to lodge there shall be given good beds with bedclothes …; and any man or woman who arrives sick shall be provided men and women to take care of them, and to quickly give them food and anything they might need, until they recover or die".

Laffi's seventeenth century diary confirms that this hospital was indeed grand. Of its size he wrote, '[I]t seemed like a city in itself. I don't think there is another like it in Spain. It holds two thousand people. They give much charity and treat them very well as regards eating and sleeping.' Clearly hospitality as well as medical care was offered. When we visited the site it was difficult for us to get a sense of this hospital, the complex now having been taken over by Burgos University and renovated to house the Faculty of Law. All that remains of the earliest buildings is the entrance to the fore-court and a bit of wall securing a large Gothic door which lead into the original church which unfortunately is now no longer standing.

The Hostal de los Reyes Católicos (The Hospital of the Catholic Royals) in Santiago was another well-endowed refuge. In the late 1400s the monarchs

Ferdinand and Isabel declared the original pilgrim hospital decrepit and in need of refurbishing. From the income obtained from their victory at Granada when the Muslims were finally defeated, the royals commissioned the lavish construction of a new building utilizing Enrique de Egas, the architect who had overseen the building of the very grand Toledo cathedral. The hospital was to be another city in miniature. Its purpose was again two-fold: to be a refuge for pilgrims as well as an infirmary for the sick. For a while the refuge also operated as an orphanage, illegitimate infants abandoned in the hostal precinct taken in and cared for and, in due time, trained to become maids and cleaners. The 1541 Hospital register listed one hundred and thirty-one such orphans.

The ground plan was square and divided into four, each quarter with its own attractive interior cloister and each built in an individual style. Two of these were used for the sick, the other two for the healthy and males separated from females. As Alfonso X had legislated three hundred years earlier for the Hospital del Rey, Ferdinand and Isabel also concerned themselves with the running of the hostal, insisting that all manner of people were to be accepted, only lepers and plague victims excluded. There was always to be one attending doctor, three lawyers, an apothecary, nurses, a cleaning woman and eight chaplains, all under the authority of one omnipotent administrator. Water was to be boiled and the rooms ventilated and perfumed. The charter allowed healthy pilgrims three days' free food and lodging in the summer. In winter the days were increased to five. The ill were permitted to remain until they had either recovered or demised. The complex operated as a pilgrim hospice until 1920 when it was taken over by the government and renovated, becoming an extremely expensive luxury parador.

I did not care for this prestigious royal building. Unrelieved by any green growth, the severity of its long, regular shape, the grimness of the stone from which it had been built and the grandness of its main entrance smack of authority and wealth and render a building supposedly dedicated to hospitality somewhat intimidating. Solid and imposing, it seems to say more of the monarchs who authorized the hospital than the people for whom it was built; that is, until one reaches the unassuming Corralón Gate at the end furthest away from the cathedral. This understated entrance leads into what looks like an old carriage house. On the wall of this building is a large placard which reads:

"All merchants bringing goods to the hospital had to enter through the Corralón Gate, where the entrance to the stables were located, as well as the slaughter house, wine cellar, oil chamber, coal storage and other service rooms. The dwellings to the left housed employees of the complex who could reach their posts via the servants' stairs which linked the alley to the apothecary courtyard. The same gate was crossed by funeral carriages removing cadavers from the hospital. They were buried in the cemetery which the institution had beyond the city walls where the parish church of San Fructuoso now stands. As occurred above with the living, the hospital watched over the body and soul of the dead below"

Having read this Terence thought it rough that pilgrims, having survived such a long and arduous journey, should not only die, but at the end be demoted to no more than 'cadavers'. Sighing, he joined me as I trespassed into a back courtyard. Unable to explore thoroughly, we were nevertheless able to gain a more realistic understanding of the complexity of running a medieval hospital. Where once there had been animal pens, as well as a jail and a medicinal herb garden, the present day enclosure is lawned. There are trees. As opposed to the imposing outside, the buildings at the rear are quaint. On the day we were there it was ordered and charming and not very busy, but it was easy to imagine fervid medieval activity, to say nothing of the smells of cooking, drains, stables and nasty diseased effluvium. There would also have been the noise of busy people going about their business: the slaughtering of animals, brewing, bread-making and the removal of those poor cadavers.

Somewhat daunted I retreated, but exiting through the stable was also sobering for I now imagined the rumbling wheels of the hand-drawn mortuary cart on the cobble-stone floor as yet another dead pilgrim was taken away. I even heard the thud as the horse-drawn carriage carrying a more notable corpse collided with the bollards on either side of the gate. Suddenly death seemed too real and Santiago too wet. I suggested we retire indoors and take strong coffee.

Not all medieval hospitals had royal patronage. Many were very modest. Near the start of the Camino I was impressed by a small fourteenth century hospice a short way from the village of Villatuerta on the outskirts of Estella. It is now a ruin. I visited this hospice on my own, having left Terence in Estella hunting the old shops for a *txistus*, a traditional Spanish pipe capable of sweet-sounding music if played correctly. Terence found one but, incapable of coaxing anything equating to sweetness, he left the instrument behind. While he was busy making this disappointing discovery, I took a taxi to Villatuerta. My quest was to walk back to Estella on a much longer, alternative route passing by the remains of the ruined hospital.

It was easily found, nestled into the side of one of the steeper Navarrese hills and remote from other habitation. Possibly it had been built under the auspices of the large Irache monastery several kilometres away. With my back to the distant bitumen and telegraph poles, I gazed upon the crumbling walls and felt confused. The fallen stone and ancient rafters appeared unyielding, affording no insight into the lives of the monks who lived there or how this hospice had offered itself to those who visited. Before the building of the highway and the erection of power lines this undulating country must have been idyllic, the peacefulness perhaps facilitating both the monks' religious calling and the healthful recovery of the inmates. Alternatively the isolation could have been daunting and the responsibility of attending to pilgrims an arduous labour. While I had no understanding of the medieval situation—the number of pilgrim beds, their joy or possible maladies—the ruin nevertheless felt alive. The hewn rock lay cushioned in a mantle of rich spring grass dotted with billowing flowers. The air was redolent with the aroma of thyme. This herb, now in luxuriant bloom, grew along the edges of the hill-side path, its scent heady and invigorating. As I walked away I asked myself, was I was simply in thrall of nature or had the essence of those dead and long gone remained behind, emanating from the ground to which they had been returned?

Another hospice that had really struggled in medieval times was located in the Caurel Mountains on the border of Léon and Galicia. Here, high on a mountain pinnacle there had once had been a Roman military station protecting Galicia from enemy invasions. There are also records of later battles, one fought in 968 in which Norman raiders were overcome. The remote settlement, now called O'Cebreiro, never flourished and could have become redundant had it not been for the advent of the

Camino, pilgrims from France on their way to Santiago having to cross this pass. In 1072 a small community of monks from the town of Aurillac in France was installed to manage a meagre hospice. It did not do well, maybe because it was difficult for the French mother-house to staff and supervise so distant a site. A record exists which indicates that there had also been various disputes over land ownership increasing the stress levels of the inadequately provided-for monks.

In 1233 Aurillac was sacked and the mother monastery was forced to sell its distant properties. Whoever bought the O'Cebreiro community failed to support it and, though most medieval hospitals were well endowed, few willing patrons could be found to provide for this almost inaccessible community. When Isabella and Ferdinand visited in 1486 they were appalled by its sorry state and made a donation of gold. They also asked the pope to bestow other unspecified privileges, which he did. The original hospice is now long gone. In 1960 a new refuge was built for contemporary pilgrims and is now efficiently run by the Galician government.

On my Camino I had made the stiff but exhilarating climb to this village and then, feeling as though I was on top of the world, decided to stay the night, but the refuge was full and there was no bed available in the inn. Because it was still early afternoon, I was forced to turn my back on the mountain splendour and walk on. In Spain with Terence I was determined to return, but mindful of my Camino experience, I decided to book a room in advance. Finding the guest-house telephone number in John Brierley's Guide, I arranged the reservation. The conversation was tortured and I could only hope I had been successful. Organizing transport to O'Cebreiro was also difficult. Unless one climbs up the mountain as a pilgrim, this village is not easily accessible from León where we were at that point, there being no direct bus route. We managed a circuitous ride to Villafranca and from there a taxi-driver was persuaded to drive us the final thirty kilometres. When we eventually reached the village I was in near-panic, so anxious was I about my Spanish telephone skills, but we were graciously welcomed. I had worried in vain.

O'Cebreiro is only of mild historical interest. It is the legends that shroud the village that mostly appeals to visitors. A placard in the village square recalls the miracle of a German pilgrim who was rescued from bad mountain weather by the sound of a shepherd's bagpipes. Of greater importance is the tradition that claims that the Holy Grail from which Christ and his disciples drank at the last supper had been hidden in in this village. Gitlitz and Davidson tell a story of how this chalice, a priest doubting the reality of transubstantiation and a fierce snowstorm combined to produce the village's most famous miracle.

The priest, possibly lonely and in crisis with regard to his floundering faith, was saying mass one bitter winter's day. Looking out into the wild weather, he was astonished to see a peasant fighting against the wind and snow in his effort to reach the church. Once in the church the priest berated the peasant, telling him that walking out in such a blizzard only to receive a bit of bread and wine was foolhardy. At that precise moment, so the story goes, the said bread and wine turned into 'real' flesh and blood. The Virgin Mary, mysteriously hidden in a statue, is said to have bent forward to observe the miracle as it happened. Needless to say, the wayward priest recovered his faith and in 1487 the truth of this miracle was certified by Pope Innocent VIII. Since then the story has been widely celebrated in Spanish painting and verse. Today, in this church, there is still a twelfth century statue of a Madonna and child and, after all this time, she is still leaning forward at an uncomfortable angle.

A beautiful twelfth century chalice is also on display, tradition claiming it as the one in use when the miracle occurred. How this vessel became associated with the Holy Grail is no longer known, but Mathew Kuefler has a theory. He claims the story began in France in Aurillac, the town of the original mother-house. Here, in the ninth century, a beautiful man called Gerald had been given a chalice by the pope himself. The vessel, claimed the pope, had once belonged to Saint Peter and so was very special. It was given to Gerald because he was an exemplary knight who looked after his peasants. He was also an exceptional warrior but went to war reluctantly, and then only to protect the innocent. Pious and in love with the Lord, Gerald eventually become a monk. In due course he was elected abbot and was eventually sainted.

At some point in his life his special chalice somehow made its way to O'Cebreiro where the French clergy were now encouraging the laity to revere the new saint. In this endeavour they dedicated the church to Gerald. It is Kuefler's contention that over time the distinction between the new saint and his chalice became confused. The chalice was then mistaken for the Grail. This confusion, thought Kuefler, was the result of the saint's name. In French, Gerald would have been known as Saint Géraud. In medieval Spanish, he was Sant Guiral. In the Galcian tongue, he would have been called Sant Gral. Kuefler then asks, 'Is it really that hard to imagine that some, shown a chalice they were encouraged to revere in a church named Sant Gral, after a man about whom they had never heard, mistook it for the Sant Grial, the Galician term for Holy Grail?' To accept this reasoning is a big ask, but the village likes the thought of having once owned the Grail and so sticks to this tale. The proprietors of our guest-house have named their establishment after this saint, but spell it in contemporary Spanish, San Giraldo.

O'Cebreiro is still a frugal village. Its few oval houses are in an ancient architectural style known as pallozas. They are built of stone with thatched roofs and microscopic windows. In days gone by humans and livestock shared this shelter. We saw no shops or other amenities except the modern pilgrim refuge on the outskirts of the village. Fortunately our guest-house had undergone a degree of internal modernization and, though icy cold, was otherwise comfortable. The meals we received were good considering the difficulty of procuring the food. For me, however, the real enchantment in O'Cebreiro was fog.

Having explored the village, Terence and I returned to the cliff edge overlooking the valley. It was late afternoon and the colours on the horizon were wonderful. As we watched we saw the fog slowly meandering up the stiff mountain slope, seemingly coming from nowhere: long, thick ropes of mist, each strand twirling round the next. The tresses reached the cliff edge and rolled into the village. It was as though this intruding blanket was not only alive but also out to consume. In half an hour everything was obliterated, soundless and the air raspingly cold. We also realized why the medieval German pilgrim, rescued by the muffled sound of bagpipes could be considered miraculous. As we retreated indoors I wondered how the pilgrims of old had fared in their inadequate hospice. I also thought of the kindly monks and the long, lonely vigils they would keep watching out for shepherds and dealing with the sick. That evening it seemed perfectly feasible that miracles of all sorts could happen up here on this remote pass.

While early medieval hospitals operated of their own accord and independent of politics, in time the nature of charity and those who deserved it became an ideological topic hotly debated by medieval theologians, moralists and canon lawyers. Early on Pope Leo I had asserted, 'No human being should be considered worthless'. Both Pope Innocent III (1198-1216) and Thomas Aquinas (1225-1274) were in agreement, claiming that the practice of charity was not only a right for the poor, but those receiving care were also ennobled by it. In a rural social order where poor people lived on the edge of subsistence, this kind of thinking was problematic. With so many poor, how were the truly needy to be identified and what would be the criteria for their assistance?

In the twelfth century the issue of impecuniousness was further complicated by Bernard of Clairvaux who now promoted the idea of voluntary poverty and so increased the number of poor. For him the distribution of alms presupposed the acquisition of wealth which he saw as leading to the sin of avarice. Opposed to ostentatious Benedictine prosperity, Bernard opted for an austere life and, in 1115, began establishing religious houses focussed on manual labour and simple self-sufficiency. At this point medieval charity was at last understood for what it was: the safeguarding of one's future place in heaven.

While this idea was attractive to many medievals, it was complicated by debate as the poor were now categorized into two sorts: those who took poverty on as a voluntary life-style to avoid supposed pitfalls in this life, and those who suffered because they were indisputably sick, disabled or dying and in need of care. While Bernard could not solve the theological tensions that arose from self-chosen and indigent poverty, he articulated the problem saying, 'It is one thing to fill the belly of the hungry and another to have zeal for poverty. The one is in

100

the service of nature, the other in the service of grace'. Were those who sought grace deserving of charity and were they still following the church's directives on the necessity to give?

In the next century Francis of Assisi established the Franciscan order. His Rule was more extreme, calling for a complete renunciation of the world and total surrender to Christ. This was symbolized by the selling of all one's worldly goods and giving the proceeds to the poor. Followers of Francis became itinerant preachers begging for their keep as they travelled abroad. By becoming poor themselves, individuals such as these escaped having to deal with the sticky theological problem of sustaining the needy.

For lay men who were well-born but unwilling to go to such extreme lengths, there were other possibilities. They could join an appropriate confraternity where giving could be more prudent. Contributing through these organizations could take the form of charitable works. Members could also gather regularly to sing Lauds and so increase the praise of God. Rather than gain heavenly favour through giving, one could purge oneself of sin by regular flagellation. While still concerned with the state of the soul, one did not have to part with one's wealth.

The increasing population in eleventh century Europe and a slowly emerging commercial economy created new hierarchies which resulted in still more tensions. Entrepreneurs now flourished, as did well organized traders and artisans. This meant that such people as unskilled agricultural labourers could no longer find employment in towns when the crops failed, and unattached women became even more marginalized. This inequality led to more discussion, this time centred round such issues as morality versus behaviour. Religion was now vying with life, particularly in urban areas, and priests found it increasingly difficult to persuade the people to continue providing generously. At this point the canons arrived to counter those from the religious orders who avoided these worldly evils by simply advocating greater asceticism and isolation.

The canons were Cathedral clerics who were very mindful of the world and its troubles. They, too, adopted the notion of poverty by organizing themselves into communities, but they remained secular in that they did not isolate themselves. Their endeavour was to redeem, or at least repair, the worst of the world's problems.

The canons chose Saint Augustine as their patron and utilized his Rule. Unlike Benedict's precise and severe model, Augustine's was more general, stipulating only that those who adopted this way pray together each day at specific times, have all material things in common, dress without distinction and obey a superior. The eating of meat was allowed, manual work was not deemed necessary and the Rule had to be flexible enough to suit the circumstances of each different community.

Sir Richard Southern, using Biblical imagery, identifies the monks in their enclosed orders as playing the part of Mary, the canons as emulating the more down-to-earth Martha. Where the Benedictines and Cistercians sought to imitate a supernatural order, the canons can be seen as addressing the broken pieces of this world. They rebuilt ruined churches and restored religious life in rundown communities, providing them with a workable routine. They established small church schools, built many hospitals and places of retirement for those unable to cope with the world. In Spain they also took trouble to rescue those who had been captured by Muslims. More importantly they redeemed large amounts of tithe money misappropriated by corrupt authorities and used the reclaimed money for the relief of the poor, sick and dying.

In the thirteenth century the canons also set about defining the poor, identifying their legal status and categorizing them according to their specific circumstances: those who travelled on dangerous roads, those who were worthy of long-term help such as widows, orphans, lepers, the blind and maimed, as well as impoverished members of the upper classes. Instead of a free-for-all as in the Benedictine houses, one now had to be deserving of charity.

In Europe generally the Augustinian canons were well received, attracting the support of the populace who saw in their life-style and religious teaching an ideal that could be comprehended. Without marks of greatness and excessive learning, not overly religious and eschewing the political arena, the canons did not intimidate. Their humbler and yet respectable way of living and their generosity in providing for the needs of the people attracted many benefactors. By the twelfth century the Augustinians were thriving all over Europe.

In Spain, however, they were unable to adopt this degree of humility. Marcelin Defourneaux provides two reasons, one being the Spanish obsession with ostentation and a focus on the impressive outward appearance of things. The other was the nature of the Spanish soul which, he claims, had become so permeated with the Roman Catholic faith there was not a single aspect of individual or collective life that was not bound by it. This meant the church not only dominated the social order generally, but great numbers of men and women were attracted to all degrees of holy orders. Monasticism flourished. The laity, too, were pious and, from every class, were willing to give generously in the form of endowments and dowries. This meant that the Spanish church became extraordinarily wealthy and outwardly grandiose. Many clergy, especially those of high rank, were prone to a lifestyle that reflected the splendour of their surroundings. While the Spanish canons were not quite so pretentious, many chose to live more affluent lives than those in the rest of Europe.

In Léon Terence and I inadvertently gained a small insight into the lifestyle of the old Spanish canons. While back home and searching for accommodation over the internet, we booked into an unusual-sounding complex called the Real Colegiata de San Isodoro. On arrival we discovered we were to be housed in the old clerical residence attached to the collegiate church of Saint Isidore, located a short distance from the cathedral. This communal house was indeed impressive. Where once it had provided for a large number of canons, the house was now reduced to eight who were accommodated more conservatively, their palatial private rooms open to the public and operating as an exclusive hotel. It was lunch time when Terence and I arrived. As we walked the beautiful upper cloister on our way to our suite, we passed a large hall furnished with an enormous table at which sat at least fifty priests and lay men. Some sort of confraternity meal was being served. This feast was impressive. The clerics in black, the formally suited lay diners, many sporting civilian and military decorations, and the handsomely laid table all exuded an overflow of patriarchal prestige.

The next morning, as part of the hotel service, we took a tour of the community complex. It was private, no other guests taking up the offer. A very polite dapper little canon with not one word of English was our guide but, with sign language, my bad Spanish and Terence's hastily recalled Latin, we got a good insight into the elegant splendours of past collegiate life. Our priest's beautifully tailored trousers, stylish overcoat and highly polished shoes indicated that though now reduced, these priests still live very well.

One of the earliest collegiate churches established on the Camino trail was at Roncesvalles. The nearby medieval Hospital of Aubric in the Pyrenees had demonstrated the need for pilgrim relief in this area. Legend has it that in 1120 a Flemish pilgrim named Adalard, at home a cup-bearer to an aristocratic lord, experienced two frightening episodes on the Pyrenean leg of his pilgrimage to Santiago. Initially set upon by brigands from whom he escaped and then almost overwhelmed by a snowstorm while crossing the mountains, he promised that if God protected him from all perils, on his return he would construct a monastery to aid the pilgrims who were to follow.

Adalard survived and eventually fulfilled his vow in 1162, becoming the first superior of the Pyrenean hospital. By then another community had also been established on the Ibañeta Mountain Pass near Roncesvalles, but, built on such high ground, violent weather had rendered it unusable. At the behest of King Alfonso I and the Bishop of Pamplona a new hospice was built to replace the earlier establishment. At first this shelter was served by a confraternity of laity and clerics, but it was soon transformed into a very prosperous community of canons.

For the time, this early collegiate community was particularly large, incorporating a church, a residence which included a pilgrims' dining hall, hospital and (as I had thought there would have been when I stayed in this hospice on my first night on the Camino), a separate guest-house for more prestigious paying visitors. Because of the severity of the crossing, all pilgrims traversing the Pyrenees stopped at Roncesvalles, so much so that during the sixteenth century the early twelfth century hospital had to be extensively remodelled and extended in order to accommodate the throng. Up to the fourteenth century Roncesvalles was also augmented by a small band of knights whose attendance there not only safeguarded the community, but also highlighted the fact that brigands and outlaws were a real threat. As Terence and I stood in front of the abbey and surveyed the green and tranquil countryside I tried to imagine the presence of something as incongruous as armed and armoured warriors patrolling this serene landscape. At such a remove it seemed an absurd notion.

Being fascinated by Roncesvalles and interested in the pilgrims who had preceded me, I was delighted to read Gitlitz and Davidson's rendition of a sixteenth century description of the Roncesvalles' pilgrim's refectory experience. Meals were a ritual affair offered at sunset. Friars would process into the hall where the pilgrims stood waiting in a long line in front of the dining tables. From the high table the prior would begin with formal prayers, first for the poor, then for pilgrims, the church next, followed by the pope, the Spanish monarchs, the nobility and then all those, Spanish and foreign, who had contributed to the monastery's support. As the prior in his pulpit called out each versicle, the pilgrim throng responded with a Hail Mary. Then another friar, or an honoured guest if one was present, went down from the high table and distributed the bread to each pilgrim after first kissing the loaf. Other friars handed out wine and then the main dish was served. The quality of the food was said to be good. It just took a long time in coming!

A twelfth century hymn called 'La Pretiosa' provides an additional insight into Roncesvalles hospitality. The first verse reads:

Its doors open to the sick and well,
To Catholics as well as pagans,
Jews, heretic, beggars, and the indigent,
And it embraces all like brothers.

Further verses describe how monks would wash the pilgrim's feet and cut their hair and beards. The sick were tended by volunteer women and those who died were reverently buried. While the hymn suggests Roncesvalles was particularly charitable, the order was, in fact, doing no more than diligently obeying the community's governing statues which demanded that the poor be treated as family and not as strangers and served as though they were lords.

Nowadays it is difficult to appreciate what the medieval hospitals were really like. In part this is because they defied generalization, built as they were to serve different purposes. Some were much larger than others. The manner in which they were endowed also varied, with some being better provided for than others. Nothing was standard, each religious order having its own system of governance. Because the general world view of this time believed disease originated in sin, the focus of the hospital was on the correction of spiritual wrongdoing rather than the treatment of the corporeal malady. Run by the religious orders and canonical houses, hospitals were therefore religious environments. Even in their architecture it was difficult to distinguish between a medical institution and a church, a chancel and altar incorporated in the infirmary hall so that the sick could view and hear the daily mass. For early medievals the emphasis was on care and not cure, and physical remedies were always subordinate to religious intervention.

By the thirteenth century the number of hospitals in Spain had not only increased, but had also begun to specialize, each catering for one particular category of the needy. Up to this point lepers had simply been excluded from the social order and forced to fend for themselves, not necessarily because they were supposed contagious, but because the physical changes in their appearance suggested that they had been visited by God's divine wrath. In spite of their supposed 'sins' they were allowed to beg on the fringes of the towns as long as they identified themselves and possessed a wooden goblet into which alms could be placed. Now they were provided with shelters run mainly by the charitable Order of Saint Lazarus. Even with the help of rich patrons these leper hospices were inadequate, twelfth century records revealing that at this time there were approximately 20,000 lepers wandering round Spain and only 200 shelters each admitting no more than twenty patients.

Another unusual category of hospital was those dedicated to helping sufferers of ergotism, the fungal infection known as Saint Anthony's Fire.[13] As there were relatively few Spanish suffering from this disease these hospitals catered mostly for the pilgrim influx from northern Europe. The mentally afflicted were now also provided with hospice shelter. Where the response to those with a mental disorder had once been a flogging and expulsion from the village, the tormented person paid to go on a pilgrimage in the hope of gaining a cure, they were now institutionalized. Starting in the 1370s they were confined in closed cells, shackles and chains used to

---

[13] Saint Anthony's fire was discussed in Chapter two.

restrain the violent. In modern terms this manner of dealing with the mentally ill would not be considered charitable, but then at least they were fed and safe from wolves and brigands. For plague victims there was no help available.

The end of the twelfth century brought improvements not only in medicine and hospitals but in education generally. Because the Christian religion had so little to say about the nature of the human body, medieval Spanish scholars at the turn of the millennium looked to Islam to update their practice, utilizing Greek philosophy and the medical texts brought to Spain by the Arabs. For a while scholarship flourished.

In 1218 the first Spanish university was inaugurated in Salamanca. It demanded of would-be physicians and surgeons a four year course of study. Where once the church had been particularly suspicious of lay doctors, understanding them as vehicles through which Satan could operate, qualified doctors now became common-place. A primitive form of science was replacing prayer and holy relics, the methods of healing favoured by the early medieval church. Even when the Catholic Monarchs, Isabella and Ferdinand, came to the throne in 1479 and forbade the new learning sweeping through Europe, the doctors qualifying from the universities, though poorly informed, organized themselves into guilds and, in a short time, established the notion of medicine as a prestigious profession with a uniformity of practice. However, as an esteemed group, they tended to serve only the nobility from whom they extricated outrageous fees. The general populace had to rely on the charity still offered by the monastic orders, or attend folk-healers, herbalists and midwives. Once caregivers had been instructed by the church to give all they could to the poor, now the focus of these secular physicians was to take all they could from the rich.

And the medieval pilgrims on their way to Santiago? Who now could assist those on that hazardous road? Fortunately by this time there were others who could help, in particular the knights, specifically those in religious orders. Before I was able to understand how these armoured warriors operated on the Camino road, I had to do a lot of reading. Because Spanish knighthood was unique, especially at the start, I had first to study the European knight generally before I could appreciate not only how those on the Iberian Peninsula helped the pilgrims, but also why they had evolved so differently.

Works cited in this chapter

Amundsen, Darrel W. *Medicine, Society, and Faith in the Ancient and Medieval Worlds*. Baltimore, Ml: The Johns Hopkins University Press. 1996.

Barber, Richard. *The Knight and Chivalry*. Woodbridge, UK: The Boydell Press. 1995.

Brodman, James William. 'Charity and Welfare': *Hospitals and the Poor in Medieval Catalonia*. Philadelphia, Penn: University of Pennsylvania Press. 1998.

_____. *Charity & Religion in Medieval Europe*. Washington, D.C.: The Catholic University Press. 2009.

Byrne, Joseph P. *The Black Death*. Westport, Conn.: Greenwood Press. 2004.

Defourneaux, Marcelin, trans. Newton Branch. *Daily Life in Spain in the Golden Age*. London: Allen & Unwin. 1970.

Freeman, Charles. *The Closing of the Western Mind: The Rise of Faith and the Fall of Reason*. New York, NY: Vintage Books. 2005.

French, Roger. *Medicine Before Science: The Business of Medicine from the Middle Ages to the Enlightenment*. Cambridge, UK: Cambridge University Press. 2009.

Gitlitz, David M. & Linda Kay Davidson. *The Pilgrimage Road to Santiago*. New York, NY: St. Martin's Press. 2000.

Kerr, Julie. *Monastic Hospitality: The Benedictines in England*. Woodbridge, UK: Boydell & Brewer. 2007.

Kuefler, Matthew. 'How the Holy Grail ended up in O'Cebreiro', *Brocar.* 36 (2012) 53-64.

Laffi, Domenico, trans. James Hall. *The Diary of a Seventh Century Pilgrim from Bologna to Santiago de Compostela.* The Netherlands, Leiden: Primavera Pers. 1977.

Lawrence, C.H. *Medieval Monasticism.* London: Longman. 2001.

Linberg, David. *The Beginnings of Western Science.* Chicago, Ill.: The University of Chicago Press. 1992.

Southern, Sir Richard. *Western Society and the Church in the Middle Ages.* Middlesex, England: Penguin Books. 1976.

4

Knights – Dark and Bright

When I began walking the Camino I never gave a thought to knights. I could have pondered them when I made the Pyrenean crossing, Charlemagne's rear-guard having been ambushed in these mountain forests as he retreated from campaigns in Spain. His knights' bloody demise was chronicled in the *Song of Roland*. At that point I had not read this poem, and even if I had, I probably would not have given much thought to Roland, my energy focussed on the stiff climb. However, when I walked out of Léon and passed the monastery of San Marcos, it occurred to me that at one time knights had been instrumental in establishing the Camino, my guide book informing me that San Marcos had been the seat of the Knights of Santiago. Having admired the monastery's splendid façade and the elegant San Marcos square, I crossed the river and walked on.

At that point my ideas of knights and knighthood were romantic, mostly formed by the Crusades, Arthurian legend and various notions of the Grail. It was only when I began researching the Santiago knights that I found out they were an amazing anomaly. In part this is because they were an amalgam of military might and ecclesiastical holy orders. Later, when I was back in Léon with Terence, I returned to San Marcos with a better understanding.

In every Western European language except English, the word for knight means horseman. This etymology seems reasonable, knights in romance literature frequently astride their steeds. In English the word knight derives from the Anglo-Saxon *cniht*, meaning servant. It is the same word as *knecht* in modern German. A knight who is, at the same time, a skilled horseman and a servant is a strange combination, but Richard Barber claims it is this dual combination that precisely defines these medieval warriors.

Knighthood had its advent in France and, to a lesser degree, in Germany in the early medieval period after the fall of Rome. Between the fifth and the seventh centuries, freemen, particularly in France, were required to fight for their king, or the king's representative, as foot soldiers in pitched battles and in small skirmishes, always close to home. In time horses were utilized and soldiers were now able to travel further afield. Because the stirrup had not yet been introduced, warriors in Central Europe always dismounted to fight but at least they arrived at the battle field fresh. As the elite soldiers were now wearing armour, the use of the horse was particularly advantageous and provided warriors mobility to react to enemy raids. Even so, fighting in the early middle ages tended to be *ad hoc*.

In the eighth century military campaigns became more complex. Charlemagne, not content to rule only France, required skilled soldiers of a higher calibre in order to establish his Carolingian Empire. With the introduction of the stirrup, brought to Europe in the late eighth century by the Arabs, warriors were now firmly seated and Charlemagne was able to organize professional cavalry to advance his various attacks. The influence of the Arabs also helped improve weaponry and equipment and campaigning in France and Germany became more effective. Because of the Arab invasion in Iberia and the ensuing struggle for supremacy, the inauguration of cavalry soldiers in Spain was very different and knighthood evolved more slowly and in its own very particular way. The ethos underpinning the Spanish knight was also unique and, to appreciate its evolution, I found it necessary first to understand the nature of French knights and then compare them with those on the Iberian Peninsula.

An army that relies heavily on cavalry is expensive. Even for a king such as Charlemagne, the price of equipping a large number of warriors with war horses and armour was unaffordable. The institution of vassalage avoided this problem. Introduced by the French, vassalage was a system involving land grants, or *fiefs*, initially given by the king to his aristocratic nobles in return for military aid and council. The estates were usually extensive and these barons became powerful men. In turn the king's men would cede part of their estate to lesser nobles who would use the entitlement to raise funds to provide themselves, and the men they drew to their following, with the necessary military equipment. Those who received land in this way became vassals. Because Europe practised the rule of primogeniture, there were many free-born noble sons who grew up without estates or assets and were willing to pledge themselves to battle in the hopes of gaining both a meaningful life style and a fortune.

The land grant was ceremonially formalized, the vassal kneeling and placing his hands in the king or lord's hands in an act of homage so establishing a strong bond of loyalty. The vassal was now honour-bound to serve his superior and the men in his following also helped to swell the royal cavalry. The arrangement usually worked, having its roots in earlier times when the Gothic tribes roamed Europe in tribal bands, each member fiercely loyal to his chieftain. In the ninth and tenth centuries these warriors, mounted and servants to a superior, called themselves knights. Today, however, historians do not categorized them as such, understanding knighthood as something more complex. Soldiers before the turn of the first millennium are now acknowledged to be no more than mounted warriors.

Tom Holland provides graphic descriptions of these minor vassals (or mounted warriors) as they roamed about France. Having to provide themselves with expensive chain-mail and maintain a war-horse to take into battle, a palfrey for everyday use and work horses for servants and baggage, vassals had to be adept at raising funds. Initially they became feuding warlords, provoking skirmishes wherever they could in the hopes of gaining battle booty or ransom money. While no doubt the warriors greatly enjoyed these endeavours, the French peasants came to dread these braggarts who trampled their crops as they hunted, looted their store-houses and callously torched their humble homes.

These noble free-born sons then demanded that the peasants help them raise funds. Where once they had been able to roam the woods and rivers, hunting and fishing to eke out a meagre existence, peasants were now expected to till the soil and reap large crops so their betters could skim off the surplus. Tolls and fines were imposed and much of the landscape was declared off-limits, the vassals needing these natural resources either for the building of their own new castles or to boost their coffers by way of sale. Life for the French medieval peasant had become intolerable. The mounted warriors, however, were having a fine time.

When I got to read *The Song of Roland* I found this poem testified to the ethos of this time. The oldest surviving work of French literature, the poem was, in its time, extremely popular. Believed to have been written between 1040 and 1090, it tells the story of a battle fought in 778 near Roncesvalles, then a small outpost in the Pyrenees. A Muslim attack is made on Charlemagne's rear guard as it marches through a narrow mountain pass on its return to France, Charlemagne having fought the infidel in Spain. The poem is also a tale of revenge and betrayal in which the tragic hero, Roland, dies. The poet tells us that upon his death he was fortunate in that angels took his soul to Paradise. Upon discovering the mutilated body of his favourite vassal, a furious Charlemagne pursues the murderers, chasing them into Spain where they all jump into the River Ebro and drown. On one level it is a moving story, but, to a twenty-first reader, the poignancy is seriously undercut by the poet's gleeful tone as he narrates his grisly tale, as well as by the extremely violent imagery. It is as though he, like the French warriors, is just as oblivious to suffering, delighted by human carnage and indifferent to death. This is one such stanzas.

Count Roland rides through the battlefields;
He holds Durendal, [his sword] which cuts and cleaves so well,
And wreaks great havoc among the Saracens.
What a sight to see body piled upon body
And all the clear blood spilled all around!
His hauberk [a shirt of chain mail] and his arms are red with blood,
And so are the neck and shoulders of his fine horse. (1338-1344)

The poet's vocabulary is positive and too cheerful for these gruesome descriptions. In this excerpt Roland's great companion fights with the hero,

Lord Oliver has drawn forth his fine sword,
Just as his companion insisted,
And he brandished it in knightly fashion.
He strikes a pagan Justin of Val Ferree,
Severing his head right down to the middle.
He slices through his body and his saffron byrnie [a sleeveless tunic of mail],
His fine saddle, ornamented with gold and gems,
And sliced through his horse's spine.
He flings him dead before him in the meadow.
Roland said: 'I recognize you brother.
For such blows the emperor loves us'.
On all sides there is a cry of 'Monjoie'. (lines 1367-1378)

The warriors are brave, strong and energetic, clothes colourful and the battle accoutrements rich and valuable. No doubt the savage deeds were appropriate for that time, but to twenty-first century sensibility they are dastardly. At the start the poem shocked me, but as I read, the sheer exaggeration and the bouncy pace made me laugh. I wondered if the readers of the time really took it seriously and if it was indeed a true reflection of the of the French nobleman's potential for violence. The story is still told today by many on the Camino, pilgrims having to navigate the pass where this battle allegedly took place.[14]

When this tale was composed the status of the mounted warrior in France was about to change. From thug he would gradually emerge as a knight proper: a rich, land-owning cavalry soldier who was expected to understand and practice the complex concept of chivalry.

Two specific medieval events helped to facilitate this shift. The first was a movement called 'The Peace and

---

[14] The poet in claiming the enemy as Muslim heathens is taking poetic licence. In reality Charlemagne's rear-guard was slaughtered by Basque guerrilla fighters.

Truce of God'. In the tenth century the church and various monastic houses in France decided it was time to control the trouble-making vassals and their various followers. Accordingly several serious proclamations were issued, all demanding peace. Initially this was to be granted to those who could not defend themselves, in particular the peasants and the clergy, but soon women were included, specifically virgins and widows. Monks were then added, as well as clerks, merchants and their servants, all chattels and various farm animals. For warriors who continued to pillage and plunder, the penalty was excommunication. However, without appropriate authorities, vandalism was impossible to regulate.

The aristocratic lords, unable to control their vassals and feeling their power was crumbling, supported the call for peace. In 972 a great rally was organized in Aurillac, the house of Saint Gerald, that pious model of how a warrior ought to behave (mentioned in the previous chapter). In 994 the influential monastery of Cluny buried deep in the Burgundian country also hosted a peace council.

The Cluny rally was truly magnificent. It was summer and rather than the constricting confines of a cathedral, an open field was chosen as the meeting place. Several bishops were invited and numerous other clergy, all adorned in rich vestments and carrying glittering crosses. From crypts all over France saintly relics were escorted to the peace site, led there by candlelit processions. Naturally there were miracles! Psalms were chanted and hymns sung.

In Tom Holland's opinion it must have seemed a magical occasion. Providing they promised to curtail their bellicose amusements, refrain from fighting for personal gain and battle instead for the glory of God, the warriors were welcomed. As knights in the service of God they were asked to make a pledge of peace, their oath sanctified by the relics. Sharing a ritual so awesome must have been compelling and they promised to comply, thus allowing themselves to become an honoured group with a specific identity. Unfortunately this glorious experience was insufficient to quell the knights' rumbustious spirits and they were unable to sustain the peace, but now as a more cohesive unit, they began to formulate a specific ideology for themselves. Chivalry was on the way to becoming an institution.

The second event that helped to elevate the status of the central European knight was The Council of Clermont inaugurated by Pope Urban II in 1095. Urban was a French aristocrat who had been raised in a castle. Now on tour in France, he not only appreciated the dire social situation, but also understood how to address the enthusiastic but morally depleted French free-born. Addressing them in their own language, his speech has been accepted as the most significant of all those delivered in the Middle Ages. He castigated the Frankish warriors for their continuing petty in-fighting and then offered the marauding troops a remarkable alternative. His address was not written down but was later summarized by Fulcher of Chartres, a chronicler who was present at the council. Fulcher's outline is long but is summed up in this paragraph.

"Let those who have formerly been accustomed to contend wickedly in private warfare against the faithful fight against the infidel, and bring to a victorious end the war which ought already to have been begun. Let those who have hitherto been robbers now become soldiers. Let those who have formerly contended against their brothers and relatives now fight against the barbarians as they ought. Let those who have formerly been mercenaries at low wages now gain eternal rewards. Let those who have been exhausting themselves to the detriment both of body and soul now strive for a twofold reward..."

The two-fold reward was the saving of the soul of each individual knight and bringing to fruition the Christian church as universally triumphant, feats supposedly achieved by eliminating from the world the 'evil and unrepentant infidel' now occupying Jerusalem. Sceptical historians also suggest there may have been a papal hope of adding to the church coffers the gains to be won by way of eastern treasure and general battle booty. To achieve this Christians, initially those from France and Germany, were now expected to engage in this 'superior' kind of warfare defined by slaughtering Muslims in the Holy Land as opposed to the French peasants. The warriors were told not only that crusading was a moral and upright undertaking, but that it was also sanctioned by God, his approval manifest that same year by way of a meteor shower.

For the warriors to be worthy of their mission, they were now also expected to become upright and honourable. Bernard of Clairvaux supported the crusading. Having already instituted the Knights Templar, he charged the would-be French crusaders to follow the lead of the Templars and not 'deck themselves in gold and silver, but with faith within and mail without and to strike terror, not avarice into the hearts of their enemies'. Because the Spanish were by this time already engaged in crusading against Islam on their own home-front, Urban forbade Spain from participating in the East, though there were some who did not obey this directive.

In the twenty-first century announcements like this seem extraordinary when issued from the mouths of eminent churchmen supposed to promulgate a religion founded on love and peace, but by the time of the Crusades, the idea of a 'holy war' had been firmly established. As far back as the fourth century Saint Augustine had claimed that war was allowable if undertaken 'in obedience to the divine command'. (I am always astonished that some people can have such certitude about what the Divine 'commands'!) Augustine also asserted that 'to put to death wicked men' did not violate the commandment, 'Thou shalt not kill'. Several centuries later Thomas Aquinas expanded these ideas, arguing that 'holy war' was permissible providing it was instituted by a proper authority and was fought with the right intentions, not for self-gain. It is easy enough to find glaring flaws in these arguments. Nevertheless, the prospect of the Crusades allowed braggart warriors to be transformed into 'Knights of Christ'.

At the start, Christ's Knights were spectacularly successful (from a Western perspective). However, Abu Sa'ad al-Harawi, a venerable *qadi*[15] from Jerusalem, having completely shaved his head as a sign of his deep mourning, arrived in Baghdad in August, 1099 to report to Islam's highest authorities the terrible calamities wrought by the invading '*Franj*', (the French). He explained they had arrived in the city that year on the 15th of July. After a forty day siege the 'blond warriors' had penetrated the city, pouring into the streets, swords in hand, slaughtering men, women and children, plundering houses, sacking mosques and raping women before murdering them. In two days not a single Muslim was left alive. Wringing his hands and lamenting, Al-Harawi claimed thousands lay in their blood on the door-steps of their homes and alongside their mosques. The last survivors were forced to perform the worst task of all: to

---

[15] An Arab judge administrating religious law.

heave the bodies of their dead relatives into vacant lots and there set them alight before they, too, were massacred. 'Never' said al-Harawi, 'have Muslims been so humiliated'.

The fate of Jerusalem's Jews was no less atrocious. In fear they had crowded into the main synagogue to pray and there found themselves barricaded in by the '*Franj*' who surrounded the entire building with all the wood they could find, torching it and burning every Jew alive. Those who managed to escape were hacked down.

Crusades such as this continued for approximately two hundred years. Five more major campaigns were launched and numerous minor ones. In spite of the first stunning success they ultimately failed, the Christians unable to gain a permanent foothold in the Holy Land. By granting Jerusalem to the Infidels one may presume Christ was displeased with his Knights, many of whom had also been unsuccessful in gaining treasure or the 'holy grace' they had initially expected. Nevertheless, at the turn of the first millennium these killers were generally understood by their contemporaries as Europe's prestigious and fully-fledged knights.

To advance to their elevated status it was now necessary for a would-be knight to undergo a lengthy apprenticeship as a squire. While still a young adolescent he would be placed in a large aristocratic household with several other squires where they all underwent extensive training in arms: learning the skills of horsemanship as well as the art of using weapons, in particular a sword, shield and lance. He would also learn the mores and culture that would eventually shape his character and regulate his status. The ideals and rituals by which he was now governed became the rules of chivalry.

Chivalry, too, had its origins in France, the term derived from the old French *chevalerie* meaning 'horse soldiery'. With time it evolved into something highly complex and difficult to define. As well as dealing with practical concerns, like battle etiquette and how to treat women, chivalry was also understood by the more astute medievals as a moral system based on nebulous ideals that combined the old warrior ethos with courtly manners, values that, to modern ears, seem unrelated. Maurice Keen goes so far as to question if the concept of chivalry and knighthood had ever been anything more than a polite veneer, a means by which a warrior could relieve 'the bloodiness of his life'. However, in romance literature both aspects, the practical concerns as well as the ideals, are important and knights spoken of in exalted terms. Not only were they expected to win battles single-handed, traverse enchanted forests and generally perform incredible feats, their general bearing had to reflect ethical and religious qualities.

In time manuals were written to explain how knights were meant to conduct themselves in battle, in court and in love. I found Ramon Llull's *The Book of the Order of Chivalry* written between 1279 and 1283 an intriguing mix. Llull, in his youth had been a one-time Spanish knight and troubadour who was heavily influenced by the French tradition. Abandoning this calling, he became a philosopher as well as a scholar within the Third Order of Saint Francis and was eventually martyred for his missionary zeal. He starts his text as a lively narrative; a young squire on his way to court and hopeful of becoming a knight, falls into conversation with 'a good hermit knight'. This hermit, in explaining Llull's philosophy, tells the squire of the knight's social function, as well as highlighting his spiritual prerequisites. He, too, insists knights be of noble birth and uphold justice. He advocates squires be of mature age before their knighting so they can 'inspire terror in ordinary folk and so prevent them from doing wrong'. He also warns that mere bodily strength and boldness will not suffice. This excerpt epitomizes his general idealism.

"Seek not noble courage in speech, for speech is not always truth; seek it not in rich clothes, for many a fine habit conceals cowardice, treachery and evil; seek it not in your horse, for it cannot speak to you; seek it not in fine harness and equipment, for they too often conceal an evil and cowardly heart. Seek noble courage in faith, hope, charity, justice, moderation, loyalty...."

Possibly the book is too didactic for general reading, except for those interested in the mores and ethos of the medieval world—or if you yourself want to become a knight!

The squire in Llull's narrative is very young but in the real medieval world a French squire, unless he came from a high-ranking family, might have to wait many years before he could afford to become a knight or gain the necessary prestige for himself by way of notable military action. When his moment did come he would be 'dubbed', the ritual by which he was elevated.

Keen, discussing the knighting ritual in France, warns that it might have been a ceremony found more often in Romance literature than in real life. The ritual is described in Geoffroi de Charny, *A Knight's Own Book of Chivalry*, written in the early 1350s. On the eve of his promotion the squire was expected to confess his sins and then take communion. He was also to bathe so that he could cleanse his body of all filth and, at the same time, recall his baptism and the fact that he has Christian responsibilities. He was then required to sleep in a new, clean bed, a hopeful emblem of his final repose in heaven should he live as a good Christian. On the morn of the ceremony he was garbed in a new white robe to remind himself always to remain distant from sin, and over this was placed a scarlet cloak indicative of the blood he was going to shed in defence of his country and church.

While these rituals were Christian in orientation, no priest was required, knights always dubbed by another knight of good standing, sometimes the king but more often the lord under whom he had served his apprenticeship. To us in the twenty-first century this ceremony may sound somewhat underplayed for such a momentous occasion. However, there were initiations that were more significant, like those made in dire circumstances on the battle field and those undergone by the Knights Templar.

The Templars were a unique and mysterious order of knights who even today capture popular imagination. Because they had also served in Spain, I took particular interest in them. Templars differed from other French knights in that their order had been specifically founded by Bernard of Clairvaux and constituted so that they were answerable to no-one but the Pope. They were also a monastic order and were expected to live as monks as well as being warriors. In the Holy Land they proved to be fighters of exceptional strength and bravery.

The Templars had also developed innovative financial techniques in Europe and managed a large economic organization, becoming exceptionally wealthy and extremely powerful. Naturally they made enemies, in particular King Philip IV of France who was deeply in their debt. When rumours began to circulate about their scandalous initiation ceremony, Philip took advantage of the gossip and demanded that the pope of the time, Clement V, excommunicate all the knights as heretics. Clement was reluctant, but, because he was ill and Philip a close blood relative, the pontiff eventually acquiesced. Contravening the conventions of the order, the trials of the Grand Master and scores of his knights were heard not in the Vatican but in France.

Philip accused them of sodomy, financial misconduct, fraud, secrecy, idolatry, cursing God and heathen practices. Tortured by the Inquisition, many were forced to confess. Burned at the stake, their deaths were unlawful, the Templars answerable to no-one else but the Pope. Nevertheless Clement, too ill to do otherwise, grudgingly disbanded the order. At the time these unfortunate knights accrued much sympathy and in a short while fantastical rumours began to circulate. Today their story is still shrouded in mystery.

In reading about the Templars I found two things of particular interest. The first was their controversial initiation ceremony. Official records reveal that initially this 'dubbing' was almost as simple as that of other European knights. In a private room the candidate was brought before a high-ranking Templar who examined him and then addressed him thus:

Sir, you see us well clothed and provided with the best horses, but very few know what our souls must withstand. If you become a Templar, you will have to face difficult challengers, hear outrageous words and accept them with patience, and obey your superiors no matter what they command you to do. Will you be able to bear the unbearable?'

The candidate replied, 'Sir, with God's help I can bear anything'. The would-be Templar would then recite the three monastic vows of poverty, chastity and obedience, remove his lay garments and don his religious garb. Once his mantle had been clasped in place, he would be a Templar knight. Believing that the ceremony was concluded, the knight in his new regalia then found himself led to secluded place, often the sacristy or behind the high altar. Here he would be told, 'Sir, all the vows you have made to us are empty words. Now you will have to prove yourself to us with deeds'. Without explanation, the new Templar would be told to deny Christ and then spit on the cross. The astonished novice was understandably distressed, but, having gained his senses, he would usually refuse. Reminded of the promise just made of total obedience, some did spit, some spat but avoided the cross, some totally refused.

At their trial some knights claimed their response to the spitting, whatever it was, had been respected, but more often there were others who said because of their botched spitting they had been threatened with prison or death. Some reported to have been beaten. Finally the new Templar was given the kiss of monastic brotherhood but scandalously on the mouth instead of the cheek. Shockingly, this was followed by the demand that the novice next kiss the master's belly and then his bare posterior. At the end of the ceremony the 'victim' of all these impositions was invited to visit the Templars' chaplain and confess his newly committed sins. The confession made and the knight absolved, the penitents were always told their offences had not been grave and that there would be no physical or spiritual consequences. They were then sworn to secrecy.

Even in the twenty-first century this ceremony seems not only immoral but also blasphemous, but it did have a purpose. This was determined by Doctor Barbara Frale. Granted permission to research in the Vatican Secret Archives in 2001, Frale discovered the Chinon Parchment, the second fact about the Templars that I found so interesting. The Parchment was a document which had been inadvertently hidden for centuries, misfiled in the Vatican's vast archival collections. The paper reveals the bitter tensions and acrimony between Pope Clement and Philip IV. At this point in the Templar trials the Pope was in France at Poitiers. He was desperately ill. He had heard the confessions of a large number of Templars and now wanted to speak with the Grand Master, Jacques de Molay and four other high-ranking officers in order to clarify the situation. He asked Philip to have these knights sent to Poitiers. Instead they were delivered to Chinon Castle sixty miles away. Too ill to travel, the Pope sent three cardinals to the Castle to listen to the officers' testimonies and confessions and directed the cardinals to compile an official record of their findings. This was the Chinon document. Ultimately Molay and his officials were found to be innocent. All five were acquitted of the charge of heresy.

From the cardinals' findings, Frale realized that the outrageous ordeal the Templar candidates had had to undergo at the time of their initiation had a dual purpose. On one level the secret ceremony was a 'test' designed to reveal the novices' true character: whether they had courage, pride, determination and a capacity for self-control, qualities necessary for front-line combat. If they had instead displayed timidity, an excessive readiness to obey or undue arrogance they would be assigned to different duties, maybe agricultural or domestic. Rather than warriors, some might also be prized for their diplomatic or administrative skills.

The initiation indignities were also intended to prepare the warrior knights for the sort of humiliations they might receive in Jerusalem should they be captured. Frale also discovered a letter written by the cardinals to Philip IV informing the king of the plenary absolution the Pope had granted to these five top officials. But Philip, bent on exterminating the Order, took no notice and condemned de Molay and one other to die a slow agonizing death by fire in Paris on the island in the River Seine. The ordeal was watched by many sympathizers.

Before their collapse the Templars also operated in Spain, there to defend pilgrims on their way to Santiago, as well as to crusade against the Muslim intruders. Passing through Ponferrada, Terence and I visited an abandoned Templar castle. It is now a ruin, but the gate-house had recently been restored. In bright sunshine and with a colourful pennant flapping in the breeze, the edifice looked more like a setting from a Walt Disney movie than a real medieval fortress. A modern museum in the ruined interior precincts also detracted from the castle's mystique. Having completed our exploration, we took afternoon tea in a café nestled outside in the shadow of the castle wall. Observed from this low viewpoint, the ruin was much more impressive, the wall at this point not only intact and towering but mightily substantial, its seeming impenetrable density protecting supposed Templar secrets and suggesting there was indeed something obscure and arcane about these fighting men.

Where it was not possible for me to imagine the Templars in the castle's interior, I could visualise these knights as I sat below that formidable wall. They were resplendent in faintly tinkling chainmail covered by pure white over-mantles, the Templar red cross emblazoned on their breasts. While I am not an admirer of the Crusades and deplore not only the carnage caused but also the unhealable breach between Christianity and Islam, I, too, have sympathy for these particular knights, not just because they were betrayed and victimized but because of their commitment and the fact that they lived the ideal to which they aspired.

So far most of what I have said relates to knights in France. They were always of noble birth and their calling in life was warfare. When not fighting, knights filled in their leisure time by listening to minstrels, wooing ladies and engaging in mock warfare practised by way of extravagant tournaments. In Spain, however, the character of knighthood was very different, particularly at the start. This was because of the Muslim invasion in 711. In a brief seven years the Moors totally scattered the entire Christian Visigoth aristocracy who, at that time, had control of Spain. Having been disbanded, it is unknown what happened to these original noble families. It is believed some were eventually integrated into the Muslim culture. Others scattered, fleeing to Asturias, a small kingdom in the far north-west. Where the French knights were always drawn from those of long-standing noble lineage, in Spain they had to evolve from out a social order in complete disarray.

Asturias is mountainous and remote, with no towns of note and the weather mostly dismal. Here the remnants of the Christian Visigoths established themselves as a new society. The Moors, used to hot desert conditions, eschewed pushing north at this point and for a while the Christians lived in peace. This is recorded fact. Folk-lore however, tells a different tale.

A tenth century Latin text, *The Chronicle of Alfonso III*, written on the order of this monarch, tells of a fearsome northern hero, Pelayo, sword-bearer to the Christian king and believed to be a distant relative of

Roderic, the defeated Visigoth ruler. Alfonso's text claims that eleven years after the Moorish invasion, Pelayo and a band of brave comrades were confronted by a massive army of 187,000 Islamic soldiers. Though counselled on the eve of the battle by the bishop of the time not to engage the enemy, Pelayo, encouraged by the Virgin Mary, remained undeterred and the following morning marched forth with his small army.

A wondrous mountain battle ensued. Saint James not yet roused, God himself stepped in, hurling back at the Muslims the rocks released from their catapults. Then a miraculous earth tremor flung those Muslims not yet slain right off the mountain. Every Moor perished and Pelayo was victorious. The chronicler then proffers a warning to possible sceptics. It reads, 'Do not think this to be unfounded or fictitious. Remember that He who parted the waters of the Red Sea so that the children of Israel might cross, also crushed with an immense mass of mountain, the Arabs who were persecuting the church of God'.

It is a good story and even contains a grain of truth. There was a real Pelayo whose small army did fight against Arabs in Asturias, but in a deep narrow valley where they could defend themselves from a frontal attack and so prevail against the enemy. This was the Battle of Covadonga. The rest is all fantasy, historians claiming that the convincingly precise casualty tally of 187,000 would have been many multiples of Spain's total Muslim population at that time. Nevertheless, Chris Lowney, who retells the tale in his work, *A Vanished World: Muslims, Christians, and Jews in Medieval Spain*, maintains its value lay in its mythic quality. After decades of retelling, a vital link was established: the Christians must not only protect themselves from the Moors, but also understand that the Visigoths had been Iberia's rightful rulers and had the duty to reunite Spain under Christian rule.

Where the skirmishes and fighting of the French warriors could be seen to have a frivolous underpinning and most French crusaders marching forth only in the hopes of gaining booty, on the Iberian Peninsula war, and the warriors who fought, were serious, at least at the start. Unlike the French Crusaders who initially travelled to the Holy Land in search of adventure, the Spaniards were fighting on home soil. Theirs was not an exciting escapade, but a grim endeavour. The foe was not imagined. In due course Spain became a frontier country, the Spaniards' purpose to reconquer their usurped land. The task was daunting but, with the Moors now on their doorstep in the north, King Alfonso's disbanded people were once more united. The small geographical extent of his kingdom was also an advantage, affording him control over his officials. His few magnates and churchmen rallied and a plan began to emerge. At the start it was little more than a dream which eventually came to fruition.

His army being small and ill-disciplined, Alfonso was unable to attack the enemy directly so his strategy had to be circumspect and turned out to be very long-term indeed. It was decided that the vast tracks of arid, uninhabited land south and east of Asturias were to be populated. By building and garrisoning many fortified castles and estates, the Christians planned to boost their army gradually and then move towards the enemy concentrated in the south. The new settlements would also act as a buffer, protecting the northern kingdom from the marauding hordes.

The colonization began in what became León and Castile, Castile taking its name from the Spanish *Castillo* meaning castle. Lacking a powerful aristocracy with grand estates, vassals and a large following, the king initially commissioned his few magnates to organize the settlement of the newly recovered land by resorting to a system of benefice: the conditional granting of land as a reward for providing soldiers by whom the Moors could be held at bay. This land was granted to commoners and so the benefice was not noble.

To combat the enemy the Spanish warriors had to be mounted. In Spain it was easier for a relatively impecunious man to mount himself and a few men, the cost of good horses being considerably less that it was in France. Many took advantage of this land offer. Unlike France, the benefice did not entail vassalage as there was no 'commending' or 'homage', no ceremonial ritual or knighthood mystique. Should a warrior not survive the battle-field, his horse and armour had to be returned to the donor. Where French knights were granted hereditary rites, Spanish cavalry-men were initially denied this privilege. Called *caballeros*, a term which translates as 'commoner-knight', they became frontier men and played a dominant role in Spanish military history, particularly after 1085 when Toledo was captured from the Muslims. This class of non-noble cavalrymen was unique to Spain.

On the frontier it was the duty of the *caballeros* to guard the villages and new small towns, as well as to fight. The new settlers gained their livelihood through stockbreeding, a more practical form of farming, the plains being arid and the animals easily moved when danger threatened. However, sheep, cattle and particularly horses were attractive booty and theft was frequent as well as lucrative for both Christians and Muslims and the *caballeros* were not only kept busy but, over time, also established a new social order; one that was conservative, grounded in reality and serious about its endeavours. Such people also had to be robust and resilient.

I wish I had known about these commoner-knights as I trudged through the central Meseta plain on my Camino walk. The thought of these unusual knights and their galloping horses would have enriched the barren landscape and could also have put me in mind of the cowboy and Indian movies I had sometimes watched as a child. Both frontiers share similar characteristics: dust, big open skies, insecurity, cattle-rustling, horse-breaking and lawlessness.

The Reconquest of Spain continued for approximately 781 years and, according to one Spanish historian, three thousand seven hundred major battles were fought before the last of the Moorish kingdoms submitted to the rule of the Christian monarchs, Ferdinand and Isabella. Over the centuries the intensity of the struggle would wax and wane and the antagonism was never consistent. This was because the north was now divided into several separate Christian kingdoms. Sometimes a monarch from one would make an alliance with a certain Muslim king in the south against a Christian rival in the north. Strife between the Christians, as well as against the Moors, was ever present and accepted as the way of life.

In spite of the unrest, a new Spanish aristocracy gradually emerged, consolidated and, like the French, became exceptionally powerful. Unlike the French, this class was neither frivolous nor irresponsible. Soon after the turn of the first millennium this privileged class had evolved into two kinds: the *ricos hambres*, who were the richer and more prestigious, and the lesser *hidalgos*. In time both were defined in terms of lineage, blood purity and an exaggerated sense of honour in one's personal worth as well as in one's social standing. The grandee *ricos hambres* who owned great estates and now also oversaw vassals, took part in palace intrigues and sought royal favours. Without great wealth the *hidalgo's* sole capital was his honour. Like France, Spain also told tales about heroes who emerged from these classes, the most famous being that of El Cid, a man who lost his honour and had to struggle to regain it.

The Cid was a Castilian Spaniard, a *hidalgo*, though the author does not use this term. His real name was Rodrigo Díaz. The name Cid is derived from the Arabic word *Sidi* meaning 'lord' or 'master' and was bestowed on Rodrigo after his death. In his day he was known as *Campeador*, a prestigious Spanish title meaning 'battle master'. He is reputed to have been born in a small town called Viver close to Burgos. The year is thought to be 1043. While the French battle at Roncesvalles was fought in 778, the Roland poem was composed more or less at the same time the Cid was alive and fighting in Spain.

The Cid's family was loyal to Ferdinand I, King of León and Castile. In his early teens, Rodrigo, astute in the practice of arms, was placed in the household of the king's eldest son, Sancho, heir to the throne, and started his career by becoming a squire. Upon Sancho's ascension as Sancho II in 1065, Rodrigo was made commander and royal standard-bearer and was soon famous for his military prowess. After a reign of seven years Sancho died and his brother Alfonso VI took the throne. Rodrigo continued to serve the crown, but he lost his status at court. Jealousy, intrigue and treachery resulted in his unjust exile to Zaragoza, a city held by the Muslims. Here he not only befriended the enemy but also learnt of their ways. These are the historical facts about Rodrigo Díaz and precede the story told in *The Poem of El Cid*.

The Cid's subsequent, and mostly fictitious, exploits were anonymously recorded fifty years or so after his death, sufficient time for a burgeoning oral tradition to have blossomed into a fanciful epic tale, but, unlike Roland's story, this one did not make me laugh. The telling is childish but straightforward and not overly emotional. The story starts with Rodrigo's exile in 1081. Before he abandons Burgos he visits the cathedral. His prayers are earnest. He is in tears, having placed his wife, Jimena, and their two daughters in ecclesiastical care, but he does not remain downcast for long. A contingent of disinherited and impecunious warriors eagerly follow Rodrigo, no doubt captivated by his charisma and eager to win a fortune.

By raiding frontier towns and conniving with the Muslims, making them pay tribute in return for the Cid's protection, this outlaw band soon becomes very rich. While he is supposedly fighting the enemy, Rodrigo's exploits can hardly be recognized as a crusade. Unlike Roland, high principles are of small consequence to the Cid. He is much too practical, his focus on the accumulation of wealth. Since he won every battle in which he engaged, Rodrigo not only gains fame and great fortune, but also claws back his lost status at court. Because he always apportions a share of the booty to the king, Alfonso mellows and is eventually placated. He even allows Jimena to join her husband.

The Cid's wealth is coveted by the two infantes, princes of Carrión. These noblemen propose marriage to the Cid's daughters. At the king's bidding Rodrigo agrees to the match but the husbands soon reveal themselves to be scheming, dishonest and cruel. As Richard Fletcher points out in his review of this text, *The Quest for El Cid*, Rodrigo takes great pleasure in ridiculing them. Cowards, they vent their shame and anger on their new wives, taking them into the forest where they are stripped, beaten and abandoned.

The two deserted brides are rescued by the Cid's right-hand man and returned to their father. Even though the Cid is quite capable of wreaking his own vengeance, he decides to sue for justice before the king. As the trial is being heard, messengers arrive from Navarre and Aragon. The kings of these two realms want the spurned daughters as marriage partners. Honour is thus restored, even though the legend makes no mention of divorce or annulment. The dispute with the two infantes is also resolved, not by royal pronouncement, but by pitting the denounced husbands against the Cid's knights in a splendid joust. Naturally they are soundly thrashed. Rodrigo returns to Valencia, the great city he took from the Moors and the tale ends with mention of the daughters' grand wedding feast.

As Roland was for the French, the Cid can be seen as an exemplar of a Spanish mounted warrior, even though the poet fails to provide the kind of battle evidence found in the *Roland* poem. Battle mayhem was part of everyday life and in all probability descriptions of it would not have interested a Spanish audience. Where Roland was a tragic gallant and capable of rousing pathos, the Cid's being is earthier and grounded in reality and not only demonstrates the Spanish as a more practical people adept at coping with struggle, but also removes from Spanish knighthood that sense of grandeur. Where the French understood the profession of knighthood as having some sort of mystique and those bearing arms as always morally magnanimous, this tale demonstrates the Spanish hero as more resolute, simply providing real facts: inside information about the difficulties of funding an army and the savage in-fighting and instability of a country continually at war.

Like Roland, the Cid is an honourable character, but he is also flawed. He swindles the Jewish money lenders and has no qualms about stealing a vast sum of money. He fights on both sides, on occasion championing the Muslims, at other times opposing them. While the Moors are the enemy, he never derogates them by calling them 'villains' or 'treacherous pagans' who 'deserve to be condemned to death', (Roland's words), but treats them as human beings. He uses cunning to get his way and is not loath to compromise his principles. But he also loves his wife and is meticulous in the treatment of his warriors, paying them well and never neglecting even the least of them. And he is loyal to his king.

Because he is a much more rounded character who exhibits nobility as well as failings, I cannot but prefer the Cid. As the tale is told I agree with King Alfonso's praise, 'by St. Isidore of León, there is no other such warrior in all our lands'. Even so, I was astonished when visiting Burgos to discover the Cid's tomb had been erected in the very centre of the cathedral directly under the dome. While a likeable being, I questioned if he had indeed been sufficiently honourable for this great privilege.

I discovered the Spanish deal with honour in a very specific way. For the nobility it was affirmed by blood and its 'purity'. Where the French demanded of their nobility a blood-line true to ancient lineage, the Spanish assessed purity of blood by the honour of being born Christian. That the Cid is of this persuasion is not doubted, and evidenced in his fulsome prayers before leaving Burgos, promises of the gifts he intends to donate to the Cathedral, his knowledge of Scripture, the fact that the Angel Gabriel appears in his dreams and his constant appeal to God throughout the tale.

Because the poem was written at the turn of the millennium, it was important for the poet to emphasize the Cid's good religious standing, not only because the Spanish placed great store on the church, but because at this time 'purity laws' had been established and nobles, anxious of attaining high office, had to produce evidence to prove that their blood had never been tainted by that of a Muslim, a Jew or heretic. Where, in the past there may have been unfortunate marital misadventures, false genealogies would be contrived. This, of course, was spared the Cid, both his blood and Christian character being exemplary. The chronicler was able to conclude the tale by saying, 'See how his honour increases, he who in a happy hour was born, for the Kings of Spain are now among his kinsmen!' Though a historical being who had fallen short of the crown, the Cid could nevertheless be framed as a mythic hero and given prestigious burial space.

At the turn of the millennium Spanish knights were dubbed much the same way as they were in France and were also expected to ride forth and prove their worth. Travelling in northern Spain, both on the Camino and later with Terence, the only time I was made aware of this sort of knight errant was in Hospital de Órbigo.

In Roman times this small town on the banks of the River Órbigo had been an important control point, but in the thirteenth century it belonged to the Knights Templar. The 'hospital' was once a medieval pilgrim hospice belonging to the Knights of Saint John but nothing of it now remains. Even in the 1500s it was non-existent, the sixteenth century pilgrim, Laffi, telling of the miserable night he spent there because he had to sleep on the ground, there being no accommodation. The town is celebrated because of its extremely long and very elegant Gothic bridge, reputed to be one of the most beautiful in Spain. Over the centuries it has been damaged by flood and battle, but those responsible for its ongoing renovation have maintained its original aspect. Unfortunately a very large and glaring neon sign advertising a hotel on the far side of the bridge detracts from its medieval mystique. In 1434 a Leonese knight of noble standing and great courage organized a very impressive 'Honourable

Crossing' on this bridge. His name was Suero de Quiñones.

Suero's story sounds like a fairy tale but it is mostly true, embellished by a little exaggeration, though in the various versions I read I found it difficult to sort out the fiction from the fact. It is a story of unrequited love. Suero had for a long time been devoted to Dona Ines de Tovar in true courtly fashion. To himself he proved his love by fasting every Thursday and on the same day wearing an iron collar round his neck to demonstrate to his lady that he was indeed bound to her. Dona Ines was quite unmoved. In an effort to further his suit, he arranged what is now considered to have been Europe's last true medieval tournament. I find it strange that an exhibition of battle tactics can prove one's love but these were medieval times and Suero went to considerable trouble with his preparations. First he gained permission from King Juan II to hold the tourney and then issued the challenge to nobility all over Europe.

In due course the very best lancers flocked to Spain to fight with him. The jousting lists and spectator pavilions were duly built beside the Órbigo Bridge and along the river bank. On the adjacent road which led pilgrims to Santiago, Suero erected a herald in the form of an opulently dressed, life-size mannequin pointing the way to the jousting site. The tournament was scheduled to begin two weeks before the feast day of Saint James, a time when pilgrim traffic would be at its most extreme. Once the tournament commenced those knights travelling on the road and wishing to cross the bridge had first to joust. This challenge was known as the 'Honourable Crossing'. If the knight refused, he had to leave a glove on the bridge as a sign of his cowardice and wade across the river.

The tournament lasted a month and in that time Suero is reputed to have broken three hundred lances. Some accounts claim that he ended the tournament jubilantly victorious; others say he was so wounded and weary he was barely alive. Whatever his condition, his lady remained unimpressed. Removing his iron collar, Suero said he was finally released from his 'prison of love' and now a free man. Greatly applauded, he departed from Órbigo, leading a procession all the way back to León from whence he had come.

In León with Terence I visited the modest palace to which he returned. It is now in poor condition but its large, double-fronted door sporting the family arms is very impressive. Once he had fully recovered, he made a pilgrimage to Santiago where he left a jewel-encrusted golden bracelet as a token of his release from the prison of love. It is on display in the cathedral museum.

Today there is a grove of poplars where the tournament is said to have taken place. When Terence and I stood on the bridge and gazed into the trees it was as though we could still hear the stamping and whinnying of horses, the musicians' blaring fanfare, the clash of arms and the jovial light-hearted banqueting. I even heard the church bells beckoning the knights to the obligatory mass said every day before the jousting began. I am glad I only imagined it as I am sure I would not have enjoyed it live.

My initial thought had been of a carefree and entertaining tournament. However, from the accounts that I have read, Spanish knighthood was governed by rigid formalism, was exceptionally stern in its ideals and practical in its achievements. As a dour people tempered by centuries of military struggle and Christian indoctrination, it is possible that Suero's tournament may well have been formal and reserved. While there were individual knights engaged in errantry, the kind of knighthood that best suited these conservative people was the sort that combined the knightly fighting spirit with monastic orders. The Templars were such knights, looked after by an abbot who attended to their spiritual well-being, as well as by a master who was in charge of the military campaigning. The knights belonging to these orders were not only expected to go forth and battle, but to do so with single-minded religious zeal. When not at war they returned to their monasteries and lived as monks.

That the church and the military could be so linked seems unusual in modern times, the church generally associated with passivity. Today we in the West are also inclined to regard peace as the normal way of being and conflict the exception. This was not the case in medieval times. Once the church became a political force somewhere round the eleventh century, it needed the military. Prohibited from engaging in battle on the grounds that all clerics were committed to prayer, pastoral ministration and spiritual needs, the church depended on knights not only for protection but also to threaten. As a consequence this institution had a great deal to say about how knights should think and conduct themselves. Eminent churchmen told them they were the 'strong arm' of the church and stridently demanded that all knights 'do the bidding of this superior order'. John of Salisbury defined knighthood as a profession instituted by God. For these men, using arms to defend the faith, as well as the poor and downtrodden, was normal. Combat was their sole function in life. When Sir John Hawkwood, an English knight at that time in Italy fighting for the Florentine Republic, was greeted by two Italian friars who wished him peace he replied, 'Peace! Do you not know I live by war and that peace would be my undoing?'

As the Reconquest advanced, military religious orders were more enthusiastically welcomed in Spain than anywhere else in Europe. The Templars were the first to come, but on Spanish soil they were reluctant fighters, complaining that the Spanish too often fought each other instead of uniting against the Islamic enemy. Local orders were soon established, all dominated by a strong chivalric ethos.

The order having the most influence on the Camino was the prestigious Order of Santiago. Its origin in the 1170s was secular, established by a brotherhood of thirteen knights who, appalled by the way the way in which their fellow Christians fought each other, renounced all earthly vanities and vowed never to unsheathe their swords against another of their own kind. Instead they promised to devote themselves to slaying heathens! The Santiago insignia is a red cross simulating a sword with a *fleur de lis* on the hilt and both ends of the cross-arm. Their motto translates as, 'My sword is red with Arab blood' and illustrates the combative temperament of these men. The order also provided a hospice for pilgrims travelling to Santiago and redeemed those prisoners taken by the Arabs.

When they were established as a religious house, these knights were formally placed under the protection of Saint James himself and the master of the community admitted as a canon of the cathedral. The order opted for the Augustinian Rule, living as canons. The Santiago knights were unique in that members were permitted to have wives, often quoting Saint Paul who said, 'it is better to marry than to burn'. Their headquarters in the kingdom of León was the monastery of San Marcos in the city of León. The sheer size of this building is sufficient to evoke awe. Built in splendid Renaissance style and standing in an extensive and very formal square, it is another intimidating ecclesiastical building that seems to contradict the edict that those in monastic orders should practise poverty.

The Order of Santiago still exists but under the Spanish crown. In 2014 there were thirty-five knights and thirty novices. As it was of old, admission to the order is open only to applicants of noble ancestry and still measured by way of 'blood purity', not by privilege or great deeds. In the Santiago cathedral Terence spotted two of these knights in the choir while mass was being said. They were identified by the bloody cross emblazoned on the left shoulder of their white copes. Hopefully these knights no longer fight.

Of course Terence and I went to visit San Marcos. The monastery is now converted into an exclusive parador. We decided to take afternoon tea in the beautiful lounge, a placard telling us this room had once been the monastery chapter-house. Our repast complete, I suggested we look through the other public rooms, but Terence is conservative and polite and decided to stay where he was. For this I was grateful because it meant I could make a much more thorough and very intrusive and impolite investigation. I was fortunate that, when I got upstairs, the cleaners were still about and I managed to see into many rooms. What I found amazed me. The building was so opulent, the beamed rooms and various suites so spacious and the rough walls so thick, the doors intricately carved and the staircases sweeping.

The church artwork and upper cloister were even more extravagant. I found no evidence of monks' cells or communal living. Instead it felt as though I was in some kind of important palace. I wondered where they could have stabled the war horses and where the monks had practised their battle skills. In my explorations I found no lingering trace of those fiery fighting medieval monks, or of the pilgrims to whom they had supposedly ministered. Later I learned that the poor had been catered for in a separate building alongside the nearby river. The noble elite did not mix with the masses!

The Camino track covers barren plains, undulating wheat fields and secretive forests. There are mountain climbs, but they are few and not too rugged. Most ranges are on the far horizon, lofty but level impersonal lines of distant rock rising steeply into the shimmering sky. Obdurate, they reveal no story. Under the spaciousness of the Spanish sky there is nothing to tell the contemporary pilgrim what it must have been like to be a *caballero* or an adventuring knight errant. Were they as brave, proud and jubilant as the Romance tales suggest? Or were these stories simply told to spur on lagging hearts? How had the military knights managed in their armour as they rode forth to face the foe? Whatever the weather, wearing a metal suit could only have been excruciating: agonizingly hot in a Spanish summer and almost unendurable in the cold. Even the sunshine on a balmy spring day would intensify the temperature inside a metallic helmet. How did they cope with sneezing and nose blowing, body smells and the scratching of prickly heat rash? Or were such irritants too trifling for men focussed only on war? When I walked the Camino I was rarely reminded of battle cries and spilt blood, mayhem and murder. Unless one makes an effort it is as though the medieval knights have melted into air. All that remains are benign knightly confraternities whose members wear ecclesiastical garb and not armour.

Works cited in this chapter

Barber, Richard. *The Knight and Chivalry*. Woodbridge, UK: The Boydell Press. 2000.

Barton, Simon. *The Aristocracy in Twelfth-Century Léon and Castile*. Cambridge, UK: Cambridge University Press. 1997.

Burgess, Glyn, trans. *The Song of Roland*. London: Penguin Books. 1990.

Charny, Geoffroi de, trans Elspeth Kennedy. *A Knight's Own Book of Chivalry*. Philadelphia, Penn: University of Pennsylvania Press. 2005.

Defourneaux, Marcelin, trans. Newton Branch. *Daily Life in Spain in the Golden Age*, London: Allen & Unwin. 1970.

Fletcher, Richard. *The Quest for El Cid*. London: Hutchinson. 1989.

Frale, Barbara. *The Templars: The Secret History Revealed*. New York, NY: Arcade Publishing. 2004.

France, John, ed. *Medieval Warfare 1000-1300*. Hampshire, England: Ashgate Publishing Co. 2006.

Kaeuper, Richard W. *Chivalry and Violence in Medieval Europe*. Oxford, UK: Oxford University Press. 1999.

Keen, Maurice. *Chivalry*. New Haven, Con.: Yale University Press. 1984.

_____. *Nobles, Knights and Men-at-Arms in the Middle Ages*. London: The Hambledon Press. 1996.

Konstan, David & Kurt A. Raaflaub. *Epic and History*. Sussex U.K.: Wiley-Blackwell Publishing. 2010.

Laffi, Domenico, trans. James Hall. *The Diary of a Seventeenth Century Pilgrim from Bologna to Santiago de Compostela*. Leiden, The Netherlands: Primavera Pers. 1977.

Lowney, Chris. *A Vanished World: Muslims, Christians, and Jews in Medieval Spain*. Oxford, UK: Oxford University Press. 2005.

Llull, Ramon, trans. Noel Fallows. *The Book of the Order of Chivalry*, Woodbridge, UK: Boydell Press. 2013.

Maalouf, Amin, trans. Jon Rothschild. *The Crusades Through Arab Eyes*. New York, NY: Schocken Books. 1985.

Rodríguez-Velasco, Jesús D, trans. Eunice Rodríguez Ferguson. *Order and Chivalry: Knighthood and Citizenship in Late Medieval Castile*, Philadelphia, Penn: University of Pennsylvania Press. 2010.

Simpson, Lesley Byrd, trans. *The Poem of the Cid*. Los Angeles, Cal: University of California. 1957.

5

God's Houses of Wonder,
God's Houses of Woe

While Catholicism is the official religion in Spain, it is Ian Frewer's contention that this faith has never come naturally to the Spanish but was imposed upon them in the fifteenth century by Isabella and Ferdinand. Too early for the people to be unified by nationality, these two Catholic monarchs united Spain by means of an enforced faith policed by the Inquisition. Even now, Frewer asserts, this religion has never taken a complete hold.

Others agree. Beebe Bahrami understands the Spanish as still essentially pagan, or at least nature-based. She claims Spain's natural and unique devotion to the Virgin Mary bears witness not only to Christianity but also to an underpinning matriarchal sensibility. For Bahrami, whose endeavour it is to seek out the hallowed places in Spain, the sacred in its traditional pagan form has always been particularly strong.

While I will accept that the native Spanish before the advent of Christianity may have been matriarchal and were certainly pagan, I cannot agree that they have maintained these sensibilities. My experience of Spanish men is that they are delightfully confident and are unlikely to be easily dominated. Though a passionate people, they are also conservative and have adjusted to the formality of Catholicism, embracing this religion with fervour and dedication. Tempered by centuries of war and decorous in disposition, they welcomed orthodoxy, particularly in the upper echelons of the medieval social order, though the peasantry could well have taken longer to yield wholeheartedly. When they did, what had medieval Spain actually accepted and how had this religion begun?

Tradition accepts that Western Catholicism began in Rome with Peter, another of Christ's three most beloved disciples. Anticipating his crucifixion, Jesus destined Peter to be the rock upon which the Christian church was to be built, at the same time giving him the keys to heaven. Since then Peter has been accepted as the first Roman Catholic pope. In spite of a few rival popes contesting the right to the papal throne, this authority has been passed on over the ages from pope to pope in one long, unambiguous line right up to the present day.

In the early days of the church the pontiff was indeed a rock because he spread the gospel and arbitrated over various doctrinal disputes. At this point he had no temporal power, his focus being on spiritual matters and the need for individuals to access heaven. Up to the eleventh century, the pope was not politically well regarded, even though he was the head of a considerable organization.

During the first part of the first millennium rulers and pilgrims from the newly converted European countries were drawn to Rome, but they did not come to consult with the pope. They came because they wished to visit the tomb of Saint Peter who was apparently still capable of ministering from his tomb. Ardent, newly converted Christians also wished to be baptised in the holy city, and the elderly and sick hoped to die as close as possible to the one who held the keys to the kingdom. It was the deceased Peter who was the active force in Rome, not the pope of the time who, at this point, did little to administer his burgeoning organization. When necessary abbots and bishops were selected for Europe's newly founded monasteries and bishoprics allocated by lay rulers. While the Pope was recognized as Peter's representative on earth, the papal mission at this time did not focus on the development of a triumphant universal church. Without some drastic turn of event the papacy could well have been made redundant. According to Sir Richard Southern, this event was the fabrication of the *Donation of Constantine*, a paper supposedly composed in 315 by the Roman Emperor, Constantine. Later it was found to be a forgery written in the ninth century.

It is somewhat startling to realize that papal power was founded on a falsified document, but these were medieval times and scholars, confident in their beliefs, had no qualms about the way in which they authenticated their ideas. The facts were never as important as the underlying intention. The anonymous author, in his attempt to legitimize the papacy and help popes settle ecclesiastical and royal disputes, provided a detailed document based on a legend. The story tells how Constantine, seeking a cure for his leprosy, was converted to Christianity and baptised by Pope Sylvester I. Acknowledging his gratitude, he bestowed upon the See of Saint Peter 'power, and dignity of glory, and honour imperial' as well as supremacy over all the Christian world. To Sylvester and his successors he also granted 'the city of Rome and all its provinces and places', the imperial insignia and the tiara, the papal crown which was only introduced as part of papal apparel in the eighth century!

While the *Donation* was, from time to time, used as a title-deed by frustrated popes to justify their decisions, it was not until 1073 when Gregory VII ascended the papal throne that the pontiff gained sovereign authority and ruled supreme in the medieval world. Up to this point the church had been extremely capable of generating fear and trepidation in individuals concerned with the welfare of their souls, but it was weak in its ability to coerce on a political level and had to depend on kingly consent and the co-operation of mercenaries and independent secular rulers to maintain order. The aristocracy were usually willing to provide this military help, mainly because in doing so they protected their own inherited interests. Up to the turn of the first millennium, church and crown had more or less governed together.

When Gregory VII took over the position of Vicar of Christ he found this reciprocity could not be sustained. Where once the church had only attended to matters spiritual, the changing circumstances in Europe meant the pope had now to embrace the temporal world. Phenomena such as acceleration in economic developments, new agricultural methods, increased population and improved infrastructure meant that life had become complex and, if the pope was to maintain his authority, he needed more than a forged document. Gregory decided to strengthen his position by undercutting imperial power. He did this by disallowing the crown to interfere in all matters ecclesiastical, in particular the investiture of bishops and abbots. Not only were they now forbidden to appoint clerical agents who would operate to the crown's advantage, but they also lost the monetary reward received in exchange for the clerical appointment, and the convenient use of the monastic houses they had founded. The various crowns were appalled.

From ancient times monarchs had ruled according to a concept called 'The Royal God-Given Right'. The origin of this 'Right' was pagan, a time when the king was often seen as some kind of god and so accepted as an unchallenged despot and answerable to no-one. With the advent of the Roman Catholic Church, this idea was overcome by the notion of the 'Two Swords', one belonging to the king, the other to the pope. In the course of the first millennium the crown, anointed with holy oils, ceremonially vested and bolstered by an impressive array of sacred relics produced to honour their coronations, felt justified in overstepping their bounds. Now, in one fell stroke, Gregory had, in effect, demoted secular rulers.

Initially the European monarchs refused to accept Gregory's edict, in particular King Henry IV of Germany. Brazenly opposing the Pope, he promptly found himself excommunicated. While he might well have been genuinely indifferent to papal intimidation, the vast majority of his noblemen were not and, within a few months, almost all had abandoned their king. Now a misfit in Christendom, Henry was forced not only to undertake a humiliating pilgrimage across the Alps to the small village of Canossa, but had also to remain on his knees for three days and three nights outside the gates of Canossa Castle where the pope was in residence while all the time a blizzard raged around him.

While history has made little of this clash, the incident was momentous, not only because the crown was abruptly deprived of divine rights, but because Gregory had effectively laid the foundations that would define the modern Western World. By separating church and state, and decreeing that these two realms should exist distinct from each other, he set in motion the advent of the secular state. Even in the sixteenth and seventeenth centuries when James I and Charles I of England and Louis XIV of France tried to resurrect the notion of monarchical absolutism, now calling it 'The Divine Right of Kings', the idea was defeated, these kings now answerable to an impressive array of political, military and cultural magnates. The existence of the Magna Carta, the

Reformation and the advent of the nation state helped to seal the division.

While this shift to the secular is indeed impressive, what I find even more amazing is that Gregory accomplished this giant sundering simply by the threat of excommunication. He then set about establishing himself as ultimate head of the church and forcefully reforming it. He forbade simony, the purchasing of positions relating to the church. He championed celibacy among the clergy and demanded that all Europe be liturgically unified. Roman discipline and Gregorian rites were to be instituted throughout Christendom. He then sent legates to oversee the task. As well as offering humanity comfort, a purpose in this world and the hope of salvation in the next, the church had also become a political force that had completely taken over the might of the collapsed Roman Empire. It is significant that more or less at this time Europe's great cathedral builders began planning and constructing awe-inspiring cathedrals. It was also at this point that the knights were encouraged to go crusading and establish the Christian church as universally triumphant.

On the Camino there is now no visible evidence of the past papal struggles for supremacy, or the Christian organization as militant, but the twenty-first century pilgrim is in no doubt that the church was a dominating force in medieval Spain. Especially at the start of the walk I loved spotting the upcoming villages. Often they were built on top of hills. The low-lying labyrinth of narrow streets and humble homes was always secondary to the church, this huge and imposing building seeming to the clasp the village to its bosom as a hen gathers in her chicks. The conventional metaphor of 'mother church' was appropriate. In the openness of the trail and under the huge Camino sky I experienced these medieval villages as comforting. In towns only slightly larger several churches could be found, though now many of these are locked and apparently abandoned.

This was the case in Uterga, a village sixteen kilometres west of Pamplona. A short way into the Camino and as yet relatively unfit, I decided to overnight here, even though it was still early in the day. Having settled into the pilgrim refuge, I set out to explore the small community. There were few people about and most of the houses lining the main street were firmly locked. When I got to the church, a large one for the size of the village and standing in fairly extensive grounds, I pushed at the door hopeful of entry. It was locked, but under pressure the insecure hinges gave way a few inches. The air that escaped was rank, heavy with the odour of mould and decrepitude. Here, in the past, this edifice had stood as a proud symbol of a mighty organization with God on its side. In the present day this grandeur had crumbled in the dust and the God supposedly within could no longer intimidate.

The earliest churches in northern Spain are Romanesque, dating from as early as the ninth century. This architectural design came to Spain from northern Italy and France arriving with the Cluny monks and the advent of the Benedictine monasteries, though in a short time Spain developed its own unique style. In Europe generally, the Romanesque tradition corresponded with a time when Christianity had become secure and theology optimistic. In Spain this was particularly so, the Reconquest (that struggle against the invading Moors), and the Cluny monks (who were organizing the pilgrimage to Santiago and financing the necessary infrastructure), imparting a decided organizational spirit. Because Spain was also populating the arid inner plains, immigrants were welcomed by both the church and the crown. Drifting in over the Pyrenees, they arrived not only as peasant labourers or infantrymen, but many also came with new artistic ideas and knowledge of different building techniques. Mostly the Romanesque is to be seen in ecclesiastical buildings, but bridges, towers, castles and palaces were also constructed in this style.

Essentially the Romanesque church was founded on the original Roman basilica. In classical times this was a large secular building, rectangular in shape and divided by a central aisle with an apse at one end. An ornate seat was placed at this point and here the magistrate presided. The Roman basilica was used for official public gatherings and was centred in the forum of the ancient Roman cities. The Christian church adopted this architectural plan for its house of worship and, over time, developed and refined the design to suit ecclesiastical needs. An altar replaced the magistrate's seat and eventually transepts were added, the basic shape now emulating the Christian cross. This basic pattern is still used for present-day Catholic and Anglican churches.

Before the turn of the first millennium the nave of a Romanesque church was covered with a barrel vault, constructed from brick. Above the transept crossing a dome was added. The single semi-circular apse was sometimes extended to three. Towers were built and the cloister became an important feature, the column capitals often beautifully carved. Decorative stone carving proliferated and were strategically placed, particularly over doorways. Initially there was no choir, the building being small and clerics few. Because the roof was weighty and rested on thick walls, windows were limited. This meant these churches were gloomy and often conveyed a sense of heaviness. However, Terence and I did not find these churches oppressive, the dimness imparting a sense of mystery and the weightiness was comforting.

This was particularly evident San Juan de Baños in Castile, a church we did not easily find. The church of San Juan is really Visigoth, its dedication taking place in 661, the date recorded in an inscription set into the wall above the arch leading into the sanctuary. While over the years renovations have been made, it retains a distinctive Romanesque character. Long, low and constructed from large well-cut stone, San Juan communicates a sense of solidarity, a feeling corroborated by the thick marble columns supporting substantial horseshoe arches. A small but exquisitely-wrought sanctuary light and a delicate filigree window on the flat wall at the back of the apse alleviate oppressiveness. Even though San Juan is now a monument and not a working church, I liked it, particularly appreciating the simplicity of the decoration.

Terence and I also loved the Romanesque art we saw in northern Spain. Primitive in style and lacking perspective and depth, these works are characterized by bright, intense colour and religious simplicity. At this medieval stage (the eighth to the eleventh centuries), papal and clerical authority were not evident and political inferences were void. Instead the Romanesque artwork illustrated reverence and divine majesty. Mary and her child were the most popular themes, followed by God in his glory and then the seriousness of the afterlife. I felt there was a solemnness about the Romanesque art that imparted a sense of devotion and pleading, making these pieces particularly appealing.

The building of a Romanesque church, even a small one, was an enormous undertaking. The project was always designed and overseen by a master-builder who had to be an intelligent man, educated in either a monastery or through a unionized masonic lodge. He would then have had to serve a lengthy apprenticeship before being offered his first contract. Once this was signed, he had in his charge the various foremen who oversaw the numerous stonecutters and masons, the glasscutters, the metalworkers, carpenters and painters and any other specialists needed for his particular project. He also had to find and hire skilled sculptures and artists for the artistic embellishment of the church and was ultimately responsible for the general outcome. He would also have to liaise with the patrons who were sponsoring the work, not only pleasing them, but also staying within their budget.

When the undertaking was large the original master-builder would rarely see the completion of his project, some ecclesiastical buildings taking decades to complete. Considering the lack of powered machinery and the primitiveness of the building tools, what the master-builder and the medieval craftsmen achieved was really remarkable.

The might of the early Christian church is best understood in the larger towns where cathedrals took over from churches. As political powers in Europe began to decline ecclesiastical institutions appropriated this secular authority and, by the eleventh century, cathedrals became not only religious complexes, but also intellectual, economic, charitable and artistic centres. Today we may well wonder how an average medieval, well tutored in the apparent ways of God, aware of the awesome mystery to be found within the liturgy, thrust into the melee of life and without insight into the political arena would have responded to the early cathedrals. Initially I thought they would have been in awe but from my reading this was not always the case, possibly because cathedrals were far too public.

The cathedral district was the hub of the city, businesses and trade flourishing along the adjoining streets and markets held in the crypts. Buildings of this size sometimes took centuries to construct and, once complete, frequently needed cleaning or repair. The surrounding town squares were always hives of activity, a multitude of builders, stone masons and artisans plying their skills. This is true even today. On both my trips to Santiago the cathedral was sconced in scaffolding, the walls being scoured and the statuary refurbished.

Records also reveal that religious services, far from being serious or pious affairs as they tend to be now, were more often social occasions providing hilarity and entertainment. To gain the attention of the congregation, quieten the gabble and alert the people that the consecration was taking place, bells had to be rung. P. Hodgson's quotation from the thirteenth century document, *Ignorantia Sacerdotum*, provides amusing insights. In translation a priest complains, 'They come not to Matins three times in a year, they jangle, they jape, they kiss women and there is no word of the service, but scorn for the priest saying he sleeps in his mass and keeps them from their breakfast'. Hodgson also records that 'fights, quarrels, conversations, or meetings could often disrupt the service'. To my astonishment he claims that clerics too were at fault, often 'singing bawdy songs during the mass!

While the general tone and ethos of the early Romanesque cathedral could well have been pedestrian and not conducive to awe, things changed in the twelfth century with the advent of Gothic architecture. This began in 1137 when Suger, Abbott of the Abbey of Saint Denis approximately fourteen kilometres north of Paris, claimed that his abbey church was dreary and failed to reflect the glory of God, or honour the French kings buried within. So he strove to renovate the church choir. His aim was to provide the world with an image of heaven.

In order to construct a heaven out of everyday material (stone, wood, glass), Suger had to imagine what heaven might actually look like. In this he was inspired by the writing of Saint Augustine, in particular an essay on aesthetics titled *De Musica.* Written in the fourth century, Augustine's work debates the nature of beauty, a phenomenon he saw anchored in divine reality. The evidence for his insight was Biblical, revealed to him while reading the *Book of Wisdom*, a philosophical treatise attributed to Solomon. A passage from chapter eleven reads, 'Thou hast ordered all things in measure and number and weight'. From this short verse Augustine concluded that the quality which best defined both beauty and the divine was the order to be found in precise mathematical relationships. As superb music is composed according to arithmetical ratios, Augustine decided all the things of the world, too, could only be beautiful if they reflected 'regular geometrical systems and principles of modulation'. He concluded, too, that numbers were the thoughts of God, each one having a divine significance. Several centuries later, Suger, living in times of chaos, as had Augustine, also perceived heaven as orderly and controlled, and his architectural design became intricately linked to geometrical uniformity.

Suger had a second major architectural concern, this time to do with light. Medieval thought generally claimed that God deliberately concealed Himself from humankind so that He could be revealed to those who chose to search for Him. Light was the means by which He could be known. This was a theology based on the work of Dionysius the Areopagite, a sixth century Greek judge who converted to Christianity and became the first bishop of Athens. His writing is considered one of the most imposing mystical constructs in the history of Christian thought. At the heart of his thinking is the idea that God and light were synonymous and that the sunlight streaming down from heaven and flooding the world was capable of connecting all creation to the divine.

This idea permeated medieval thinking. Accepting this, Suger's new architectural endeavour was to have light penetrate every corner of his church. His quest was to achieve greater openings. Innovative pointed arches, flying buttresses and ribbed vaults all worked together to permit the building of larger, more spectacular windows. Thus the harmony of heaven was emphasised in the lofty height of the ceiling vaults, architectural precision and the greater infiltration of light. This was the advent of the gothic cathedral and all over Europe there was a sudden rush to rebuild or update churches in Suger's new style. These design changes resulted in vast buildings of astonishing splendour that sharply contrasted with the general messy smallness of medieval life and were deliberately built to inspire awe. For Robert A. Scott, the medieval Gothic cathedral was one of the West's most impressive accomplishments.

Because I grew up in a part of Africa devoid of splendid cathedrals, my first experience of one took place when I was visiting England at six years of age. On a delightful summer's day my family and I were bike-riding, our destination the town of Ely located a fair way from our holiday home. Here we intended to visit Ely's large Gothic cathedral. I was happy cycling through the yellowing East Anglian wheat fields, but happiness turned to joy when my sister's front wheel fell into a rabbit-hole and she sailed over the handle bars, landing in a thick clump of nettles. My sibling is seven years older than me and she had always managed to organize our relationship to her advantage. Observing her woe on this particular day I felt as though I had suddenly become the favoured one.

Eventually her pain and tears subsided and we were able to resume our ride, but my euphoria was soon quelled.

Turning a corner the cathedral suddenly loomed out of the billowing wheat. Never in my short life had I beheld such magnificence; a splendour that was at the same time somewhat daunting. Once I entered, this feeling was exacerbated by the sheer size of the lofty ceiling, the brilliant colours, the splendour of the stained-glass and the hushed, echoing ambiance. Overwhelmed and incapable of comprehension, I came to the conclusion that I had in some way been responsible for my sister's tumble. Gripped by guilt, I began to weep. My mother, embarrassed by the noise and excessive moisture, told me I was desecrating God's house and ordered me out.

I was eighteen when I suddenly understood what had happened to me in Ely. Again I was in England and standing in another splendid church, this time the chapel in King's College Cambridge. It was a particularly fortunate visit because I had arrived in time to hear the massed choirs practice for the forthcoming Christmas celebrations. On this occasion it was not only the architecture that overawed but also the power of the music. The cadence, the choristers' pure voices and the swelling vibration of the organ resonating in my chest, all seemed unworldly. I felt as though I had been taken to the brink of eternity and was about to vanish. However, I was now more mature and not quite so easily overcome. I also realized that what I had felt as the six year old in Ely had not been provoked by guilt, but by a profound sense of having been taken over by something much greater than me.

Travelling in Spain with Terence I found it difficult to recapture that same degree of sublimity. There were two reasons for this, the first being the twenty-first century tourist throng, particularly those who came *en masse* with tour guides who rattled off a requisite script in very loud Spanish. When such a group entered Terence often walked out. The second was because of the Spanish choir.

A cathedral choir is that area that accommodates the clergy during divine services. The seating is arranged in hierarchical order, each cleric having his own private stall where he keeps his books and where he can engage in private devotion. Because it was thought this was a place where clerics were most likely to reach God, the choir was considered a holy space, reserved only for choristers and those in holy orders and made worthy by way of exquisite carving and furnishings. In English cathedrals the choir is beautiful but discreet, usually placed against the wall of the chancel between the nave and the sanctuary and, if one enters through the main door, does not impede the often very impressive sweep up to the high altar and the 'Holy of Holies'.

In contrast the Spanish choir is very large and imposing, organized in a wide 'U' shape, faces the altar and sits heavily in the middle of the nave. From the main door this construct blocks the view to the sanctuary. To my way of thinking this tends to spoil the visitors' sense of wonder when entering. On festive occasions the Spanish choir also makes it difficult to accommodate a large congregation. A German tourist told me the reason the choir has been so drastically removed from the side walls and squarely placed on the west end of the crossing was because the supposed busyness amongst the massed clerics could well impede the 'terrible mystery' that was supposed to take place on the altar during the mass. 'The Spanish priest and the sacrament', said my German guide, 'must always be protected from possible distraction or impurity'.

In spite of tourists and a bulky choir, there is one cathedral in Spain that conforms to Suger's precise architectural criteria. It is in Léon and dedicated to the Holy Mother. On my initial visit I was not particularly impressed by this building, thinking it too dingy to warrant its reputation. Two years later when I was there with Terence, the windows had been cleaned, allowing a flood of light to penetrate. The difference was astonishing. As a pilgrim I had noticed only the lower windows. I thought they were not only dark but too pagan-like with their vegetal design. With the added brightness I had a change of heart and was able to focus on the towering walls, the simple arches branching into a multiplicity of exact and graceful curves, the ribbed vaults offset by the now visible plain but textured brick ceiling. I wondered how the hardness of stone could create such an astonishing sense of flow. I accepted the beautiful fluidity and the elegance of the ribbing as a triumph, the spiritual world able to take over everyday reality and by doing so, delightfully dazzling me. I am sure Suger would have approved the soaring, ribbon-like windows peeping forth from a forest of flying buttresses, allowing the filtered light to create the soft, mellow atmosphere.

On this second visit I was also astonished that, as a pilgrim, I had been immune to this beauty even though it had been marred by dirty glass. Possibly my focus had been on walking and open space rather than the sights to found within the confines of the towns.

It is claimed that there are seven hundred and thirty-seven windows in Léon's cathedral, taking up approximately one thousand, nine hundred square metres of space. It is said, too, that this cathedral contains more glass and less stone than any other in Spain. Some see it as a delicate house of glass poised between buttresses. As a consequence, Léon is known as a 'Cathedral Without

Walls' and this allows the guide book to claim it as 'The Dream of Light Realized'. It is also a construction that complements the theory of Dionysius the Areopagite who claimed God and light were synonymous. As a modern traveller rather than a pilgrim, I thought the stained glass allowed visitors to feel as though they had accessed a colourful and translucent parallel universe.

Where Léon's cathedral can be termed God's House of Light, I see Burgos as its antithesis. While classified as Gothic and utilizing builders and craftsmen from France, this cathedral does not emulate the delicate French style. On the Camino I had walked into this city in the height of summer. From a distance and in the strong sun this building looked like a thrilling, giant wedding cake.

A medieval traveller coming into Burgos could well have had a different reaction. In the thirteenth century the cathedral did not stand among multi-storeyed constructions, but would have risen hugely from more modest surroundings, its beautiful pinnacles and spires as though soaring up to heaven. Mighty and imposing it could well have reinforced the notion that God was almighty and the church sufficiently powerful to operate on God's behalf, excommunicating the culpable or exonerating the worthy. With God's power so clearly demonstrated, the church was a force to be heeded. However, when I eventually entered, the awesomeness diminished. Finding the cathedral depressing, I was happy to continue my Camino walk.

On our second visit Terence and I examined the cathedral's interior with greater care, but I still decided this was a gloomy church. Jan Morris is more robust in her criticism. While she acknowledges the splendour of the cathedral treasure, she describes this edifice as 'gnarled', 'dour', with 'no fun or flare' and reminiscent of 'an old American battleship'.

Not every-one is so derisive. David Gitlitz and Linda Kay Davidson enthusiastically describe Burgos as 'the richest anthology of medieval art and style pilgrims will find along the Camino road'. They claim several visits are necessary in order to appreciate all the gems. Had I visited this cathedral only to admire individual pieces of art I might agree, but I want cathedrals to be more than art galleries. Built over several centuries and consecrated as sacred spaces, I believe these buildings should also be capable of reflecting the glory of God as he once might have been perceived. Once inside I need to glean some sense of what it means to be holy.

I found two writers who attempt to explain the nature of a Spanish cathedral. The first was Charles Rudy. In the introduction to his book, *The Cathedrals of Northern Spain*, he points out the hybrid nature of the church, as well as the people, claiming both have been victims of conquering hordes: first the Romans, then the Gothic tribes, the Moors, the influence of the Bourbons and finally the ravages of the French during the Napoleonic Wars. As a consequence, he says, the native northern Spanish have been unable to develop either a sense of patriotic nationhood or a distinctive art style. The early Gothic tribes had accepted Christianity, seeing it as a religion that complemented their fierce sense of independence by teaching that all people were equal in the eyes of God. Christianity was also a religion that allowed the worship of pagan deities by the simple expediency of disguising these gods as Christian saints. Always adapting to foreign ways and alien ideologies, Rudy maintains the development of a unique Spanish art style has not only been hindered but also disadvantaged by an early social order composed of too many illiterates and almost devoid of a middle class, rendering them indifferent to the fine arts. Those who were wealthy enough to commission art all too often had to import artists, sculptures and architects, or purchase works from France and Italy.

Because Christianity had taken over all of Europe and art everywhere was dominated by this religion, I find this criticism harsh. Executed and organized according to strict rules, most painters had to conform and were unable or reluctant to heed the dictates of individual imagination. As a consequence artistic outlay, particularly in the form of painting, tended to be uniform throughout medieval Europe.

The second explanation was offered by Havelock Ellis. In his work, the *Soul of Spain*, Ellis contradicts Rudy by claiming the Spanish style as unique and the result of climate and the landscape. Both, he says, are inhospitable, with sharp contrasts, strong colours and vast skies, producing a hardy and resilient people who best express themselves in dramatic sculpture and architecture. When they did paint, Ellis saw the works as passionate, with strong expression and extravagant boldness and, at the time of execution, not generally appreciated. Because Spain in the tenth and eleventh centuries had been a frontier country, colonizing an isolated, sparsely occupied interior and focussed on fighting, the delicate aesthetic sensibility could not have been an aspect of their reality. Living a vigorous masculine life-style with a realistic grasp on the world, the early pioneers were very probably disdainful of the refined artistry found in the softer European north and seemingly favoured by Rudy.

The unyielding harshness of the bare plains and the ravages of past, ongoing battle can also be seen to have made their way into Spanish cathedral design. These buildings are often fortified, as in Pamplona and Santiago.

Even when classified as Gothic, the massive square shape of the building and the heavy towers impart strength, not the elegance to be found elsewhere in Europe. It is for this reason that Rudy disapproves of Léon. While admiring its beauty, he says its gracefulness does not represent Spanish sensibility. Instead of French delicacy, both Rudy and Ellis claim the Spanish are more impressed by 'mass, weight and quantity', an assertion borne out in the love of heavy, wrought-iron screens and the placement of massive, highly ornate retablos.

Stupendous retablos are a feature in all Spanish cathedrals. Placed as a back-drop behind the high altar, they often cover the entire east wall. These wooden structures consist of niches filled with large, often brightly painted biblical scenes or statues, sometimes life-size. They are flanked by thick, gilded columns. Some incorporate polished marble and precious stone and are executed in a variety of styles. These retablos can be recognized as awe-inspiring displays of incalculable wealth. The Burgos retablo is Renaissance in design and remarkably golden. It is comprised of seven very tall vertical columns, the paintings in the horizontal inserts narrating the life story of the Virgin. Though ostentatious, I thought it was also tasteful.

The iron screens in the Burgos cathedral were a different matter. They were plentiful and used to close off the numerous chapels, and to isolate the large choir and high altar. While I acknowledge the metalworkers' craftsmanship (the casting of complex and often intricate scrolls and floral or geometrical designs), I find this form of art not only too precise but also claustrophobic and reminiscent of prisons, the harshness of the iron inappropriate in a house of prayer. Where once there would have been several ways to access the cathedral, today one must enter through the south door. In this transept the visitor is faced with a tall restraining grille that, unlike medieval times, disallows direct access to the high altar. A large arrow printed on a piece of hardboard directs visitors round the extensive choir until an opening in the north facing iron-work is reached. Only then is one allowed to stand in the centre of the crossing and view the altar and the magnificent geometrical design of the central dome. When I finally reached this point I was at last able to appreciate this beauty, but I did not feel in any way welcome. Back home and reflecting on Burgos, I decided it was this heavy ironwork that imparted the oppression I had felt in this cathedral. Possibly it was also the reason why Jan Morris felt as though she had visited 'an old American battleship' when she was in Burgos.

As Gitlitz and Davidson point out, the artwork in Burgos is spectacular. Most of the paintings are illustrative, depicting Biblical scenes or characters. This is true of all churches on the Camino. It is popularly believed these pictures in medieval times served a pedagogic purpose, allowing the illiterate access to the Bible. However, church art is also highly iconographic. Each medieval artist had a master from whom he learnt the various artistic codes. These would then be piously perpetuated. Most medievals would have been *au fait* with this iconography, understanding both the codes and the illustrated stories.

In Australia, the older generation may still have knowledge of the Bible stories and Christian principles underpinning them, but younger age groups are mostly ignorant. For many of us the artistic codes are also unknown. Without this information one's appreciation of church art is curtailed. Émile Mâle explains some of the hidden medieval symbolism in his book, *The Gothic Image*. For instance, how characters are placed in a picture is always important. The right being the accepted side of honour, an artist illustrating the crucifixion would be severely castigated if he painted John on the right side of Christ as this would dishonour the more important Mary.

Codes also allow the viewer to recognize characters. Saint Peter, for example, is always given a short curly beard and a tonsure and he holds a set of keys; Saint Paul is bald with a flowing beard and has a book in his hand. Statues often stand on small crouching figures. These are strangely decorative and each figure is in vital relation to the sculpture above. Apostles tread upon the kings who persecuted them, Moses stands on a golden calf, angels step on dragons from the abyss and Christ and the Virgin trample the serpent. Everything a medieval artist placed in a picture meant more than is conveyed by superficial viewing. Unless a contemporary viewer is conversant with these values it is difficult to fully appreciate what the picture is about.

Mâle also explains that, in order to understand the external statuary, it is useful to be conversant with the general ecclesiastical ground plan. For example, both churches and cathedrals are constructed so that the altar is always placed on the east wall, the side of the rising sun and symbolic of Christ and new life. Usually windows alone embellish this outer wall. The opposite west wall faces the direction of the setting sun and represents death and judgement and this explains why such a large number of monstrous beasts and demons are to be found in the west tympanums.[16] The north wall, the region of cold and darkness in the northern hemisphere, is dedicated to Old

---

[16] Tympanums are the large semi-circular, highly decorative alcoves above the main church doors, bounded by the lintel below and the arch above and containing rich bas-relief sculpture.

Testament iconography and the south wall, bathed in warmth and sun, is devoted to the New.

Even with Mâle's considerable help, I feel it is impossible to truly grasp the ecclesiastical medieval world. For instance, when viewing the artwork, I found I would always juxtapose the antiquity of the bygone age with modern sensibility. This disallowed impartiality, my ideological conditioning always intruding, making me overly judgemental. I tried to overcome this by simply trying to appreciate the art, but this, too, was difficult because of the horror or excessive cruelty, medieval artists so frequently focussing on suffering.

In the Burgos cathedral for example, there was James, the saintly Moor-slayer, magnificently wielding his mighty sword as he hacked down dark-complexioned Muslims. Saint Roque displayed his gory plague wound, the dog by his side about to lick this lesion hopefully back to health. There was a statue of Saint Sebastian liberally pierced with the arrows of persecuting Romans. A canvas portrayed Saint Agatha, unconcerned as a soldier sliced off her breast. A painted Saint Victoria was bleeding from a mortal neck wound, an angel behind her right shoulder overseeing her holy demise. We saw Saint Bartholomew who achieved sainthood because he was flayed, his skin sliced from his body while he still lived. I remember a canvas of Saint Jerome as he examined a book, probably a Bible, his forefinger pressed upon a grisly skull, a reminder of the eventual fate of all mortals.

For me the most eerie statue was the Santo Cristo de Burgos, a cruelly lacerated thirteenth century black Christ supposedly sculptured by Nicodemus, the man said to have assisted in the preparing of Christ's body for burial immediately after the crucifixion! Legend has it that the statue was found floating in the sea. It was originally housed in an Augustinian monastery, only arriving in Burgos in 1835. The nails, thorns, hair and skin are said to be real and apparently the image once required shaving every eighth day.

It is also Mâle's assertion that one can glean much about medieval interests and concerns by viewing the content of the artwork. In Spanish art Mary is particularly revered. The works also contain the major Christian landmarks: the last supper, crucifixion, the last judgement and the ascension, but my attention was always drawn to the vast number of paintings depicting the martyred saints. Even understanding that the martyrs were crucial to medieval sensibility, their suffering gaining for the populace direct access to the bosom of God, I regretted that the medieval and renaissance artists focussed on their excessive suffering as opposed to the benefits the saints were supposed to have won. I wondered if this was simply the legacy of Christianity or if the plight of the martyrs may have reflected the brutality, harshness and misfortune of everyday medieval life and if viewing these works provided the folk of that time with the hope that they, too, might eventually be lifted up to the Everlasting Arms.

To be fair not all the treasure in Burgos was gruesome. In the cloister, now a museum, I was delighted to behold in a small chapel a large, colourful chest pinned high up onto the wall. It is reputed to be the one in which the Cid had passed off sand for jewels and gold coin when he deceived the Burgos Jewish moneylenders before setting off on his unjust exile. I also really appreciated the Santa Ana chapel. Here the general theme was conception. The retablo is unusual in that it features a sleeping Jesse, father of King David and ancestor of Mary. From his chest a large tree grows and various kings of Judah can be seen in the spreading branches. Towards the top Mary appears with Jesus. Ana and Joachim, Mary's parents, stand in the centre affectionately embracing each other. Around the tree are charming three-dimensional bas-reliefs depicting details in the life of Mary and Christ. I particularly appreciated the soft expressive faces and the domestic detail. Overall this was a chapel that did convey a sense of piety.

Nevertheless it was a relief to walk out of this Cathedral and be greeted by warm spring sunshine. Terence and I walked down a lane-way named after the Virgin. We were on our way to the Plaza Mayor in search of restorative refreshment. As we rounded a corner, we were met by the strains of music, seemingly sent straight from heaven. A singer from Madrid, made redundant by worsening economic times, was busking in the shadow of the cathedral, her husband providing the accompaniment. Ironically her song was Puccini's '*O Mio Babbino Caro*', (Oh My Beloved Father). While not a King's College rendition, her voice swelled in this narrow Burgos street and filled me with incredible sweetness. It was an uplifting conclusion to this particular cathedral visit.

In retrospect I realized I had also been dissatisfied with Burgos because I felt as though I had visited a museum and not a house of God. The Chapel of the Condestables illustrates this notion. This is an octagonal mausoleum independent of the cathedral. It is described by Gitlitz and Davidson as one of Europe's greatest treasures. To a point I agree. The chapel is indeed bright and beautiful. Though ornate, it also exudes elegance and a wonderful sense of harmony. The starry dome, deceptively simple, is exquisite. However, I took exception to this chapel because it has nothing to do with ecclesiastical reality but instead honours a family who had enriched itself by way of Burgos' burgeoning wool trade and then set out to display this wealth to the world at large.

Terence, too, claimed Burgos as no more than a museum, but said it was the placement of the choir and the need to perambulate the huge amount of space taken up by this ornate construction. Rudy contends there is simply too much treasure in Spanish cathedrals generally, visitors prompted to spend all their time looking and examining.

Gianni Vattimo, however, claims the general redundancy of the cathedral as a central power was inevitable and unavoidable, the ultimate result of the Christian acceptance of the incarnation. Where, in Judaic times, philosophers and theologians had struggled to interpret the meaning of the Bible and the nature of God as they searched for His truth, once the 'truth' had been provided in the form of God's apparent manifestation on earth, the scriptural canon was fulfilled and the church, without the need to search further, would over time, have to reform or become obsolete. Those not satisfied with simple pastoral care or the administration of sacraments and obsessed with the need to find ultimate meaning, would now have to look elsewhere. This may well be true of Australia and in parts of Europe and is confirmed by severely diminished congregations. However, in the lesser churches in northern Spain I witnessed sufficient of the Christian devout to make me think that in Spain the Catholic Church is still viable.

When Christianity was a vital religion with a God firmly ensconced in heaven and cognizant of humans, it was understandable that people would want to honour that God by giving expression to their belief. The later medieval churches achieved this by embellishing their sacred houses, obsessively overloading the holy vessels, the hallowed texts and ceremonial vestments with colour and gems and covering the furniture and walls with rich murals and carving, even in places concealed from the public eye. It seems God not only demanded art, but work from only the finest artists. Anxious to curry heavenly favour, the church was willing to provide the best. Suger, writing about his Saint Denis renovations said, 'everything that is most precious should be used above all to celebrate the Holy Mass'. By offering only the finest, the bishops and priests believed the divine spirit would be encouraged to enter and occupy the building, succouring the congregation, as well as themselves, and providing blessings and boons. The artwork and sculpture we saw in Spain's cathedrals, as well as the rich treasure housed in various cloisters and chapter-houses, confirmed this medieval assertion.

In the fifteenth century with the advent of the Renaissance and the reforms promulgated by the Protestant Reformation, the Italian and the Spanish church in particular, set out to counter the new restructuring of Catholicism. It was at this time that the Spanish monarchs, Isabella and Ferdinand, inaugurated the Spanish Inquisition whose purpose was to banish protestant heretics and establish Spain as wholly Catholic. This Counter Reformation, lasting from the fifteenth to the seventeenth century, was helped by a newly founded religious order whose members were known as Jesuits.

As well as reinforcing established Catholic doctrine, the Jesuits also became patrons of the arts, forcefully promoting the inflated and overstated Baroque style in order to restore the church's pre-eminence. Reacting against Protestant severity and restraint, Baroque artists were encouraged to be dramatic and grand. The works produced were large, exaggerated and sumptuous, focussing on the mysteries of the faith, as well as the role played by the Virgin Mary and the saints, aspects of church doctrine the Protestants wished to ignore. Proficient artists combined an extreme outward realism with a sense of inward spirituality, often creating forceful,

175

breath-taking canvasses. It was in the Baroque period that many of the retablos behind the high altar became their most flamboyant. Over the centuries the various styles of art and architecture have surprisingly blended together. The cathedral in Santiago, however, was, to my mind at least, an exception.

In other Spanish churches new styles were accommodated by the simple expedient of building a new chapel. This was the case of Saint Cernín in Pamplona. Constructed on the site of a Roman temple dedicated to Diana, Saint Cernín has pagan origins. Nothing remains of this temple. At the time of Charlemagne the early Romanesque church was considerably damaged because of the tensions between the French, the Basques and the Muslims, and a new fortified building was erected with thick walls and two tall towers. Over time various military skirmishes have necessitated more renovations, resulting in a confusing structure.

Entering, one steps into the oldest and most appealing part. Here the spacious nave is mostly Gothic, with some pieces of Romanesque art. The pews are few, allowing a visitor to appreciate the vast expanse of a superbly polished floor. Two types of wood were utilized and laid in a simple regular pattern. The grain and smoothness of these ancient slabs is beautiful. Where the Gothic cathedral puts one in mind of a nebulous heaven above, in Saint Cernín one is grounded by this floor and made to feel secure. Over the street door a mounted Crusader knight, directed on his way by the hand of God, can be seen. This picture is unusual, Spanish nobles ordered by the pope to fight the Infidel only on home soil. The few side chapels and altars are all small and insignificant except for the newest one built into the south wall. Not only is it very large, but flamboyantly Baroque and gives the visitor the impression that another church had been built and squeezed into the original one. This strange chapel is dedicated to the Virgin Mary.

Saint Cernín is also a working church, the congregation utilizing Mary's chapel, leaving the older part of the church peaceful and empty. When Terence and I visited we were fortunate enough to arrive on a day when the local confraternity of Mary were to renew vows and rededicate themselves to their queen. A statue of Mary was on prominent display. She was resplendent in a magnificent robe of gold brocade and illuminated by a halo of sparkling stars. She completely outshone her holy son who was sitting on her lap, his minute silver image barely visible in the folds of her gown.

Legend claims this statue as 'Mary of the Camino'. In 1487 she mysteriously appeared in Saint Cernín, found high up on one of the roof beams. The effigy was the property of a small church in a faraway village called Alfaro. Though it was repeatedly returned, the statue kept reappearing. After two years of backwards and forwards shunting, it was decided the recurrences were miraculous and it was agreed that Mary had best remain in Pamplona. The Baroque extension was built to provide her with a new ornate home, at that time deemed suitable to her divine standing. In the short while we spent in this church, Terence and I were astonished at the number of people who arrived to kiss the base of the statue and submerge their faces in the folds of her sumptuous gown. I have no affinity with the holy Virgin, but observing the apparent comfort she provided for these worshippers, I wished I had.

As we left I decided what I really liked about Saint Cernín was the way the exuberant colour and decoration in the Virgin's chapel emphasized the simple beauty of the older part of the church. Where for some the Baroque was the age of magnificence, I personally prefer the simplicity of earlier centuries.

Before I conclude this chapter I would like to comment generally on the cathedral's contribution to education. As well as social centres, this institution was also a highly politicized centre of authority and learning. Within the ecclesiastical precinct bishops established cathedral schools in order to provide the church with educated clergy. In time some of these evolved into early medieval universities. The earliest evidence of such institutions was in Visigoth Spain and focussed on the welfare of the male children of nobility who were expected to make an ecclesiastical career. Such schools became a testing ground for future bishops, as well as for the training of royal chaplains. Demands were also made for the teaching of government bureaucrats and other church officials and thus cathedral training became an essential requirement for all those wishing to hold higher office in both secular and episcopal courts.

A successful pupil handled a demanding curriculum covering the study of scripture and pastoral theology, as well as the seven liberal arts: grammar, rhetoric, logic, arithmetic, geometry, astronomy (including astrology) and music. Students would graduate as knowledgeable and articulate, adept at resolving contradictions, able to speak Latin, propose and defend an argument and engage in quantitative reasoning. This curriculum was scholastic and heavily focussed on church doctrine. It seems the emphasis in the cloister and chapter-house was on intelligence and political prowess rather than simple piety.

When we were travelling Terence and I saw no evidence of cathedral schools but, from the grand old chapter-houses we visited, we were able speculate on the worldliness and wealth of the bishops and church dignitaries. In old, stately rooms with imposing doors, heavy rafters and sweeping staircases it was easy to imagine the scheming of staunch clerics and politically ambitious men. Those who searched for spiritual or mystical dimensions were most likely directed to the monasteries, the subject matter for my next chapter.

Works cited in this chapter

Bahrami, Beebe. *The Spiritual Traveler: Spain: A Guide to Sacred Sites and Pilgrim Routes.* Mahwah, N.J.: HiddenSpring. 2009.

Charles, Victoria & Klaus H. Carl. *Gothic Art.* Vietnam: Parkstone International. 2012.

Ellis, Havelock. *The Soul of Spain.* Westport, Conn: Greenwood Press. 1976.

Frewer, Ian. 'Weird and Wonderful: Witchcraft in Spain'. *Expatia.* March. 2005.

Gitlitz, David M. & Linda Kay Davidson. *The Pilgrimage Road to Santiago.* New York, NY: St. Martin's Press. 2000.

Holland, Tom. *Millennium: The End of the World and the Forging of Christendom.* Great Britain: Abacus. 2011.

Icher, François, trans. Anthony Zielonka. *Building the Great Cathedrals.* New York, NY: Harry N. Abrams Inc. 1998.

Mâle, Émile, trans. Dora Nussey. *The Gothic Image: Religious Art in the Thirteenth Century.* London: The Fontana Library. 1961.

Morris, Jan. *Spain.* London: faber & faber. 2008.

Rudy, Charles. *The Cathedrals of Northern Spain.* Boston, Mass: Colonial Press. 1905.

Scott, Robert A. *The Gothic Enterprise: A Guide to Understanding a Medieval Cathedral.* Berkeley, Cal: University of California Press. 2011.

Strafford, Peter. *Romanesque Churches of Spain.* London: dlm. 2010.

Stemp, Richard. *The Secret Language of Churches and Cathedrals*. London: Duncan Baird Publishers. 2010.

Swaan, Wim. *The Gothic Cathedral*. London: Elek Books. 1969.

Vattimo, Gianni, trans. David Webb. *Beyond Interpretation: The Meaning of Hermeneutics for Philosophy*. Stanford, Cal.: Stanford University Press. 1997.

Whitehill, Walter Muir. *Spanish Romanesque Architecture of the Eleventh Century*. London: Oxford University Press. 1968.

6

Getting Away from it All?

In the previous chapter I found it necessary to do much circuitous reading in order to understand the church generally, as well as how it operated in Spain. I found it no different when trying to appreciate Spanish monasteries. My research took me to Egypt and the deserts of Syria and Judea, the birthplaces of European monasticism, Christianity having initially arisen and prospered in the teeming cities of the Eastern Empire.

In the first few centuries after the death of Christ, the city of Alexandria on the Nile Delta was a major centre for Christian intellectual life, its scholars a unique blend of erudition and devotion. The question that most preoccupied these early Eastern Christians, steeped as they were in Greek philosophical learning, was how to live a good life and access the one great God. The general consensus at that time claimed this was only achievable through celibacy, the disciplined mortification of the flesh, rigorous fasting and solitude.

By the fourth century hundreds of Easterners, forsaking personal property, the pleasures and comforts of ordinary life and overly ardent in their desire for God, had migrated to the deserts of Egypt to live either as simple hermits or as the more dedicated anchorites who not only lived in isolation but also took vows to ensure they remained steadfast. Committed to a secluded life, they had to battle loneliness, boredom and poor health. Known as the Desert Fathers, they were the founders of the monastic way of life, Saint Anthony the Great being the most famous.

Anthony was born to wealthy landowning parents in Lower Egypt in the year 251. When he was eighteen years of age both his parents died and Anthony, disenchanted by city hordes and the superficial worship of many Christians, abandoned his lucrative inheritance, placed his younger sister in a community for Christian virgins and took himself into the deep desert where he became an anchorite. His story was later recorded by Athanasius, Bishop of Alexandria. Gathering his information from villagers and the many pilgrims who had visited Anthony, Athanasius wrote his biography in Latin. It was translated into several languages and became popular reading. This book was partly responsible for bringing the idea of monasticism to Western Europe.

Athanasius tells his readers that initially Anthony lived in the open where he was tormented by the Devil. To avoid this malevolent being he first took cover in an empty tomb. Then he sealed himself into a remote and abandoned Roman fort. Peasants fed him through a hole in the rock. No matter where he went, the Devil would follow, imposing upon the Saint boredom and laziness, as well as presenting to him visions of desirable women. Anthony remained chaste and undaunted. On one occasion the Devil apparently beat him unconscious, but still Anthony remained staunch. The Evil One then unleashed upon Anthony a variety of monstrous wild beasts: wolves, lions, snakes and scorpions, all anxious for battle. The saint overcame these creatures by scorning them. In the face of such resolution the Devil had to withdraw. Ultimately at peace, the anchorite became a renowned counsellor and was visited by many seeking his wisdom, communicating with him through a crevice in the fort wall. While these stories may well be fanciful, Athanasius' text proposes that living alone in a remote landscape allows one access to divine truth through the overcoming of extreme temptations.

Another ascetic famous for his suffering was Simeon the Stylite. Withdrawing to a small platform erected on the top of a pillar in the Syrian Desert, this man never again touched the ground. His austerities included exposure to blistering sun, severe fasting and praying in bizarre and uncomfortable positions. Admired by many ecclesiastics and commanding awe from the general populace, Simeon remained on his pillar for thirty-seven years. He, too, dispensed wisdom to clerics and distressed folk who used a tall ladder to access his platform. A vast numbers of sightseers also visited, anxious to view this strange man sitting upon a perch.

In time the more scholarly ascetics became distrustful of those who were so ostentatious in their practice, wondering if these hermits were driven by pride rather than holiness. Pachomius was one such monk and advocated that these desert dwellers should forsake the cruel rigors of the solitary life and instead form themselves into loose communities. In 318 he founded his first desert monastery. Though a cohesive group the monks were, at this point, not bound by a rule but lived independently, assembling every day at set times for communal worship and meals. Pachomius' monastery became the model for western monasticism. Growing in wisdom, the monks were visited by many who journeyed into the desert to seek advice. In time the sayings of these hermits were committed to paper. The work is still in print, titled *Sayings of the Desert Fathers*.

Women, too, were attracted to the desert. In some texts they are honoured with the title, Desert Mothers.

Though also of great courage and determination, they tended to be more conservative. Theodora of Alexandria, anxious to do penance for an undisclosed sin, had to disguise herself as a man so that she could join a band of Desert Fathers, 'mothers' not yet having founded communities. She remained with them until her death when her true identity was at last discovered. Melania the Elder was more fortunate in that she was graciously received as a woman. A Spaniard married at the age of fourteen and living with her husband in fourth century Rome, Melania opted to retreat to the Egyptian Desert when her husband and two of her three sons died. She served the Desert Fathers for five years, then relocated to Jerusalem and there founded a convent. Fifth century Sarah of the Desert chose to live as a hermit near the banks of the Nile where she remained for sixty years. As a discipline she never allowed herself to look upon the beauty of that vast waterway. Records of her sayings indicate she was of a particularly strong personality.[17]

By the end of the fourth century the call of the wilderness had been heard by vast numbers, so much so that Athanasius claimed 'the desert had become a city'. The reasons are debateable. The patristic father, Jerome, also inspired by thoughts of the wilderness, claimed the hermits were refugees avoiding Roman persecution and seeking safety in the wild. Dennis E. Tamburello, a twentieth century theologian, argues that the move arose from a basic tension that followed the 313 Edict of Milan in which Constantine recognized Christianity as a

---

[17] On one occasion Sarah is reputed to have said, 'If I prayed God that all people should approve of my conduct, I should find myself a penitent at the door of each one, but I shall rather pray that my heart shall be pure to all'. At another time, two old men, great anchorites, decided to humiliate her, telling not to become conceited because she, a mere woman, had been visited by two important men. She replied, 'According to nature I am a woman, but not according to my thoughts'.

legitimate religion and forbade the persecution of Christians. Up to this point the followers of Christ had been illegal, seeing themselves as beings 'in' the world but not 'of' it. Their focus was on God, not the social order in which they found themselves. When legitimized and part of a large number of nominal Christians, those who were more deeply committed felt obliged to remove themselves because they feared association with the general populace would make them less watchful and they would come to neglect God. Where once it was martyrdom that enabled one to be redeemed, renunciation of the world now became a popular option.

C.H. Lawrence offers a more orthodox view. He claims the Christian rejection of normal life was rooted in the Gospels, John the Baptist crying in the Wilderness and Christ's sojourn in the desert providing examples. Lawrence also quotes the parable of the rich young man who was told to give up all his worldly wealth if he wished to be saved. I find this explanation simplistic, many other religions also promoting the ascetic life.

Considering the dilemma of many post-modern young girls who also withdraw from everyday life by way of anorexia, I feel the answer to the Desert Fathers is more fundamental and psychologically deep-seated. Were the hermits, who were also indifferent to food, like today's anorexic patients? Both are disempowered, lack autonomy and may be daunted by a changing world, but can at least exert control over their own bodies. Whatever the reason for this early withdrawal, these Desert Fathers triggered my imagination. What was the desert like sixteen hundred years ago? As barren as it is today? Medieval painters imagined a lusher terrain. Was the sojourn as harsh as we believe it to have been or did many cheat? To sit for years aloft a pillar or locked away in a cave must require extraordinary fortitude. Today, if we believed in something as devoutly as they did, would we have the resilience to endure so long?

By the fourth century the concept of communal monastic living travelled westward to Europe, initially brought there through the teachings of the church fathers, Augustine and Jerome. Both were interested in communal life as a means by which to search for truth. Augustine, converting to Christianity after having read the life of Saint Anthony, eventually became a bishop, established a monastic house in North Africa and devoted his life to preaching and writing. Jerome's theological writing was also influenced by the several years he had spent in the Egyptian desert. Because at that time it was generally believed that the search for truth could only be accomplished if one avoided the pursuit of wealth, honour and sexual pleasure, the teaching of these two patristic fathers quickly spread.

John Cassian was another influential monastic ambassador. A monk, cleric and theologian from the East, Cassian was invited to Italy and Gaul where he established an Egyptian-style monastery near Marseilles. His work, *Collations: Conversations with the Desert Fathers*, written more or less at the same time as Jerome and Augustine were putting out their texts, is said to be particularly persuasive and is even now considered a supreme masterpiece of early Christian Literature. I was not able to access an English copy of this work, but I am told it includes wise sayings from the more enlightened Desert Fathers, as well as addressing theological and practical issues raised by the ascetic life. It lays before would-be monks a strenuous yet feasible attempt to answer the appalling challenge, 'Be ye ... perfect'.

Even in Visigoth Spain the hermitic lifestyle flourished, archaeologists having found many cave churches and solitary stone cells built into the porous rock that is prevalent in northern Spain. Walking through Tosantos on the way to Villafranca it is possible to see the white façade of Our Lady of the Rock, a church built into the side of a cliff and surrounded by numerous caves, creating a sanctuary for ancient hermits. Legend holds that a year after the Muslim invasion an image of the Christ child was hidden under a bell in this church. As the hermitage is only a short distance from Tosantos, I decided to visit but unfortunately it was late evening and I had no time to explore this fascinating complex properly. When travelling with Terence we also found hermit caves in the cliffs of Nájera and in the small mountain at Castrojeriz. Even today there are several people who live permanently in the Castrojeriz caves. I do not know if they consider themselves ascetics.

While most of the stories of the early Spanish hermits are now lost, *The life of Valerio of Bierzo* (630-695), written by his own hand, has survived. Bierzo was a monk who took up communal living but, distracted by his brethren, opted for more solitude. Withdrawing to a church in mountains near Astorga, he set himself up in a small stone cell near a church altar. Here he took upon himself the pattern established by his forerunners: he was tormented by the Devil, fed by locals, grew in wisdom, resisted ordination and dispensed wisdom to those who asked for it.

A more entertaining, but much later story, is that of Saint Juan de Ortega, an eleventh century hermit who travelled to the Holy Land. On the return voyage he was almost shipwrecked and promised that, if he survived, he would donate himself to God. He did indeed endure and, home once more, lived in holy solitude until he felt God's call telling him to help pilgrims on their way to Santiago. He did this by building hospices. After his death he became the patron saint not only of hospice keepers but also of children and barren mothers. The reason for the latter was because, when his tomb was opened at a later date to translate his bones, there was a powerful issue of sweet odours and the release of a small swarm of white bees. The locals who witnessed this disinterment interpreted the bees as the souls of unborn children who were in the saint's safekeeping while they awaited their incarnation into the wombs of earthly mothers. Among those who visited the deceased Juan was Isabella, Queen of Castile. Having produced a daughter she was not exactly barren, but eight years had elapsed since that birth and she was anxious to produce a son and heir. After praying at this tomb in the fifteenth century she finally conceived and the hoped-for son arrived. She named him Juan. The monastery of San Juan de Ortega is on the Camino trail and Juan's tomb can still be visited in the church crypt.

The earliest communal monastery Terence and I came across in our travels in northern Spain was the twin complex of San Millán de la Cogolla. The newer and much larger part is called Yuso meaning 'lower' because this building stands in a valley. The other, Suso, means 'upper' and was built upon the mountain-side at an earlier date. This monastery is not on the Camino trail but close by. As I had not visited this World Heritage site when walking the trail, Terence booked us into a small hotel in Badaran, a village approximately eight kilometres away. Our hotel room was strange in that no wall separated our bedroom from the bathroom, but the proprietor was friendly and showed us how to access a walking track that would lead us to the monastic complex nestled in this remote, sparsely populated valley in the heart of Rioja.

The trail followed a boisterous stream that flowed through poplar groves, the leaves sparkling in the sunshine. On either side were rich, green wheat fields surrounded by a ring of mountains, one still snow-capped. It was an idyllic walk. Eventually arriving at eleventh century Yuso, we found we were too late to enter, the last tour of the morning having commenced and the afternoons reserved for supervised visits to sixth century Suso. We were relieved. Yuso's cavernous vestibule, over-run with busloads of tourists, their many voices magnified by the marble walls, was singularly uninviting and after our sublime walk the raucous din was unnerving. Terence wanted to flee, but I was not totally daunted and hastily bought tickets for Suso. While we waited for the bus that was to take us up the mountain, we sat in the sun and ate oranges. Eventually we were counted into a coach and commenced the steep hair-pinned ride.

On arrival I was surprised at the unpretentious smallness of the monastery basilica. A path led us to a front porch, its eight symmetrical arches overlooking the magnificent valley and open to the weather. In this portico we were greeted by eleven tombs, seven supposedly containing the headless bodies of the Princes of Lara. The story of the de Laras, a prestigious Navarrese family, is recorded as a ballad. It is a revenge tale revolving round the betrayal and ambush of the seven Princes by their uncle, Ruy Velazquez de Lara. At a wedding feast the Princes had apparently insulted de Lara's wife, Doña Lambra. Feeling her family had been belittled, she beseeched her husband to avenge this wrong. He acquiesced, selling the princes to Muslims. Knowing the young prices had no hope of winning, they were nevertheless cajoled into fighting their Muslim captors and, losing the duel, each boy was then decapitated. The ballad, even in translation, makes good reading, the father's lament at the end being particularly moving. I had thought the story a legend so I was surprised to find this poignant line of simple tombs covered with flat stone slabs. Their deaths were grisly, but their mountain repose is splendid.

We found Suso fascinating. This mountain rock is porous, creating another multiplicity of small caves. In the sixth century San Millán chose one of these for a hermitage. A hundred years after his death his life was recorded by Braulius, Bishop of Zaragoza. Born of poor Roman parents in the nearby village of Berceo, Millán looked after sheep. One day, while watching the flock, he fell asleep. As he lay upon the ground God breathed on him and when he awoke he realized he was no longer a shepherd. 'Enlightened', he abandoned the sheep and went in search of learning. In time he became a priest, but a very reluctant one. Eventually, after giving away the assets of the church to which he had been assigned, he retired to the nearby cave to take up his true calling: that of a hermit.

In time Millán grew in holiness and fame and pilgrims of that time came to him in search of healing as well as for the exorcizing of demons. It is said that on occasions when the crowd was large, Millán was able to multiply bread to feed the worshipers who gathered round his cave. During his life he attracted a small group of disciples who occupied the many caves found in the mountain-side. Now a religious community, they built the small basilica. Millán, however, favoured solitude and found another cave some way away to which he would often retire. In the thirteenth century Gonzalo de Berceo, Spain's most famous poet as well as a monk at the monastery of San Millán de la Cogolla, retold the saint's life in poetic form.

Millán lived to be one hundred and one years old. Upon his death he was buried in one of the caves that opens into the Suso church. His sarcophagus is strikingly carved, the ancient life-size stone saint reclining in his strange ecclesiastical robes. Round his recumbent figure are carved monks and pilgrims kneeling in devout worship. Four angels, one at each corner, guard the tomb. In this ancient, primitively built basilica and against the natural mountain rock, the Romanesque vault seems oddly sophisticated and extraordinarily beautiful. The church no longer contains Christian symbols such as crucifix, pulpit, choir etc. Much of the architecture is Islamic, the site apparently shared by a few Muslim hermits. The rituals and vestments would have been Visigoth, so it was impossible for me to imagine how these old monks would have conducted themselves. Against the backdrop of mountains and valley and open to the elements, Suso felt animated, not by an ancient Christian tradition, but by spirits preceding Christianity. Maybe it was the sunshine and the rustling of trees, but these spirits felt friendlier.

Millán's tomb is now a cenotaph, the saint's body having been removed from Suso in 1053 and his bones provided with a new reliquary. This was installed in the Yuso basilica. Records claim the appalled Suso monks considered the removal as a theft.

The Suso tour over and tired of being organized by the monastery's officials, I persuaded Terence to hide with me in a clump of bushes on the other side of the church and allow the bus to drive away without us. Terence, an anxious lad, is uncomfortable doing the wrong thing, but he had no need to worry. While we had been conscientiously counted onto the bus at Yuso, at Suso the departure was much more cavalier, the passengers bundled aboard and our absence unnoticed. As the vehicle trundled away we were now at large to amble round at our ease and so found additional caves at the rear of the basilica. Though it was difficult to see into these because of railings, it looked as though these passages had been shaped and the floor smoothed. The roof was low and, unable to stand up straight, I wondered how those old monks had endured the discomfort. A short way away we also found the remains of an ancient wall suggesting that the complex had once been more extensive. There were also one or two gnarled old fruit trees and beyond these, deeply hidden in the undergrowth, encrusted with moss and overrun with ivy, we found an ancient cistern. We wondered just how old it was and if it had served those old monks. The natural spring, still flowing into and out of the tank, was icy cold and crystal clear. While committed to prayer and contemplation, it seems the monks still had to attend to the mundane, the needs of everyday life always intruding. Fortuitously our exploring also revealed a well-defined walking track which eventually led us round the mountain-side and back down to Yuso.

In Australia I had read about San Millán's second personal retreat hidden away in mountains a distance from the communal hermitage. In Badaran I decided I wanted to find this cave. Terence was agreeable and the following day we walked back to the monastery to search. With difficulty we discovered the signpost that supposedly pointed the way to this shelter. However, the mountain track soon became faint, indicating that the cave was seldom visited. After some aimless rambling Terence became daunted and, mindful of his fragile knees, I reluctantly agreed to abandon the quest. The terrain, even today, is steep as well as wild and devoid of all signs of civilization. In spite of Terence's company I felt lonely. I wondered how Millán had endured the solitude. No doubt his medieval confidence in a heavenly afterlife and his religious convictions allowed him to accept God as a companion and the ecstasy of prayer may have been a fulfilling consolation. Having no such sustaining beliefs, I wished I could have been, in some way, touched by this saint. I left the mountain disappointed.

By the time we got to the road and hiked back through the wheat fields we were hot, sun-baked, dog-tired, and appalled to find we had apparently been locked out of the Badaran hotel. It had been a special festival day for the village, something to do with the approaching harvest, and every last person was in the plaza having fun. After a search we discovered an unlocked back door leading us through a laundry, a utility room and a store. Once in, we felt no compunction making for the bar where Terence pulled us both a long, delicious beer. That night dinner was served at a very late hour.

Western monasticism shifted from the Egyptian desert to Italy. Here, since the fifth century, monasteries had been controlled and governed by an anonymous document regulating communal life. This was the *Regula Magistri*. In the sixth century Benedict of Nursia used this as the base from which to formulate his famous Rule. Fuller and more carefully thought out, Benedict's Rule became the model for Western monasticism. We know of Benedict and what preceded his Rule from the *Dialogue*, a text written by Gregory the Great, a pope much impressed by Benedict's erudition. His work is a collection of four books about Italian saints and the signs and wonders they performed. Exaggerated in style, the stories are told by way of a dialogue, Gregory's interlocutor lamenting that he had never heard of anyone in Italy famous for their virtue. To set him straight, Gregory offered this series of stories. They made popular medieval reading.

The second volume of the *Dialogue* is devoted entirely to Benedict. Born in 480 in a small hill town in

Umbria, Benedict was sent to Rome to receive a classical education. Despising formal learning as well as the depraved life-style of his fellow students, Benedict abandoned Rome and returned to rural Italy with his nurse, settling in a small mountain town called Enfide. Here he met and befriended a monk called Romanus. When Benedict discovered the entrance to a cave hidden at the bottom of a deep and gloomy valley, he was encouraged by Romanus to use the shelter as a hermit's retreat. Forsaking his nurse, he spent the next three years there foraging for food and sustained by the occasional loaf of bread brought to him by his new friend. Gregory claims that in this cave Benedict matured both in mind and character, becoming wise beyond his years. His pious life attracted pupils and sympathizers. Now famous, he was asked to act as abbot in a nearby religious house. This venture proved unsuccessful. Later he established his own monastery on the top of Monte Cassino just outside Rome. It was here that he formulated and wrote his Rule.

Influenced by Pachomius, Augustine of Hippo, and John Cassian, Benedict writes with extreme exactitude. In seventy-three chapters he presents the monastic constitution and addresses various aspects of everyday living: the duties of the monks, lapses and punishments and the regulations governing eating, fasting, work, dress and the admission of new brethren. The monks were to be self-sufficient and live as one family under one roof, the rigors of the solitary life frowned upon. The most important task of the day was participation in the communal prayer and study. This provided the monks' basic framework. Starting at midnight, seven services known as offices were to be sung at intervals throughout the next twenty-four hours.

While strict, the Rule is also compassionate and calls for moderation. For instance, Benedict insists that the monks' fasting was not to impede their prayer. Two dishes were to be served at the main meal, providing the diners with a choice. Allowances had to be made for climatic conditions and the different abilities of individual monks, especially in the case of illness or age-related problems. Guests were to be welcomed as though they were Christ, but housed in a separate guest-house lest they disrupt the cohesion of the brethren. Prospective monks were not allowed easy entry, but had to undergo a trial period so they could ascertain their suitability for the demanding lifestyle. After this apprenticeship they took vows of obedience (placing oneself under the direction of the abbot/abbess), stability (committing oneself to a particular monastery) and "conversion of manners" which included the forgoing of private ownership and the commitment to celibacy. Whatever property the new monk still had was distributed to the poor or given to the community. Outside of communal prayer, the monks' day was divided into periods of manual work and the compulsory reading of sacred texts. Upon the death of the abbot it was the monks' responsibility to elect a new leader from amongst those in the community.

It has generally been suggested that monasteries in the Middle Ages proliferated because the monks were provided with a safe haven in a chaotic and hostile world. Because all their needs were met, the monks were also criticized for failing to take responsibility for their lives, opting instead for an easy life. This assertion is debatable. In the preface to his Rule Benedict states, 'We must create a *scola* for the Lord's service'.

The historian, C.H. Lawrence, provides a sixth century interpretation for the Latin *scola*, understanding the term to have a military as well as an academic meaning. In Rome it was a term used for a special defence regiment, a *corps d'élite*, stationed outside the city walls.

Benedict defines the nature of his monastery in this sense of *scola*. It was not to be a quiet sanctuary nor a school in the academic sense, but 'a kind of combat unit where the recruits were trained and equipped for spiritual warfare under an experienced commander—the abbot. The object was the conquest of sensuality and self-will so as to make a man totally receptive to God'. A life dedicated to such an end is the complete reversal of everyday experience and could hardly be seen as easy. The strength of mind required for this commitment is reflected in the architectural style of the Benedictine monasteries as they evolved over time. By the tenth century and viewed from afar, the monasteries looked formidable.

Benedictine houses came relatively late to Spain. In the sixth and seventh centuries communities had been established but operated according to different rules. Inspired by the Visigoth rulers and missionaries from England and Ireland, there was a mixture of regimes. Isidore's system, heavily influenced by eastern tradition, was popular. It was not until the advent of Cluny (the monastery established in Burgundy in the tenth century), that the Benedictine Rule was introduced into Spain. In the space of time between Benedict's life and the establishment of this particular monastic house, Benedictine influence had waned. Cluny's astonishing achievement was the manner in which this Rule was reinstated all over Europe.

Cluny owes its existence to Odo, a cleric comfortably ensconced in a French canonry in Tours. One day Odo had been glancing at the Benedictine Rule and was overcome because he suddenly realized Benedict's text had made him dissatisfied with his life. There and then he decided to become a monk instead of a simple cleric. He set out to find a monastery where this Rule was observed, but such a house was difficult to find. Eventually he arrived at a remote abbey in Burgundy. The abbot was Berno, a monk who had been commissioned to re-establish a Benedictine house. Berno, impressed by Odo's zeal, allowed him to take up the monk's habit. A few years later in 909, Berno was visited by Duke William III of Aquitaine. Old, childless and with murder on his conscience, the Duke decided he needed to found a monastery for the sake of his soul. Taking the abbot he set forth to survey his Burgundian estate, searching for a suitable site. When Berno chose a richly wooded valley, William protested, claiming this forest as his favourite hunting ground. Berno replied with a question, 'Which will serve you better at the Judgement, the prayers of monks or the baying of hounds?' William yielded and signed over the land. Because the document preceded Gregory VII's reforms, the Duke was also able to provide a foundation charter that forbade any lay or ecclesiastical interference. Cluny was built and remained totally autonomous. Unhindered by outside pressures, the monastery grew to be a formidable power and dominated the religious life of Western Europe for the next several centuries.

In his book, *Millennium*, Tom Holland describes Cluny as 'a glory', its valley protected from the outside world by sheltering forests and hills. He claims the monks' genuine and obsessive drive for 'purity of heart' had created something miraculous. This monastery became a refuge from the evil of the times, so much so the papacy, in 'naked awe', claimed Cluny as 'Christendom's most impregnable sanctuary'. In violent times it offered 'the rarest and most precious of all balms: order and clear-sightedness'. Odo was the one responsible for this revitalized Benedictine ideal. Berno's abbacy had been short and Odo, as his replacement, was astoundingly successful because, even more than Berno, he truly lived the Benedictine ideal. Worship as opposed to manual labour now became the work of the monks. Every hour of every day the monks sang praises to the Lord in the form of prayers, hymns, anthems and responses. They sang even as they were shaved. The entire monastery seemed shrouded in holiness. Rudolf Glaber, a tenth century monk and chronicler writing for the laity claimed, 'so reverently are the masses performed, so piously and worthily, that you would think them the work, not of men, but of angels'. The piety appealed to the aristocracy and endowments flooded in. Cluny became very rich.

The abbots of Cluny were not only holy men, but also astute administrators, excellent arbitrators and perceptive politicians. Cluny was soon called upon to assist with the troublesome affairs in Rome. Wholeheartedly endorsing the Gregorian reform movement initiated by Pope Gregory VII, the monastery was frequently approached by various popes and asked to help settle disputes, restore clerical discipline and generally assist in the reform of the church by alleviating the abuse and exploitation that had been metred out by lay rulers. The abbots were also asked to reorganize old monastic houses and establish new ones according to Benedict's Rule. Because the relics of Saint James had become popular, and pilgrimage to Santiago seen as spiritually and financially advantageous, Cluny also turned its attention to northern Spain, founding monasteries and hospices and providing much of the necessary infrastructure to secure the way to the holy city.

Many of the Benedictine monasteries I saw on the Camino have not endured the passage of time. In Sahagún only a few poignant ruins survive of a once powerful monastery dedicated to the third century saints, Facundo and Primitivo, martyrs who were tortured and beheaded on the banks of the nearby River Cea. According to legend after their decapitation milk as well as blood gushed from their necks. Strategically built on the agricultural plains of the Meseta, this monastic house bore witness to the fierce wars fought between the Muslims and Christians. In spite of constant friction Sahagún became one of the most important religious and economic centres in eleventh century Spain. The very impressive fifteenth century arched gateway still stands, its past splendour blemished by today's civic guard who have utilized part of the ruin to build a very uninspiring brick barrack. Terence, who on occasions, also has an unquenchable curiosity, found evidence of further ruins near the river, suggesting the complex was indeed large. We also stumbled on an ancient-looking, extremely tall, stone wall completely enclosing an area about an acre in size and standing alone on the edge of the town. The enormous and ancient wooden double doors were securely locked. To Terence's exasperation I walked every inch of this wall and nowhere could I find a peep-hole or foot-hold that would allow me to see over. I left Sahagún with my curiosity unassuaged.

To leave Sahagún one must cross a pretty medieval bridge that spans the river. Immediately one enters Charlemagne's legendary Field of Lances, a site where once a battle against the Muslims had supposedly been fought. The night before this clash an amazing miracle had occurred. At that time Charlemagne was in Spain under two pretexts, firstly to safeguard the way to Santiago, making it safe for pilgrims, and, more importantly, to secure his own territory in the north. The night before the battle the Christian soldiers, having prepared their weapons, stuck their lances in the ground forming a straight line in front of the camp. At dawn the following day they were amazed to find these weapons had grown into full-sized trees. Astonished at this great wonder, purportedly wrought by God, they felt compelled to cut the trees off at ground level. The battle that followed was a disaster. Turpin, Charlemagne's archbishop in

Rheims, recorded the tale of this battle in Book IV of the *Codex Calixtinus*. Prone to exaggeration, Turpin wrote that on that fateful day forty thousand Christians fell. Of the tree roots that remained in the ground after the mysterious felling of the trees, a great forest was born, becoming a memorial to those who had been slain. We entered this forest. Observing the relatively immature trees growing in remarkably straight lines, Terence decided that Charlemagne's troops must have been overseen by a very firm and bossy sergeant major!

Terence and I also called in at Leyre, one of Spain's oldest houses and seemingly the first to convert to Benedict's rule. It still operatives as a monastery. We arrived on foot, hiking in from the small village where we had lodged the night before. It was a stiff, uphill walk, Leyre built against the impressive backdrop of the Sierra de Leyre, a long austere mountain range of forbidding rock. It is remarkable how ecclesiastical authorities in medieval times found this secluded location, oversaw the clearing of the dense forest and organized the onerous task of building a large monastic complex.

Apart from the very ancient crypt and some aspects of the Romanesque church, I was sad to find that most of the buildings had been destroyed and rebuilt and now radiate little sense of its medieval past. Nor does the monastery make much of Virila, an extraordinary abbot who, in ancient times, could not comprehend the concept of eternity. Following the call of a sweetly singing nightingale, Virila went into the monastery garden to meditate and there he fell asleep. When he awoke and returned to the monastery he was astonished to see how it had increased in size. When he knocked at the door the monk who answered did not recognize him. Puzzled, then concerned, the monks decided to consult the monastic records. It was found that Virila had been the abbot, but three hundred years had lapsed since his abbacy. The records revealed that he had not died but had simply disappeared. Having been miraculously returned, they all praised the Virgin who suddenly appeared at the window in the form of the nightingale, so confirming Virila's identity. Alfonso X, King of Castile, León and Galicia, tells the story of this miracle in his superb *Cantigas de Santa Maria*, a collection of medieval poems set to music and exquisitely illustrated.

Samos is yet another still operative and once very splendid monastery. Walking the Camino and entering the village it was as though I had come upon an enchanted land. I first saw this religious house in early morning sunshine set against a backdrop of Galician forest and built beside an idyllic river. It glowed. Ducks on the water, geese strutting in the grass and hay stacks in a nearby field could only charm. In medieval times Samos played a central role in the history of Galicia. Its wealth was so well known that it was sacked on several occasions by pirates. Favoured by monarchs, it once controlled two hundred towns, one hundred and five churches and three hundred monasteries. Fire marred its fortune. In 1536 it was almost gutted but rebuilt. In 1951 another fire destroyed the library.

The monastery now conducts tours. One enters by alighting a steep monumental staircase more in keeping with a palace as opposed to a monastery. The monk who was my guide was impressive, not only because of his immaculate Benedictine robes, but because he was so tall, extremely handsome and exuded a profound sense of presence. Unfortunately he only spoke Spanish. I know the monastery church he showed us was splendid, but the impact of the modern mural painted on the walls of the upper cloister was so forceful I have no memory of this church. The paintings depict episodes in the life of Saint

Benedict. The art style is stark and dramatic, showing larger than life monks dressed in black and looking down at the viewer with severe expressions. As opposed to the gentle being I knew from Gregory the Great's *Dialogue* and the splendid monk who was my guide, these painted beings were reminiscent of the infernal realm. I left Samos unnerved.

What impressed me about the monasteries we visited in northern Spain was their mysteriousness and secrecy. Abandoned religious houses are always baffling. They also make me sad, the unknown monks or nuns who once lived and prayed there now vanished and forgotten. In communities which had withstood the passage of time, visitors are only allowed to visit the church and cloister; the rest of the complex is always strictly out of bounds, doors securely locked. This is understandable in those houses still operative, but why could we not have been allowed the run of the slowly decaying Irache?

Monasteries are also enclosed by an enormously high outer wall, the stout wooden doors always bolted. On the Camino I liked to stay in monastic refuges, but here, too, pilgrims were accommodated separately and the guest-house staffed by lay people. I never once saw into the monastery living quarters. In part I think this exclusivity, together with the arcane lifestyle, imbues those in holy orders not only with the inexplicable, but also with a sense of tremendous power. This was particularly evident when Terence and I visited the Convent of the Saint Clares just outside Castrojeriz.

As an enclosed contemplative order the Saint Clares have no access to the outside world. We called on a damp spring day, the air so loaded with misty moisture that the walled convent seemed to waft in and out of the surrounding fields of wheat. When we arrived the gates were open and we made our way through the neat forecourt to the church beyond. Inside it was gloomy, the only light a glow on the far west wall opposite the altar. Terence recognized the discreet beam was illuminating a monstrance, the receptacle used to display the consecrated host. We soon realized that what we had taken for the back wall was a grille separating the nuns' choir from the church. This choir was dark and partly curtained and in the shadowy depth it was just possible to discern the slightest of human movements. We concluded the nuns were venerating the exposed sacrament. As quietly as we could we looked over the church and just before we left I could not help myself; I walked up to the monstrance and knelt. The gesture was ignoble as my intension was not to revere but to spy on these mysterious, unreachable women hidden in the deep gloom behind the grille. I saw very little, but the sense of numinosity in those choir stalls was palpable.

I am fascinated by those who choose to live such committed and austere lives and, because I wonder at the power monastics are capable of exerting, I appreciated Jean Leclercq's, *The Love of Learning and the Desire for God*, an historical work providing insight into monastic sensibility. A one-time Benedictine monk and now an author and scholar, Leclercq claims monastic strength is a faculty dependent on study. Contradicting the popular notion of the jolly, illiterate monk or nun bent simply on singing God's praises, Leclercq reminds us that in medieval times those in Holy Orders were of aristocratic birth and thus cultured and well-versed in sophisticated medieval manners. They were also educated, capable of reading and writing as well as speaking Latin. For those who had not learnt these arts, and for the children dedicated to the monastery early in life, schooling was provided. However, monastic training differed from the scholarship offered in the cathedral schools. Where those students were taught to question dogma and texts and debate issues, monks and nuns were forbidden to query or dispute. Instead they had to master the art of meditation. Like the cathedral scholar, a sound grounding in grammar had to be gained, but then the monk or nun assumed a position of 'intelligent ignorance' in order to free the mind.

The practice of monastic meditation is complex and always based on a text. The process combined two Latin concepts, one being *meditari*, which translates as 'thinking the mind' or 'reflecting'. The second was *meditatio*, a meditation exercise that implies thinking on the specific thing one had just read about with the intention of assimilating and becoming it. Leclercq states each meditative session would involve first preparing oneself by setting aside what one already knew about the text and opening oneself to God, allowing Him to speak through the words. The wisdom gleaned from the text had to be desired with all the heart. The next step was the endeavour to integrate that wisdom into one's very being.

At the turn of the millennium monastic reading was slow but at the same time active. For a start it had to be audible, silent reading forbidden. This meant the monk heard the words as well as saw them. Like chant or writing, the body was involved, the mouth pronouncing the words, the memory fixing them, the intelligence understanding the message and the will desiring to put it into practice. The true end was always the search for God and the motivation spiritual. With practice and time a successful monk would undergo a gradual, profound transformation. This was how it should have been, but sometimes an intelligent or more mature postulant found it difficult to be so constrained, and the training of the monastery would vie with cathedral humanism. The monastic struggle was therefore arduous and not all monks succeeded. The successful one, gaining an elusive knowledge unknown in the everyday world, would no longer be of the norm. It is little wonder that those in holy orders, austere and withdrawn, are usually understood as other-worldly and, for some, disconcerting.

As literature assumed a place of unparalleled importance in the monastery and convent, the only texts appropriate for monks and nuns were those that would further their knowledge of the divine. In his Rule Benedict recommended only the Bible, Cassian whose *Collations* introduced Egyptian asceticism to the West and Saint Basil, a renowned early Eastern theologian. These texts could be read in the refectory, in the choir and before guests. Later monastic libraries added commentaries on the Bible, the writings of the patristic fathers, biographies, hagiography and, in some monasteries, a selection of the classical authors, these texts introduced to Europe by the invading Muslims or else resurrected from old monastic archives because of the new Islamic influence.

For some abbots the classics were problematic, the ancients unacquainted with Jesus and their work therefore considered unworthy or heretical. Other abbots thought these writings commendable and decided that if the authors had lived at a later date they would have made an exemplary Christian. In her book, *The Medieval Vision*, Carolly Erickson records a legend circulating in the thirteenth century which demonstrates how the ignominy of paganism was removed from the teachings of Plato. According to her story Plato's tomb was, at one point, opened. Miraculously found on his corpse was a golden inscription proclaiming his belief in Jesus who was soon to be born of a virgin and, after suffering for the human race, would rise up to heaven. For some this story legitimized Plato's writings.

All monastic texts were written in Latin. In early medieval times the Romance languages had barely taken form and the Germanic language poorly expressed Catholic dogma which was already rich in nuance. The Latin favoured was a Christianised form, less vigorous than that of classical times. Flexible and more musical, it was better suited to expressive poetic writing, like parts of the Bible. Latin was also a language known to the elite because it had been part of their education.

Sacred learning of this nature may well have been easier for the medieval monk and nun, their minds accepting without question the reality of other realms and the primacy of incorporeal forces. God and his angels were understood as real. Both Leclercq and Erickson acknowledge the medieval imagination as both active and vigorous, not only allowing access to visions, but also granting monastics the ability to 'make present' the literature they read. Where many post-modern minds are almost one-dimensional, limited by logic and scientific scepticism, the medieval imagination was unbounded. As I perused Erickson's text I wondered what kind of God the medieval monastic mind saw. The didactic artwork in the Spanish cathedrals depicted the great Old Testament Judge and Patriarch lording it over his broken son and accepting the martyrs only because they had suffered so. Did the monasteries know of a kinder God? The writings of Saint Bernard of Clairvaux suggests that they may well have.

Bernard was a Benedictine monk and abbot who sought to reform the extravagances of the Benedictines by establishing the more modest Cistercian order. To achieve this shift, he wrote prolifically. In his text *On Loving God*, Bernard spoke of a Divinity that is compassionate as well as sympathetic towards humanity. Bernard also understood people not as fallen beings and in need of grovelling, but only as 'distorted'. He saw humanity, created in the image of God, as 'tarnished', never beyond repair and able to once again reach out to accept that original 'Likeness'. In his Sermon on the *Song of Songs*, Bernard's concern was to move a quailing people away from the fear of God to a more mature sensibility where they could reach out as Solomon's bride who, 'in confidence, kisses His mouth and joins Him in the sweet embrace of love'.

Many post-moderns would probably cringe at this, seeing it as either too mystical or as sentimental. They may also bulk at the thought of having to consider the nature of God. For these folk 'God is dead'. However, not all contemporary thinkers accept this Nietzschean assertion, one being George Steiner. In his work, *Real Presences*, God is indeed real, but neither as the cantankerous old man nor as a 'fossil still embedded in the mind and yet to be relinquished'.

Steiner's God is a 'Presence', without form, never directly addressed but to be found in language and the way language performs. He asserts that humanity's need to find meaning in existence, in particular in the abstruse meaning communicated through literature, the arts and in musical form, is always rooted in 'the transcendent'. It is his lament that in today's cultural landscape, dominated as it is by politics and technology, we have been insulated from this sensibility. Deprived of primary texts and insensitive to syntax, poetic language and aesthetic experience, many of us possess only an 'absence of presence'. Intangible and elusive, this kind of literary God emerges as a 'wager', a gamble on the part of both creator and reader as they search for 'the meaning of meaning' found in the encounter with that nebulous 'other' strangely located in the text. Steiner claims if we recognize this encounter we can either be shaken out of complacency or provoked to examine our humanity more deeply.

It is not that the transcendent infuses all art, but rather the search for meaning and the drive to create as God created become the powerful moving force. It seems Steiner's complex insights are born out of an aversion to post-modern nihilism and the contemporary propensity to refuse meaning. His insights affirm a belief that the *logos*[18] is still to be found and remains meaningful. Such a God is not sentimental. It simply 'is' and need not be articulated, just recognized and appreciated so that life may be enriched.

Another academic fascinated by the production of 'presence' and tired of the contemporary world is Hans Ulrich Gumbrecht. His discipline, too, is the humanities which he understands as dominated by a 'meaning culture', a term he uses to describe a Cartesian worldview that places higher value on the interpretation of texts and phenomena than on material presence. In his book, *The Production of Presence: What Meaning cannot Convey*, Gumbrecht argues that the 'meaning culture', while acknowledging humanity, disallows that humanity to be part of the world. For academics in particular, thinking takes them beyond, or below, everyday reality. Western culture he says is merely 'a progressive abandonment and forgetting of presence'. To remedy this Gumbrecht advocates a 'presence culture' in which humans refrain from interpreting the world and instead attempt to become part of it. Gumbrecht does not wish to replace the

---

[18] At its most basic *logos* translates as 'word', but it has a much broader meaning. In philosophy it is a term for order and knowledge. Aristotle used the term to refer to 'reasoned discourse'. Steiner uses the term in its Biblical sense in which the apostle, John, identified *logos* as that through which, in the beginning, all things were made. John also identified Jesus, or the Divine, as the incarnate Logos. As I read Steiner, he seems to suggest that the 'presence' he finds both in language and beauty can be correlated with that which is divine.

'meaning culture' with that of 'presence', but wants these sensibilities to oscillate, always in a state of tension, the one informing the other.

To explain himself Gumbrecht uses medieval culture. In much the same way as the truth of God was to appear for the monks, he suggests we, too, refrain from imposing meaning and simply allow an 'unshaped' knowledge to be revealed, a knowledge that is not exclusively conceptual, prior or dependent on interpretation. Like Steiner, Gumbrecht encourages an appreciative approach. For both theorists, aesthetics plays a significant role, the viewing of art manifesting in epiphanies or 'moments of intensity', an experience that seems similar to monastic meditation. For Gumbrecht this is not religious in the usual sense, but is instead understood as 'a surrogate religious experience'.

Having read these two authors I finally understood why I had been so impressed with my visit to Cartuja Miraflores in Burgos, a monastic house of the Carthusian order. The Carthusians are an unusual religious group founded in 1084 by Saint Bruno of Cologne. Initially Bruno was a diocesan administrator of exceptional intelligence. His future was potentially brilliant, but Bruno had no taste for ecclesiastical politics and took himself, as well as a small number of friends, to a remote uninhabited private house in the Alps. A man of remarkable austerity, he and his friends chose a life of isolation dedicated to poverty, prayer and study. The community he eventually established operated according to its own unique Rule. The monks, though living communally, consider themselves hermits, working, eating and praying alone except for the daily mass which they sang together and a joint Sunday meal eaten in silence.

The Carthusian Rule provided each monk with a small individual living area containing a stove, a workshop and space for praying and sleeping, as well as a small walled garden where they were expected to grow flowers for themselves and vegetables for the common good. As it was in the eleventh century, so it is in Burgos in the twenty-first. Far from the Alps twenty-two Spanish hermit monks live here in a one-time royal palace and hunting lodge donated to the order in 1441 by King John II of Castile. Over this lodge the order built a remarkable monastery. Though the vast grounds were surrounded by the usual impenetrable wall and the complex devoid of all evidence of monks, Terence and I felt an intense sense of their holy presence. This was a complex that clearly took no part in Gumbrecht's 'meaning culture'.

Terence and I walked out to Miraflores on a wet, blustery day. Terence grumbled a lot about the mud, but on our arrival he found the door-keeper's hearty welcome wonderfully restorative. Sheltered from the weather in the monastery's austere atrium, we read the provided literature written by a monk whose sincerity and love for his order were clearly evident. As well as explaining the Carthusian lifestyle and aims, this unnamed monk offered an insight into another unique way Carthusians reach God. As well as contemplation and manual work, these contemplatives find artworks a sound pathway, not only because of the spirituality discerned within the content, but also in the beauty and form of the actual painting. It was explained that the art displayed in the church and in the small adjacent gallery fulfilled much of the monks' liturgical and devotional needs.

In the small Miraflores gallery I found a painting which confirmed the monks' beliefs and Gumbrecht's assertions. It was a picture of the Annunciation. The Carthusian order is dedicated to the Virgin and the devotion they profess to her each day is deeply felt throughout this church and, in particular, in this painting. In my travels in Spain I very rarely noted the names of the painters or sculptors whose works I examined, but I was so taken with this Annunciation I recorded the artist's name. He was the fifteenth century Pedro Berrugete, a Spaniard famous for his transitional style between Gothic and Renaissance. He painted for kings and the great cathedrals.

In this canvas Berrugete has placed the Archangel Gabriel and Mary within a home setting. In the immediate foreground is an ornate arch protectively framing the protagonists. Two connecting rooms are seen with a beautiful Gothic window in the background overlooking a distant treed garden. A superb sense of perspective has been achieved, not only because of the clear passage from foreground to the remote garden, but by way of the geometrical detail in the carpet. The colours are rich and vibrant. Light floods in, suffusing all with a warm yellow glow. The painting looks golden even though no gold paint has been applied. Mary has a delicate refinement, her robes gracefully drawn round her slim form. What I particularly liked about this picture was the fact that Mary and the angel make no eye contact. While the angel's attention is on Mary, Mary looks down, her face contemplative. It is as though she is not only unaware of the angel, but the angel is a figment of her imagination, manifesting as a sudden realization of the profundity of her pregnant condition. This notion is supported by a small, almost unnoticed white dove flying in from the top left of the picture and aimed at Mary's head. For me this makes the story in this picture plausible. All this, as well as the illusion of space and clarity of purpose emphasized by the clear glass vase holding three white lilies, are not sufficient to explain the magic in this picture. It was as though Mary was alive, so much so that when I turned my head I thought she had moved. All I can say is this picture has an ineffable quality and for me, this confirms Steiner's notion that some art is indeed inspired by something over and above the paint and the painter's hand.

The sense of holiness that I searched for in the cathedrals of Northern Spain but could not find, I gleaned in the Spanish monasteries. Though many of the communities in the north are now abandoned or in ruins, it was as if those bygone monks and nuns, in their quest for the Divine, had not only been successful in their search, but had also infused these old buildings with the insights they had discovered, somehow leaving behind traces of that ineffable reality which can only be felt and never articulated. I cannot agree with those who think monasticism had been an irresponsible way of life or an unfortunate renunciation. Though they did withdraw from the world, it was possibly from a shallow existence. What they aspired to instead could have been, for at least some of them, a world of greater richness.

Work cited in this chapter

Bernard of Clairvaux, ed. Emilie Griffin. *Selected Works*. New York, NY: HarperOne. 2005.

Brooke, Christopher. *The Age of the Cloister: The Story of Monastic Life in the Middle Ages*. United Kingdom: Sutton Publishing. 2003.

Butcher, Carmen Acevedo. *Man of Blessing: A Life of Saint Benedict*. Brewster, Mass.: Paraclete Press. 2012.

Erickson, Carolly. *The Medieval Vision: Essays in History and Perception*. New York, NY: Oxford University Press. 1976.

Gitlitz, David M. & Linda Kay Davidson. *The Pilgrimage Road to Santiago*. New York, NY: St. Martin's Press. 2000.

Görg, Peter H. *The Desert Fathers: Saint Anthony and the Beginnings of Monasticism*. San Francisco, Cal: Ignatius Press. 2011.

Gumbrecht, Hans Ulrich. *Production of Presence: What Meaning Cannot Convey*. Stanford, Cal: Stanford University Press. 2004.

Holland, Tom. *Millennium: The End of the World and the Forging of Christendom*. Great Britain: Abacus. 2011.

Keller, John & Annette Grant Cash. *Daily Life Depicted in the Cantigas de Santa Maria*. Lexington, Ken.: The University Press of Kentucky. 1998.

Kerr, Julie. *Life in the Medieval Cloister*. London: Continuum. 2009.

Krüger, Kristina. *Monasteries and Monastic Orders: 2000 Years of Art and Culture*. Potsdam, Germany: hf ullmann. 2010.

Lawrence, C.H. *Medieval Monasticism*. London: Longman. 2001.

Leclercq, Jean, trans. Catherine Misrahi. *The Love of Learning and the Desire for God: A Study of Monastic Culture*. New York, NY: Fordham University Press. 1998.

Merwin, W.S., trans. *Spanish Ballads*. Port Townsend, Washington: Copper Canyon Press. 1961.

St. Benedict. *The Rule of Saint Benedict*. New York, NY: Random House. 1998.

Steiner, George. *Real Presences*. Chicago, Ill.: University of Chicago Press. 1991.

Tamburello, Dennis E. *Bernard of Clairvaux: Essential Writings*. New York, NY: Crossroads Publishing. 2000.

Vattimo, Gianni, trans. David Webb. *Beyond Interpretation: The Meaning of Hermeneutics for Philosophy*. Stanford, Cal: Stanford University Press. 1997.

Ward, Benedicta, trans. *The Sayings of the Desert Fathers*. London: Mowbrays. 1977.

7

Death – Damnation or Delivery?

As I perused various texts trying to glean yet more of the essence of medieval Spain, I discovered that, allegedly, the Spanish have a predilection for death. Travelling on my own as well as with Terence, I was never made aware of this disposition, possibly because I could not converse with the Spanish at a deep level. To understand this propensity I realized I would have to consider the ancients and their various burial places and practices.

As a pilgrim and gazing upon royal tombs, I had taken it for granted that the kings of old died simply because their time had come. I never considered the drama that may have preceded the demise. However, looking at the extravagant effigies in the various cathedrals I visited, I was critical of what I took to be the aggrandizement of medieval royalty. Ultimately, I thought, the end of life should render everyone equal. I decided that, for the Spanish in particular, death in those violent times could be seen as no more than a moral corrective for the ills of castle and court. Later, when I returned with Terence, I had a better understanding of the Spanish throne, as well as the symbolic role of the medieval king.

In the Middle Ages the king was not only the authoritative ruler of a certain people in a certain place, but also an agent of order in a world of chaos, the final arbiter of political disputes and the supreme representative of the secular values and beliefs of the people over whom he reigned. For the medieval historian, Carlos Eire, this meant that the king was central to the social order and supposedly able to maintain stability, security and prosperity because he had been endowed with a certain mystique, his anointing at his coronation supposedly having granted him wisdom and secret power.[19] His death was therefore a momentous occasion and his funeral became a state affair, demonstrating to the common people the continuity of kingly authority. His elaborate tomb was a visible sign not only to honour the dead king, but also to demonstrate to the general public the hierarchical nature of the social order, those at the lower end of the spectrum reminded of their insignificance. Funerals were also linked to the coronation soon to come, ensuring the dynasty's ongoing hold. It was therefore necessary for mausoleums to be ostentatious and effigies to be revered. In Eire's words, tombs were not 'mere ceremonial trappings', but 'primary components in the symbolics of power'.

As we travelled along the Camino trail, Terence and I found several remarkable ceremonial grave sites. The strangest was in the monastery of Santa Maria la Real de Huelgas just outside Burgos. Formally a royal holiday retreat, this religious house was founded in1175 by King Alfonso VIII whose main goal was to create the world's most sumptuous convent for the use of widowed royals and other notable women. Here they were to retire, the term Huelgas derived from *holgar* and meaning 'to rest'. As opposed to the nun's habit, these ladies continued to wear plush court apparel. Surprisingly, Alfonso placed the convent under Cistercian rule, but decreed that the nuns were to answer to no-one but the crown. From the start the ruling abbess was granted extreme power and able to

---

[19] This royal mystique refers to 'The Royal God-Given Right' discussed in Chapter 5.

exercise ecclesiastic, civil and criminal jurisdiction over the convent, the immense King's Hospital nearby and all the villages and estates that the nobility progressively contributed to this house. There was, however, a catch. The convent and church was not for the exclusive use of the women, but also had to serve as a mausoleum for the Castilian and Leónese royals.

The church plan is Gothic. Though built in the form of a Latin cross, the sanctuary and high altar are small and tucked into a single apse. The crossing predominates and is walled off from the nave and aisles. These, too, have been separated, one from the other, the divisions forming a trilogy of long, hollow-sounding halls. Here, parallel to the walls, lie thirty-six royal tombs. A number of unnamed knights recline in the atrium and the dead abbesses in the cloister. Most of the coffins are constructed from plain white stone with a gabled lid, others are intricately carved. The choir, of walnut wood and of simple design, is in the nave and so is disconnected from the high altar. There are fifty stalls against both side walls, one line facing the other, the founding abbess having limited the number of incumbents to one hundred.

Prominently displayed in this space is the lavish double tomb of the convent's founder, Alfonso VIII, and his queen, Eleanor of England. This grand sarcophagus is richly decorated with the castles of Castile and the three Plantagenet lions. It has a central position and is located below the choir and far from the elaborate golden altar on the opposite wall dedicated to Ana of Austria, wife of Philip II. High above the retablo is a long, plain glass window, rounded on the top. If one stands at the foot of the royal sarcophagus, the distinct lines made by the regular, highly polished floor boards direct the eye all the way along the nave, up to the altar and the window above. When I was there the light flowing in was blinding, making me feel as though I was on the cusp of Judgement Day. I was happy to move on.

Most of the tombs lie in the galleries on either side of the nave. Sixteen tombs can be seen against the walls in the aisle dedicated to Saint Catherine, thirteen in identical plain stone and three richly carved. Pictures of saints decorate these walls, the most unnerving depicting a female in luxurious satin robes, eyes raised to heaven and about to slice off the head of a man lying at her side. Already she had his hair in her grasp.

In size the convent is vast, its outer architecture complicated. The inner church stonework is plain, the slender pillars unfluted and the vaults simple. However, opulent artwork flouts the simplicity of the Cistercian tradition. It sports much gold and combines the extravagance of the Western Renaissance style with Islamic vegetal and geometric design. Three small chapels entirely fashioned by early Muslim artists put one in mind of the Crusades. Paintings of battle, coats of arms, pennants, walls hangings depicting Roman emperors and the presence of the anonymous knights, one sarcophagus still draped with an original tabard,[20] convey a distinctive military air and could be seen as representative of Eire's 'symbolics of power' supposedly imparting strength and authority. However, the fact that this was the domain of women somewhat undercuts this assertion.

The nave and aisles are light and airy, but still there is a gloomy feel to this convent. Death is an inescapable reality, but to face it every day as one sings the office must have been intimidating and, for those of the twenty-first century, oppressively morbid. This sense is exacerbated by the fact that the spaciousness one should feel in a church has been contracted and compartmentalized into

---

[20] The short emblazoned garment worn over armour.

what I thought ought to have been private spaces. Even though it was appropriate for medievals to be constantly reminded of death, I still felt sorry for these long dead women. Once powerful, and then locked away from the world in the company of the dead, I thought they had got a raw deal. In las Huelgas I gave more thought to those distant nuns than I did to the royal dead. This is not how it should be in a mausoleum.

Where I found the Huelgas convent tombs problematic, the Royal Burial Vault in the Romanesque Basilica in León delights and astonishes. This church, first built in the tenth century, was dedicated to Saint Isidore in 1063. Queen Sancha of León commissioned the building. Here she intended to lie in death, her dead husband beside her.[21] Constructed in the portico of the church as it was then, the mausoleum is small, approximately eight metres square. Two robust columns divide the area into three spaces, all vaulted and supported by six round arches resting on the two central pillars, on wall columns and on the exterior arcading. The capitals that finish off the short, thick supports are exceptionally beautiful and said to be the first Romanesque sculptures to appear in northern Spain.

What really dazzles in this mausoleum is the bright Romanesque painting that festoons all the arches and the low ceiling. Whether because of the location, humidity, temperature or air-flow, this artwork has maintained its colour and definition, making it the most striking and extensive Romanesque work I saw in northern Spain. The subject matter is diverse. There are the usual New Testament scenes from the life of Jesus, an enormous Christ as ruler of the universe, the evangelists represented

---

[21] The building of this basilica, the commissioning of the tomb and the installation of the saint have been discussed in Chapter 1.

in symbolic form, angels, the holy spirit as dove, as well as mundane shepherds and farm workers, servants waiting at table, the famous and charming farming calendar and other anecdotal details of Leonese medieval life worked into the various Biblical compositions and keeping a protective watch over the bodies of the kings and queens lying at their rest. For some this vault could be recognized as an expression of power and authority because of the vibrant colour and artistic richness, but for me the everyday touches painted into the serious scriptural compositions seemed to make this royal burial house benevolent rather than authoritative. As well as the ardent medieval desire to access the divine and immortality, I also felt a lingering sense of the pagan and this, too, dissipated the sense of ongoing power.

The royal effigies found in the Monastery of Santa Maria la Real in the town of Nájera were a more apt expression of royal authority because they were formally arranged. As one enters, the monastery church is not particularly impressive. The entrance is near the high altar and, having admired this, I turned to wander into the depths of the basilica. There, in hushed dimness, I beheld the ancient dead. There are thirty in all, their graves decorously arranged in straight lines. Bar one, they are all royals from the kingdom of Navarre, their tombs dating from the tenth to the thirteenth century. However, in the mid-fifteen hundreds they were all exhumed and each monarch and his queen, as well as several uncrowned offspring, provided with exquisitely carved effigies.

The Navarrese royals belonged to members of two historic dynasties, the Jimena, an indigent Navarrese family and who governed from Nájera from 918 to 1076, and the other dynasty founded by Garcia Ramirez who held sway from 1135 to 1234. Over three centuries members from both lines were tormented by personal jealousies and an insatiable greed for military and political might. The twelve most important tombs rest in a dark recess along the back wall of the church facing the high altar. The line is broken by a narrow, arched passageway leading to a cave in the cliff face against which this monastery is built.[22] Examining each effigy I was amazed by the sculptor's skill. Though stilled by death, each expressive face was unique, the clearly defined features revealing very separate identities. Small details extended their characters: a dog at the foot of a queen, a sword laid crosswise over a breast instead by the side, possibly indicating that this particular knight had been a crusader, one queen ornately dressed and jewelled, another demurely veiled, a king with a luxuriant flowing beard, others with cropped facial hair, one royal clasping a breviary, another a rosary. Because their personalities were portrayed so specifically and seemed historically accurate, I decided to find out who they were.

After much searching I discovered the oldest tomb in the pantheon belongs to Sancho Garcés II, ruler from 970-994, lying on the left-hand side of the cave passage as one faces the altar. Sancho Garcés was son of the founder of the Nájera dynasty. His queen, Doña Urraca Clara, occupies the grave beside him. Next to Doña Urraca lies Bermudo III of León, a kingdom at odds with Nájera. At the tender age of twenty Bermundo engaged in territorial disputes with Nájera and was slain. The year was 1037. I have not yet found out why one of Nájera's enemies lies here in Navarre. Sancho the Wise, ruler from 1150-1194, and his queen, Doña Beatriz, lie to the left of Bermundo. Flanking the cave passage, one on either side, are Garcia Sánchez III, 1035-1054, fighter of Moors and founder of the Monastery Santa Maria la Real, and his wife, Doña

---

[22] The story of this cave and the statue that was there found will be told in the following chapter.

Estefania, whom he deeply loved. As opposed to lying recumbent, their effigies are piously kneeling. Beside Garcia Sánchez is Sancho IV, 1054-1076. Gaining the throne at the age of fourteen, he battled to maintain his position as king. Led by his brother Ramón, his siblings conspired against Sancho, forcing him over a cliff and usurping the throne. Sancho's queen, Doña Placencia, lies beside him. Ramón, the traitorous brother, rests two graves away. On the left of Ramón is Doña Blanca Garcés of the House of Jimena and grandchild of El Cid. Aged sixteen, this Navarrese princess was married to Sancho III of Castile, a gesture designed to reconcile the two houses. Doña Blanca died in childbirth. She was nineteen years old. Her death was a grievous blow to her husband, so much so his pain is mentioned in the inscription on her tomb. (The gabled lid of her original tomb has survived and is displayed in the church as a free-standing monument.) Beside her effigy is Ramiro, a prince in direct line to the throne. On the death of the king, Ramiro could find no supporters and, another victim of political intrigue, his throne, too, was wrested from him. The annals claim he died heroically in battle in 1083.

And so it was in Navarre; brother who had been pitted against brother, son against father, assassins as well as victims of family feuding, war and sorrow, they now rest here one beside the other, finally silenced. In the quiet of the church there was no feeling of hatred or grief. Though the ambiance was gloomy and chill, the sense of death was difficult to grasp. Initially, and from afar, I thought the formal arrangement of the tombs suggested order and authority, but close up I had a change of heart, the effigies unable to communicate the over-riding power of kingly icons. Instead of representing might, I saw beings recumbent seemingly peacefully breathing as though quietly asleep. Terence suggested this was because these royals had been disturbed and were not now lying in their original graves, but I decided the felt absence of death and military turmoil arose from the craft of the Renaissance sculptor. His work was just too beautiful. Exposing so much personality these people could not be read as mere symbols. Carved with delicate sensitivity, each likeness seemed to say more about the artist who had fashioned the stone than the dead royals he was attempting to portray. Working on these graves several centuries later it felt as though he was attempting to find a solace for the past political mayhem, as well as consolation for human mortality. The Romanesque lid to Doña Blanca's original tomb depicting her soul, carved to resemble a little baby received into heaven by angels, her grieving husband looking on and a procession of woeful mourners, was the only piece that communicated loss and sorrow, possibly because in the stone there was a narrative to be read. Even in this mausoleum the machinations of medieval power games escaped me.

Terence and I spent a long time in the Nájera pantheon and it was late when we eventually made our exit. Having examined the exterior of the monastery and the strange way it backed into the red cliff of conglomerate stone, we intended to make our way back to our pension, but the weather was balmy and we decided to dine *al fresco* beside the murmuring river. When we took our places in a restaurant the swallows were gracefully gliding in the deep dusk. As the kindly restaurateur took our order, it was difficult to believe that this small town, strategically placed in the fertile region of Riojas, seat of the royal house of Navarre and at one time capital of all the Christian lands from the Atlantic to Catalonia, sandwiched between warring kingdoms and always taking the brunt of the past military mayhem, could now be so tranquil and sleepy.

Because it is difficult to find primary documentation concerning common folk, those who wish to study death in medieval times have to resort to examining the manner in which the elite exit this world. I found Carlos Eire's understanding particularly illuminating, his research influenced by the manner in which the Spanish have embraced Catholicism. For all Catholic Europe before the Enlightenment, death was the moment when salvation was decided and the soul began its unseen spiritual journey. It was a moment orchestrated by the church, and Spain, being the staunchest defender of the Catholic religion, allowed its ecclesiastics complete control over the people, utterly shaping social behaviour. Reading the various Spanish ascetics, Eire came to believe that a normal person's understandable denial of death had, in medieval Spain, been overtaken by an ardent desire for this final departure, and this to a degree unseen anywhere else in Europe. Eire understood Philip II of Spain (1527-98) as a prime example of this sensibility.

This king died in the Escorial, an austere and gloomy edifice of gigantic proportions built by Philip on the instructions of his father, Charles V, the Holy Roman Emperor. Lacking what he thought was a sufficiently prestigious burial place, Charles wanted his son to provide a mausoleum appropriate to the might of the Hapsburg dynasty which had by this time reached the zenith of its power. Philip acquiesced and in twenty-one years built not only a royal pantheon but also a grand palace, a school and a monastery run under the auspices of the Hieronymite monks, an enclosed order particular to Spain. The location for this Palace of Death was a lonely village, once the site of an iron foundry on the grey and sombre slopes of the Sierra Guadarrama and remote from the bustle of Madrid.

At the time of its construction the complex was recognized as a 'new Temple of Solomon', 'a monument of military might' and an 'expression of a sacralized monarchy'. It is also the site of the world's largest collections of holy relics and books printed before AD 1500. In its time it was understood as a shrine to God as well as to the current kings and so I find it ironic that the name, 'Escorial' means 'slag-heap'. In the twenty-first century it can be viewed not only as vast and imposing, but also grim, reflecting a power-crazed people preoccupied with decorum, protocol and intrigue. The Spanish philosopher, José Ortega y Gasset, writing in the first half of the twentieth century, recognized the Escorial as strange, saying of it, 'We apprehend here better than anywhere else the Spanish essence, that subterranean spring from which has bubbled up the history of Europe's most abnormal people'. According to Eire an aspect of this abnormality was the Spanish attitude to death.

Philip's departure from this life was truly gruesome. Gout, arthritis, dropsy and a remorseless fever meant he suffered unrelenting pain for fifty-three days before succumbing to death. His skin erupted into boils and ulcers and diarrhoea meant he practically rotted away in his own excrement. Every detail of his agony was recorded, this death receiving more attention than that of any other European monarch of that time. This was because the Spanish believed Philip's fortitude and indifference to pain and suffering promoted advantageous attitudes from which the social order could benefit. His death was to be understood as a lesson in the art of dying.

Philip prepared for his transition to the afterlife by first ordering the building of his coffin. When complete it was brought to his room, a dark chamber plainly furnished. Much earlier Philip had looked ahead to this day and procured the necessary material, a particularly durable Eastern wood salvaged from a shipwreck and brought to Spain from Portugal at great expense. A month before he died he ordered monks to descend the black marble staircase leading to the Escorial burial vault below the high altar and there measure his father's casket, his own to be constructed according to the same dimensions. He asked, too, that it be lead-lined to 'prevent bad odours escaping'. He allowed the inside to be covered with white silk, but the outside was to be draped in black and trimmed with gold. He also requested they open his father's coffin to observe the garments in which Charles had been laid to his rest. In like manner Philip in death wore a simple white gown, was wrapped in a winding sheet and laid out with a plain wooden cross around his neck.

Before his demise Philip asked that the small box bequeathed to him by his father be brought out. This receptacle contained two candles from the Shrine of Our Lady of Monserrat and a small crucifix which had comforted Charles in his final moments. Philip was now not only preparing to console himself with this same cross, but he also requested that it be restored to its box upon his demise and brought out once again at the time of his son's death. This was the future Philip III. Unlike Charles, the dying Philip did not participate in a trial run of his funeral ceremony while he was still alive, but he did have three confessors with whom he constantly prayed. His death chamber was also adjacent to the monastery chancel and Philip was able to observe and hear the daily mass from his bed. Finally, this stern king ordered that his son witness his death as a lesson in mortality. He died gazing at the high altar.

In part Philip's funeral anxiety could be read as a consequence of his pain and not necessarily as a drive to embrace death. However, in medieval times preparations for death were a major preoccupation for dying monarchs and were duly recorded in the annals. In her biography Sister Maria del Carmen Fernández de Castro Cabeza, utilizing these annals, tells of similar arrangements made for Ferdinand III of Castile (1199-1252). Before receiving his final mass Ferdinand requested that he be dressed in 'the beautiful white and gold rich silk shirt he wore on feast days'. Now focussed on the afterlife and not wanting to see his earthly crown and sceptre, he asked that all his royal paraphernalia be removed from his chamber and bade them erect instead an altar covered with 'beautiful purple damask and fine linen whiter than snow'. This was to be placed opposite his bed. 'A sacred crucifix and six great candlesticks with lighted candles' were set upon this altar.

The chronicler of the time describing this mass tells that, when the king observed the elevated host, he felt a great surge of love, so much so he was able to lift himself from his bed and kneel upon the hard marble tiles. Because he believed himself to be a miserable penitent, the king had prepared himself for the moment. Humbling himself before God, he took a length of rope from a pocket which he tied around his neck. Then, 'contrite and humiliated', he made an extremely lengthy confession as well as lamenting his weaknesses and pleading for forgiveness. Having received the host, he asked for his rich garments to be removed and his body once more placed upon his bed. He then addressed his sons, bade all those he loved farewell and gazed upon a statue of the 'Virgin of Battles' which a priest had placed on his bedside table. Praying and imploring, he entered his last agony, a choir intoning the Litany of Saints. Then, in a 'rapture of joy', he asked the choir for the *Te Deum* and thus gladly departed. The chroniclers of the time recorded that 'there above the white roofs of Seville (the city where he died) in the star-filled sky of that May night, they say the angels were heard to sing a song that human ears had never heard before'.

We know nothing of what happened to Ferdinand's soul, but his body proved to be incorruptible and can still be seen today in the Cathedral of Seville enclosed in a very splendid gold and crystal casket. In 1671 this king was canonized.

Clerics, too, took care that they die well. Alban Butler, an eighteenth century hagiographer, provides a description of the demise of Saint Isidore, archbishop of Seville, claiming that as his end drew near he:

'... entreated two bishops to come to see him. With them he went to church, where one of them covered him with sackcloth and the other put ashes on his head. Clothed with the habit of penance, he stretched his hands towards heaven, prayed with great eagerness, and begged aloud the pardon for his sins.'

Then, having received the last sacrament, Butler tells us he 'remitted the bonds of all his debtors, exhorted the people to charity and caused all the money he had not yet disposed of to be distributed among the poor'.

I cannot be sure of the royals from León or Nájera, but in terms of medieval thought, the departure of this archbishop and these two kings would have been understood as a 'good death', in spite of Philip's horrendous suffering. This is because all three had been appropriately prepared. A very real fear at this time was to die suddenly without warning. I have no insight into what the common people did to safeguard themselves against this possibility, but we know that knights and pilgrims took care to confess and celebrate the mass before jousting, marching forth to battle or setting out on a pilgrimage. Royalty and the nobility, too, protected themselves by employing full-time chaplains who could minister in times of crisis. Accordingly Philip, Ferdinand and Isidore were all confessed and shriven and fortunate enough to die with the Viaticum.[23] In early Christian understanding accepting the Viaticum meant that Christ would accompany the newly dead on the journey to the next realm, comforting them and assuring salvation. The affairs of the crown would also have been in order.

In medieval Spain it was not possible to die well unless one's earthly concerns were satisfactorily organized. This was accomplished by the making of a will, an undertaking demanded from everyone no matter how rich or poor the estate. The consequences for those dying without this document were dire, the deceased person denied not only a Christian burial, but also hope of salvation, a disclaimer the rest of early Europe reserved for those who had been excommunicated, declared a heretic, suicided or considered a hardened criminal. With time the harshness of this decree was lessened, especially in rural areas and in cases of severe poverty, providing the family of the deceased offered some form of alms and made a few pious bequests, usually in the form of masses which naturally had to be paid for. When illness was deemed serious and the dying person conscious but still without a will, a notary could be called in at the same time as the priest and the necessary document quickly procured.

A Spanish will was formulaic, divided into two distinct sections, the first part dealing with the spiritual estate of the one about to die. According to the medieval church, no-one could anticipate salvation without the help

---

[23] The Viaticum was the host offered in the final mass and placed on the dying person's tongue.

of the living who were expected to assist the dying person's passage to the afterlife by the use of intercessory prayers. The will specified the nature and duration of these prayers, as well as the masses that were to be said for the one just dead. The document also stipulated the necessary payment. At least one requiem mass was deemed necessary. The wealthy demanded many more, Philip II apparently requesting and paying for daily commemorations for the next two centuries!

In the medieval church there were clerics whose sole function it was to celebrate ongoing votive masses. Because it was Biblically decreed, alms also had to be offered to the poor and the will stipulated what these were and provided the authorization for the payment. The second part of the document dealt with the legal distribution of one's material property. Finally, when one's time came, a representative of the church arrived to take a *pro rata* cut. For us today these wills not only reveal the excessive attention the medieval Spanish devoted to death, but the writing of this document could be seen as initiating the death ritual.

Medieval death rituals have been widely studied. The twentieth century French ethnographer, Arnold Van Gennep, identifies a good medieval death as having a tripartite pattern. As death is a change from one state to another, Van Gennep uses the term 'liminal' to describe the actual death phase, liminal derived from the Latin *limen* meaning threshold. Preceding the actual death, the dying person would undergo certain preliminal rites. Postliminal activities would conclude the translation. The preliminal stage focussed on rituals designed to help the person detach from his or her personal world, as well as from the social order generally. To face the afterlife it was necessary to be physically clean and the soul purged of sin and so purification ceremonials would be offered. The body would be washed and confession heard. Specific prayers were offered and the priest would then administer the laying on of hands and an anointing with holy oil.

The anointing of bodies is not particular to Christianity, but has been an ancient practice found in all cultures and in all eras, even among the Aborigines who used kidney fat and such ancients as the Incas who anointed with blood. For the Jews in Biblical times the practice was reserved for the ordination of Jewish priests and for the consecration of Tabernacle articles. Later, anointing was extended to kings and prophets. The Hebrews used pure olive made holy by prayer and the addition of myrrh, cinnamon or cassia. The purpose of the anointing was to cause the person or the object to become 'most holy'. Cyril of Jerusalem, a fourth century Doctor of the Christian Church, adopted the practice, explaining that when applied with due reverence, the oil could to be understood as an outward sign indicating that the Holy Ghost had been called. All Christians could receive this 'ghost' providing they had been made worthy by way of appropriate ritual and prayer.

In later medieval times the oil was known as Chrism, a word derived from the Greek meaning to daub or rub. Initially a small amount was smeared onto to the head, but after the teaching of Cyril it was also applied to places associated with the senses: the eyes, mouth, ears, hands and feet. According to Frederick Paxton, Spain was the first Christian country to add healing herbs to the oil and to perfume it, usually with balsam, sweet smells indicative of wholesomeness and remote from the cesspit associated with hell and the underworld. Once a year there would be a blessing of this oil, usually on Holy Thursday when God was asked to strengthen the mix with power from the Holy Ghost. Kept safe, often in exquisitely wrought containers, this oil could only be administered to the laity by clerics. In the early Middle Ages one could expect salvation if one had been appropriately anointed.

Once the liminal stage was reached the Viaticum was administered. In medieval Spain a good death was always a public affair and those who were to attend to the dying now gathered to offer supporting prayers. They became the official mourners and chief funeral attendants. It was at this point that a carefully laid out will was appreciated. All being well, this document would also have specified the body's final resting place. In medieval times the only acceptable place for burial was in consecrated ground inside a parish or monastery church, or sometimes in a cloister. Outdoor cemeteries were introduced at a much later date, possibly when the churches had finally reached full capacity.

Where one's remains were placed in the church was of utmost importance. For the well-born the choicest spot, if it could be afforded, was near the altar or close to the Eucharist. If one was royal, aristocratic or of high clerical office, a cathedral burial would be anticipated. For lesser mortals the chancel of the local church or Baptistery was acceptable. Lay tombs were usually found in the atrium and in the periphery of the church complex. In Spain the burial of the lay was also a family affair, no-one expecting to lie alone in death, each family sharing the same cramped space. This meant that the dead were routinely exhumed and their bones gathered up and crushed into smaller containers and pushed aside to make room for the newest arrival.

I found the thought of these communal graves somewhat macabre and suggested to Terence that many of the churches we had visited in Spain may have been little more than charnel houses rather than ecclesiastical buildings. To my surprise Terence, usually a fastidious man, was quite unperturbed, reminding me that, as a young lad, his grandmother had conveniently inured him against death when she sometimes took him to the family vault in Glasnevin Cemetery in Dublin to visit dead ancestors and chat with them, often asking advice regarding sticky family problems. As he spent his time playing amongst the tombstones in this vast graveyard while his grandmother did the talking, Terence had no idea what these sticky problems were, or if the dead provided answers, but he opines that 'chumminess in death' is appropriate. At this point I was envious, wondering if I, too, would have been less squeamish with a different and more formidable grandmother.

The cortege following the funeral service heralded the postliminal stage. The Spanish made much of this procession. While there was a universal pattern to all medieval funeral marches, the Spanish added their own unique embellishments. Typically the cortege had a three-cluster configuration: the coffin in the middle, with two distinct and hierarchically ranked groups, one on either side. Marching in the front were the clergy, led by a crucifer holding aloft the processional cross. As the function of the cortege was supposed to be intercessory, the presence of confraternities marching behind the clerics was of utmost importance. By the fifteenth century these lay Spanish associations, devoted as they were to acts of charity, were not only understood as essential to the cortege but came to resemble burial clubs, being seen as the ones responsible for opening the gates of heaven, duty bound to rescue suffering souls and helping to allay the fears of the living. For a well-born Spanish man to die alone and without the help of his confraternity was a frightful fate because it was thought that such a person could well be denied entry once on the other side. I do not know what was likely to happen to the female elite!

Trailing the coffin were the mourners, family first, then friends and acquaintances. Behind them came a gaggle of orphans and poor. Relief of the poor was a significant aspect of a Spanish funeral. This was not because they were a particularly altruistic people, but because giving to the needy was a Biblical requirement. One's final act of charity was making provisions for the destitute and disadvantaged and this was recorded in one's will. Not only were the poor then asked to join the cortege, but they were also provided with alms and appropriate clothing which they could keep. Orphan children were particularly favoured because, as all medievals knew, the prayers of orphans and the poor were more readily heard in heaven! Eire claims royalty sometimes invited an entire orphanage to attend. The less prestigious nobility often summoned twelve as a gesture to the memory of the apostles. There was no set alms fee, testators offering according to their estate. It was also believed that heaven would favour those who could provide candles and torches, light accepted as a triumph over the darkness of death. It is not surprising that the funeral marches of the rich were often of extreme length, the crucifer sometimes arriving at the church before the last of the mourners had left the house. At the conclusion of the burial the Spanish poor were invited to participate in the funeral feast.

This feast signalled the final postliminal stage of a good death. Paxton claims this meal was essential, helping the family to re-establish equilibrium and integrity and providing an opportunity for the mourners to organize their grief. The meal, often lavish and raucous, took place at the graveside, the church becoming a banqueting hall. Because it was seen as an extension of a past pagan ritual, the clergy objected to these feasts, frequently quoting Augustine of Hippo who had stated that if food was to be outlaid it should be distributed among the poor rather than for 'the unruly ingestion at the grave'. Augustine also wanted the money laid out for funerals reserved for the exclusive use of 'the living poor', possibly for the first time linking almsgiving with burial, a custom Spain heartily endorsed. The Spanish, addicted to ostentation, ignored Augustine's admonitions.

In 1541, a bishop from Madrid tried to forbid the use of churches for banqueting, complaining, 'They eat and drink, and put up tables within the churches; and even worse, set plates and pitchers on the altars, turning them into sideboards'. In spite of his protests the feasting continued, possibly because food eaten in troublesome times can be comforting. As well as objecting to these ceremonial meals, Spanish authorities tried to put restraints on mourning. Eire quotes from the 1323 Synod of Toledo where a halt was called on the 'lugubrious excesses', the 'execrable abuses' and the 'indecencies' practised after a funeral had taken place. This decree, too, was disregarded. Even as late as the 1500s the 'terrible and loud lamentations' and 'the pulling out of hair' was still going on.

These funerals, as described by Eire, were for the Spanish elite, the poor unable to outlay such expenses. I have not yet found out how the disadvantaged and impecunious were buried, but I have read merchant families saved for years so that they could satisfactorily dispatch the head of their house.

It appears to have been easier to die a good death in earlier medieval times. At this point the church was triumphant and congregations, optimistic that they would be purged of sin, could anticipate a secure place in heaven. This is an insight gleaned from Frederick Paxton's examination of ancient liturgical texts and breviaries where he found the prayers preceding the first millennium had been encouraging, not only revealing a longing for God, but also demonstrating confidence in His mercy. Unfortunately, in the 1100s this certainty was undercut by the introduction of Purgatory, a nebulous intermediary place located beyond this world and seemingly before the next. Theologians of this time had decided that those souls destined for Heaven could not travel there directly, but would have to undergo additional purification by way of suffering for an indeterminate period before they were able to face the 'Wondrous Beatific Vision' and enter the 'Joy of Heaven'.

It was preferable that those intended for Purgatory die in a state of grace achieved by undergoing the prescribed death rituals. Naturally, those who were pious and of an exemplary character had a better chance. The wise who had accrued indulgences by way of pilgrimage, or by becoming monastic patrons, were also at an advantage. Those who had committed a mortal sin, however, and had been unable to confess, were always allotted Satan's infernal depths.[24] Once Purgatory had been accepted as a place where the fate of the newly departed soul was always in question, a fearful responsibility was placed upon the already fraught mourners. It was as though the destiny of the departed soul was now placed in their hands and they knew their intercessions had to be convincing and sincere. The reality of Purgatory also robbed mourners of the comfort derived from the belief that the newly departed beloved had been received into the Everlasting Arms.

I find it strange that a culture in possession of a positive vision should have, at a certain point, suddenly

---

[24] Mortal sins were those specified in the Ten Commandments and deliberately committed with the sinner's full knowledge.

opted for something as agonizing as Purgatory. The idea that such a place existed had been accepted by the early church fathers, in particular Ambrose of Milan, Augustine of Hippo and Gregory the Great, but had always been obliquely referred to and not taken seriously. In twelfth century Spain the idea now flourished. That the optimistic teaching of the early church had been put into jeopardy can be observed in the paintings produced at this time. As well as a tormented Christ and his various broken saints, Terence and I often observed portrayals of souls suffering in Purgatory. These pictures were nearly always painted in two or three horizontal tiers. At the top were visions of the Heavenly realm, usually with Mary at the pinnacle, the souls at the bottom, mostly depicted in a murky groundless realm. Often in naked human form they floated as they lamented in one messy mass. In between there would be angels sometimes reaching down into the nebulous depths to haul one or two fortunate ones up into Heaven's midst.

Purgatory was only in a small way responsible for the change in attitude in the second millennium. Death by way of plague had a much greater impact. Believed to have started in the 1330s in central Asia, this disease arrived in Spain in 1348, Barcelona being its portal. Then, as an un-named pandemic, it was referred to by a variety of names: 'The Pestilence', 'The Great Death', 'The Epidemia' or 'The Terrible Malady' (the term 'Black Death' only coined in the nineteenth century). The Spanish Muslims applied more poetic metaphors: 'The Cup of Poison' or 'An Invading Army', victims taken by an 'Arrow', a 'Sword', a 'Snake' or by a 'Lightning Bolt'. The disease is characterized by swellings in the groin, followed by an horrendous fever, delirium, diarrhoea, bloody eyes and finally coma, one symptom following the next in rapid succession. Death came suddenly and all too often victims vacated this world without the necessary preparations that would ensure salvation, either because the priest was too busy to come or because he, too, had been targeted. Priests, because they attended to the dying, were the hardest hit. All too often people died unexpectedly far away from home. For this reason citizens in France took to wearing identity tags if called away on business. Malignant and virulent, the disease swept through whole towns and cities. No-one was immune. Communities soon ran out of coffins and authorities had to resort to common graves in unhallowed ground, a resting place calamitous to Christians ardently seeking heaven. To die of plague was to die a bad death.

The medievals claimed the various outbreaks were always preceded by earthquakes, floods, fire, comets or eclipses. For a long time it was thought that the disease was the result of corrupted air and fumigation by way of smoke or holy water was recommended. In 1345 the medical faculty of the University of Paris, at that time the most prestigious in Europe, announced that the sullying of the air was astrological, caused by a conjunction of Jupiter, Saturn and Mars. A bishop named Isidore said the corruption was caused by excessive dryness and heat. However, Spain in the fifteenth century discovered the real cause!—apparently plague arrived at the instigation of the Jews and with great flourish the Catholic monarchs, Ferdinand and Isabella, banished them all. The expulsion took place in 1492. In 1494 another epidemic struck, this time lasting for five years!

Mostly the Spanish accepted plague as God's wrath in action, the Divine Being using natural powers to punish a sinful people. Many fled to the monasteries to pray for forgiveness and there anticipate death. Others gave all they had to the church in the hopes of making things right with God. Yet more flocked to the confraternities who had no cures but could offer comfort and support for frightened medievals as they waited for the deadly assault. The brotherhoods also organized prayer meetings, processions and, importantly for Christians wanting to die well, they guaranteed an appropriate burial. Because of the culture's emphasis on sin and the need for repentance, confraternities also endorsed flagellation. After fasting and participating in the daily mass, groups would re-enter the church stripped to the waist and soundly beat themselves. They did this so enthusiastically the church eventually forbade the practice. The edict was ignored. In 1349 Pope Clement had to denounce the practice as heretical.

Whole villages were wiped out and towns took years to recover. Where the nobility were decimated, communities were left without leadership. The drop in population not only meant a general economic decline, but also a shortage of labour. This meant peasants could demand higher wages. Others found themselves with more goods and property than they had before. The lower classes were becoming destabilized. In the sixteenth century the aristocracy were also rebelling against monarchical authoritarianism and people were beginning to question the primacy of the church. In Spain there was a new eruption of Arab armies from the south and, because the military, too, had been devastated, this enemy was able to penetrate up into France. At this point the continual outbreaks of war, as well as famine, left Spain at a very low ebb. According to Joseph Byrne, plague not only retarded the social, political and cultural growth of Western Christendom, but was also a major cause of the demise of feudalism. The decline can be observed in the literature of the time.

The distress of the 1500s was able to produce saints such as Teresa of Ávila and John of the Cross. It also resulted in a myriad of sermons, ardent prayers and poetic works revealing anxiety about the prospect of sudden death, disbelief that it could happen and the crushing experience of suffering and loss.

Spain in this century was also responsible for the advent of the picaresque novel. In these works the protagonist, replacing the noble hero of the old romance, was a nonchalant rogue of low social class who lived by his wits in a corrupt society. Picaresque novels were realistic, humorous and often satirical. They contained no overall plot or character development and were unconcerned with moral issues or traditional norms. The first, and possibly the most popular novel, was *Lazarillo de Tormes* written in 1554. The anonymous writer tells of the adventures of Lazarillo, a protagonist who finds himself abandoned and alone in the world and must now work as a servant. He becomes guide for a miserly blind beggar, house servant of a destitute priest and assistant to a fraudulent seller of papal indulgences. Lazarillo then gains employment with a young nobleman who turns out to be so penniless he has to beg bread for both of them. As a reward for marrying the mistress of a lecherous archpriest, Lazarillo is made the town crier. In this text, and those that followed, the idealism of the earlier Romance literature has been made redundant. These novels could suggest a social order that had lost its way.

The mortality rate because of plague was overwhelming. In the 1600s the disease claimed approximately 1.25 million Spanish lives, Seville and its rural districts being hardest hit because the authorities in this city chose to ignore the quarantine. Maybe it was such circumstances, together with the destructiveness of famine and flood, which prompted the composition of the *Dança general de la Muerte*, or the Spanish *Dance of Death.*

241

Death being so pervasive, 'dances' focussing on the subject were popular, not just in Spain but throughout Europe. Written in poetic form, these old literary 'dances' were actually dramatic works acted out in cemeteries. The enactment opened with a serious sermon on the inevitability of death delivered by a cleric or monk. At its conclusion, a figure humorously personifying Death, would burst forth from the charnel-house costumed in a dark, tight-fitting suit painted to resemble a skeleton. Holding a lantern in his right hand and ringing a bell with the left, he would start the drama by addressing a selection of 'victims', asking them to dance with him. Knowing they were to be taken beyond the grave they naturally refused, offering instead various excuses. These were always declined and Death's quarry was authoritatively led away. He never engaged in debates about body or soul. Nor was hell ever discussed. Death's only concern was with the gates into the other side, not what lay beyond.

Illustrations of this macabre figure can be seen all over Europe in texts, on canvases and in murals on church walls. As opposed to being grim, the portrayals are disconcertingly cheerful. Though his message is serious and denotes finality, Death is paradoxically filled with energy and vitality. He laughs and his antics are entertaining, possibly demonstrating that people had either become inured to his overwhelming call, or that the artists' light-heartedness in the face of Death was an apparent brave put-down, the belittling of Death reducing the fear generated by his pervasiveness.

The Spanish *Dança gereral de la Muerte* follows the general European pattern. However, Florence Whyte's research on this literary piece claims that in Spain the drama was not only acted but also actually danced, probably in a circle. Where ecclesiastical authority banned dancing inside churches, they allowed this one because the gravity of the message undercut the frivolity. Dancing was also favoured by pilgrims who helped to enrich the church coffers and this may have allowed the church to disregard the pagan connections. Whyte's research also revealed that the genesis of the dance was a folklore superstition. She does not elaborate, stating only that the story concerned certain rural dead who rose from their graves at midnight and led away the reluctant living.

The message to be gleaned in Spain's dance poem is not about the terror of impending death, but the bitterness of being separated from cherished earthly existence and the various occupations that are here on offer. The written text is organized into seventy-nine stanzas. Instructions state that the dance must commence to the sad strains of a flute. The first dance is performed by two maidens. Unwilling brides of Death, they symbolize not only their sex but also the beauty and vanity of earthly life. Death as husband spirits them away. In the next stanza Death becomes female and remains so for the remainder of the poem. Her subsequent victims, all male, are examples of a patriarchal social order, both lay and ecclesiastical. They are arranged in the fixed social categories defining each one's external life. Death starts with the top rank and descends in hierarchical order, an ecclesiastic alternating with a layman, seventeen estates for each.

As they dance Death points out the weakness of each group: the Emperor has amassed treasure through the waging of tyrannical wars, the Cardinal plots to usurp the Pope, the Squire is ruled by amorous passion, the Canon loves his fine linen vestments too dearly, the Merchant refuses to give up his ill-acquired profits, and so on. All deny the charges laid against them or else find excuses not to leave. The final ones to be rounded up are the bearded Rabbi, the *Alfaqui*, a Mohammedan teacher of Islamic law, and the *Santero*, a Moorish hermit. The Rabbi is accused of only examining the Talmud and thus failing to find Christ; the *Alfaqui* is told he is a hedonist and too fond of his wife. The *Santero's* life style, in spite of his begging, is deemed too easy, his cabbages growing too well. The Benedictine monk, however, is happy to accept Death and the Christian hermit also commends himself to the God he has served in a life of poverty and contemplation. Death treats these two kindly. In contrast, his attitude to the Friar is contemptuous. Though also taking holy vows and preaching to the populace, friars are mendicants and so given to begging. Whyte supposes the favouring of the Benedictine indicates the anonymous author was a monastic from an enclosed order. Death also softens his tone towards the hard-working farmer.

I am sure I would have greatly enjoyed this poem had I been able to read old Spanish, or if I had found a good English translation. The only copy I could procure was dreadful. However, Whyte's commentary, pointing out that the gestation of this piece was from folk-lore, put me in mind of a story I was told by a fellow Spanish pilgrim as I trudged through Galicia towards the end of my Camino. It was the tale of the *Santa Compaña* and kindly told to me as a warning against walking in the dark in this part of Spain. At the time, and with no explanation, I was somewhat mystified but later discovered that the *Santa Compaña* was a deep-rooted belief about unhappy souls who, for some reason, could not leave this world but wanted to, and so were severely tormented.

At midnight, my English-speaking story-teller told me, the souls wander round the local parishes, a living person leading the procession carrying a cross and a small phial of holy water, the imprecise phantoms following with ill-lit candles. The benighted cross-bearer can never renounce this duty unless he frees himself by persuading another to take over the onerous task of leading. To avoid this imposition the person unfortunate enough to chance upon the leader could defend himself by either making an appropriate hand gesture to ward off the pleader or by drawing a magic circle on the ground in which to stand and so be isolated. However, these protective strategies were not always known to those travellers merely passing through. The *Santa Compaña* could be dimly observed by sensitive mortals. The insensitive who failed to see them would know of their presence because of the smell of hot candle wax and the breeze created by their passing. As a sign of impending death, the odour of burning candles in the remote Galician forests may well have created panic among foreign pilgrims, as well as for the Spanish people focussed on death.

Back home I wondered if the *Santa Compaña* illustrated a medieval anxiety about sudden death without due preparation for what lay beyond. Weary of this world but terrified to discover what awaited them, did the poorly prepared anticipate remaining forever in limbo? I also marvelled at the longevity of this enduring story told to me by a young man in the twenty-first century.

Graves of the common Spanish medievals are almost impossible to find. The only ones I came across were in the precinct of the Irache monastery. I had already been to this monastery with Terence but, because I wanted to check the small relic I had earlier spied in the chancel, I made a second trip on my own. When I arrived the basilica was unfortunately locked. Turning my back on the great sun-drenched doors I ambled round the dry-stone wall enclosing the monastic complex hopeful that I might discover something interesting.

The day was balmy, the warm afternoon sun countered by a fresh spring breeze. The wall was solid, seemingly held together by the grasp of bramble and ivy.

At first I could find no way of climbing over. As I admired the stonemason's craftsmanship I spied an overgrown breach in the wall, the gap fitted with a simple wrought-iron gate. Scrambling up a steep bank and finding no lock, I entered a small, high-walled grave-yard. Not being able to read the dates on the tombs, I am not sure if this cemetery could be classified as medieval, even though it gave the appearance of being extremely old. Gazing at the haphazard arrangement of old tomb-stones, some precariously leaning over or else totally collapsed into the luxuriant spring growth, I felt confused. The dead had clearly been laid here, but it felt as though time had dislocated them from their simple memorials, the weather almost obliterating the old Latin inscriptions and human hands lifting some of the stones and standing them against the wall.

To one side there was a simple metal crucifix attached to a wooden tabernacle possibly erected there in the hopes that the dead would be divinely supervised as they journeyed to the other side. Once this cross would have been pristine, but with the passing of time it is now a sad derelict. For the medievals for whom it may once have provided comfort, this neglect may have been seen as a catastrophe, but for me these graves, resting under the blue sky of early afternoon amidst dancing wild poppies, seemed to negate medieval death angst. Unlike the doubting dead of long ago, unsure of their destination in the afterlife, these dead seemed confident and at peace.

Death is a grim reality. Associated with disintegrating bodies and stench, it is a menace we always set aside so that we can live. Hunting down the medieval dead in northern Spain, I never once thought of those long gone dead in this polluting way. This was not the case with the modern Spanish. As opposed to the English who have allowed their dead to rest in deep graves surrounding a serene church in a well-groomed church-yard, contemporary Spanish now seem to favour communal, above-ground sepulchres. The one that particularly comes to mind I chanced upon while walking the Camino. As I recall, it was in the vicinity of Villafranca. Here, on a steep-stepped incline, was constructed what looked like a double row of low 'tenements' for the dead.

Built of concrete, each 'apartment' was white-washed and flower-adorned, many of the pediments surmounted by a Christian cross. As cemeteries go I had never before seen one like it. I did not stay long. At the time I thought this was because I should respect those newly interred, but on reflection I walked away because the site was both confronting and uncanny. It was also claustrophobic: too many bones clustered too tightly together and the vaults stacked one on top of the other and all above the ground. Where death in the Irache grave-yard and in the mausoleums in León and Nájera seemed poetic, the dead trailing memories just beyond my grasp, here it was too literal and, to my imagination, the odour of corrupting flesh still almost detectable. Obviously time conceals death's horror and, thankfully, either nature or beautifully wrought sculptures take over.

Because the afterlife was believed by all, death in medieval Europe had profound implications and was always treated with respect and awe. However, theorists claim the phenomenon became a personal obsession in Spain. The only scholar I came across who disagreed was Marcelino Menendez y Pelayo, writing in the late nineteenth century. It was Pelayo's contention that the Castile sun is too potent and so could dissolve those gloomy concepts of death that were proper to the foggy lands of the north.

Ernest Hemingway, in love with northern Spain, had a contrary view. He claimed it was this same brilliant sunshine that allowed the Spanish, particularly the Castilian peasant, to fully understand death's profundity. This was because the peasants were able to observe death's horror each time they watched the matador fight bulls in the bright light of day. With stark clarity they could observe death as it was 'given, avoided, refused and finally accepted', and all for the admission price to the bullfight. For them death was unflinchingly acknowledged with the support of a religion that allowed them to understand that death had to be accepted and, because it was much longer than life, one had to prepare for it. While Terence and I were never made aware of this predilection, it must be there. Too many write of it. In the early 1930s the great Spanish poet, Federico Garcia Lorca, declared that Spain was 'a country of death, a country open to death'. In his 1933 lecture on the *duende* Lorca also wrote,

In all countries death is the end. It arrives and the curtain falls. Not so in Spain. In Spain, on the contrary, the curtain only rises at that moment, and in many Spanish poems there is a ramp of flowers of saltpetre over which lean a people who contemplate death.

Saltpetre is a chemical compound used in fertilizers, rocket propellants, fireworks and, in the Middle Ages, as a food preservative. I wonder which use Lorca had in mind when he wrote these words.

Works cited in this chapter

Bentley, James. *The Way of Saint James*. London: Pavilion Books. 1992.

Binski, Paul. *Medieval Death: Ritual and Representation*. London: The British Museum Press. 1996.

Byrne, Joseph P. *The Black Death*. Westport, Conn.: Greenwood Press. 2004.

Eire, Carlos M. N. *From Madrid to Purgatory*. Cambridge, UK: Cambridge University Press. 1995.

Ellis, Havelock. *The Soul of Spain*. Westport, Conn.: Greenwood Press. 1976.

Fernández de Castro Cabez, Sister Maria del Carmen. *The Life of the Very Noble King of Castile and León, Saint Ferdinand III*. New York, NY: The Foundation for a Christian Civilization, Inc. 1987.

Geary, Patrick J. *Living with the Dead in the Middle Ages*. Ithaca, N.Y.: Cornell University Press. 1994.

Gitlitz, David M. & Linda Kay Davidson. *The Pilgrimage Road to Santiago*. New York, NY.: St. Martin's Press. 2000.

Hemingway, Ernest. *Death in the Afternoon*. London: Jonathan Cape. 1958.

Lindberg, David C. *The Beginnings of Western Science*. Chicago, Ill.: The University of Chicago Press. 1992.

Paxton, Frederick S. *Christianizing Death: The Creation of a Ritual Process in Early Medieval Europe*. Ithaca, NY: Cornell University Press. 1990.

Stamm, James R. *A Short History of Spanish Literature*. New York, NY.: New York University Press. 1979.

Whyte, Florence. *The Dance of Death in Spain and Catalonia*. New York, NY: Arno Press 1977.

8

Mary Mary Quite Contrary

Travelling in Northern Spain, it is impossible not to be conscious of the Virgin Mary. Images of her are to be found in every church, chapels are dedicated to her and cathedrals named in her honour. And she is worshipped, many people seen reverently kneeling before her shrine. By all appearances she has been, and still is, much loved. Growing up in the Anglican tradition, I had not given much thought to Mary. While we acknowledge her, the Virgin is not central to Anglican worship. Now I wanted to become better acquainted with this timeless mother.

As my Irish-born husband started life as a Roman Catholic, I began my Marian investigations by asking him if he had ever loved Mary as a boy. Love was too strong a word for Terence, but he grudgingly supposed his grandmother might have felt some sort of attachment. As a member of the Sodality of the Children of Mary she had promised to devote herself to the Holy Mother, serving her by way of prayer and charitable works. Followers of this society identified themselves by wearing a blue cape. Borrowing this garment had greatly enhanced Terence's childhood games, making him a splendid Francis Drake and a very effective Superman. For a little boy it was good to have a grandma who loved Mary. However, as an adolescent schoolboy his attitude changed. Reciting the Angelus at speed every midday made the boys slipshod in their pronunciation. When they got to, 'Blessed be the fruit of thy womb', all Terence heard was 'blessed be thy iron womb'. Not only did Terence regard the womb as a dubious bit of female anatomy, but having one constructed from metal made the Virgin particularly suspect. He decided she must be 'weird'. I was staggered by this revelation and wondered what a Freudian analyst would make of such a pronouncement. In Spain, when I gazed upon images of Mary, she never impressed me as weird but, at times, she did make me ponder.

The first time I came upon a Marian shrine was as I walked into Roncesvalles after having crossed the Pyrenees. Gathering my breath on the crest of the Ibañeta pass I must have found the view distracting because when I again took up the trail, I missed the way-makers and walked the final kilometre or so on the main road. Thus it was that outside the abbey precincts and at the foot of a steep hill I came upon a shrine. A serene and peaceful Virgin sat there watching over travellers on the twisting mountain road. The stone from which she had been fashioned was weathered to soft dove grey, all harsh lines smoothed out by time. In the narrow space between the shrine and the hill a tiny mountain stream trickled, feeding into a fountain which gently gushed from below Mary's feet. She was flanked on either side by flowers. I found her charming. When I returned to Spain with Terence we went directly to Roncesvalles. The shrine was one of the first places we visited. She was there and, evidenced by the fresh flowers, still loved.

While the contemporary Spanish seem devoted to Mary, my reading indicated she has not always been accepted as a revered figure. She did not feature at all in early mainstream worship, possibly because the canonical New Testament is bland with regard to Mary, suggesting she is not really worthy of worship. She appears only briefly in the four gospels fulfilling a limited number of roles. She is portrayed as the mother of a son destined to become important. She is also recorded as a passive observer, one who reflects as she watches. In the 'Gospel of Luke' Mary does initiate one momentous event in Cana: she persuades Jesus to perform his first miracle, changing water into wine. She is present at the crucifixion and finally, in 'The Acts of the Apostles', she is recorded as being among the followers who had reassembled in Jerusalem after the death of Jesus. Bearing a child, supporting that child in life and grieving for him after death are conventional roles readers of the Bible, and those who listen to sermons, might well have expected of any mother. At this point her story is not significant.

When I discovered the apocryphal gospels I found the laity in early Christian times had not been so dispassionate. Written for common consumption, these gospels tell popular stories by filling in the tantalizing gaps left in the official records. In Mary's case we are provided with details of her family, her everyday life and explanations of her uniqueness. The 'Protevangelium of James' is one of the earliest of these gospels. The author reveals himself in the final chapter, claiming to be James, son of Joseph by his first marriage and thus a half-brother to Jesus. Based on the style of the language and the fact that he describes certain activities as contemporary Jewish custom that did not exist at the time of Christ, scholars dismiss James as the author, instead assessing the work as a mid-second century text written by someone now unknown. Particularly popular in the East the 'Protevangelium', first written in Greek, was translated into a number of Middle-Eastern languages.

Initially the focus of this short narrative is on Mary's parents, Anna and Joachim, and their grief at being childless. A visiting angel sorts out this problem and nine months later Mary is born. While an angel tells Joachim the child will be of his seed, the writing, or translation, is grammatically confusing and the reader is not certain how Anna actually conceived. We are told, too, that prior to conception Anna was cleansed of all original sin and thus Mary is born without blemish. In an effort to maintain this purity the child's feet were not permitted to touch the ground and, for her first few years, she was confined to her bedroom, attended there by 'daughters of Hebrews who were undefiled'. At three years of age Mary was taken to the temple. Accepted by the priests, she was further removed from the world and made to lead a strict monastic life. When she became pubescent she was betrothed to Joseph lest her monthly flows 'pollute the sanctuary of the Lord'. At this point the text implies that Mary was unable to maintain her pristine purity.

The manner in which Joseph was chosen as the future husband made Terence and me laugh. Joseph had not only to be a widower, but one chosen by the Lord. So that the Lord's will could be known, widowers from all over were ordered to the temple, each bringing a 'rod'. Once assembled the high priest took the rods and prayed over them. As each one was returned it was deemed no good, or, thought Terence, possibly too good. When Joseph's rod was given back 'a dove came forth and flew upon his head'. This symbol of softness and tranquillity was the needed sign and Joseph was proclaimed the winner, but not a happy one. As an old man he feared he would become 'a laughing-stock to the children of Israel' and Joseph had to be bullied into accepting Mary. He avoided criticism by abandoning her for four years while he attended to various building projects in distant parts. Fortunately Mary was cared for by the Lord. When Joseph returns, Mary is sixteen, had been visited by the Angel and was huge with child. Where in the canonical gospels Joseph remains quite passive about this legal breach, the apocryphal Joseph 'smote his face and cast himself down upon the ground on sackcloth and wept bitterly'. Mary, too, does a fair bit of wailing, so much so the temple priests step in. They do more 'tests', angels visit and eventually all are placated.

In due course Jesus is born in a cave on the way to Bethlehem. Mary is on her own because Joseph has gone off to find a Hebrew mid-wife but, because the whole world stopped still for one moment while he was away, people, animals, 'even the fowls in the air were all without motion', Joseph knew the child had arrived. When he returns with help Mary is examined. Astonished to find her new patient still a virgin, the mid-wife goes outside where she finds Salome, another mid-wife who refuses to believe the first one's diagnosis until she herself prises Mary's legs apart and makes her own examination. Yes, says an astonished Salome, Mary is still a virgin.

My curiosity not yet sated, I found another apocryphal text, 'The Gospel of Pseudo-Matthew'. Ascribed to the apostle Matthew, this work, too, was written several centuries after the time of Christ. The anonymous author prefaced his narrative with several letters supposedly exchanged between the early church father, Jerome, and a number of bishops. The bishops request that Jerome translate this Hebrew manuscript into Latin. (Translating biblical manuscripts had been Jerome's speciality). 'Pseudo-Matthew' too was well-liked, this time in the West. The first twenty-four of the forty-two chapters tells Mary's story in much the same manner as the 'Protevangelium'. The second half is devoted to entertaining anecdotes relating to the early childhood of Christ. The details concerning Mary provide the reader with more particulars of her astonishing goodness and maturity, her prayerful piety, her repetitive, monastic routine and her ability to heal, a feat achieved only when someone inadvertently touched her. In these two texts it is Mary's perpetual virginity that is particularly emphasized.

While I enjoyed the two gospels, what really impressed me was the amazing non-entity of the recorded Mary. Even before she is born her destiny is decided. Promised to the temple and to God, and imposed upon an unwilling spouse, Mary is, at every point of her life, guarded and protected by parents, by 'undefiled Hebrew daughters', by priests and even the Lord himself. Shunted backward and forward, she is subjected to accusations and has to be tested, all without protest or opinion. Rather than a flesh and blood woman, the apocryphal Mary comes over as an artificial construct designed for a specific purpose. Apart from the purity of her virginal body she, as a person, seems to have been of little consequence, the stories only written to satisfy the curiosity of the people of the time who simply wanted more biographical facts. In the first few centuries of the Christian era Mary functioned in this way. In both the canonical and apocryphal gospels she appears as a passive being, more done unto than doing. However, at the Council of Ephesus in 431 she became the centre of ecclesiastical mayhem.

The Council hosted an ecumenical debate in which a problem that had rocked the church for at least two centuries was finally settled. Initially the quarrel had nothing to do with Mary, but centred round the question of Christ's true nature. Was he God or was he man? In the first century the Gnostics asserted he was simply a divine phantom, nothing more. A century later Arius, an ascetic from Egypt, claimed Christ as an ordinary human who had simply been adopted by God at the time of his baptism in the Jordan. Over the years the church fathers, still trying to establish official ecclesiastical doctrine and intolerant of alternative views, tried to counter each theory as it presented itself. The pivotal point in these arguments was always the manner in which Christ had been born. The nativity, which had not interested the clergy at the start, now became the focus and in this way Mary was forced to the fore. Yes, the church fathers told the Gnostics, Mary was human and of the blood line of David and therefore so, too, was Christ. To the Arians who declared God was too infinite to be contained on Earth, they trotted out Mary's unbroken virginity, the means by which the laws of nature could be suspended to allow the divine to manifest. Increasingly it became necessary to stress this strange virginity.

By the time a feud had begun between Nestorius, the archbishop of Constantinople who held the view that Jesus was not truly God, and Cyril of Alexandria, who offered a contrary opinion, those who denied Mary's perpetual virginity were excommunicated. The bitter battle climaxed at the Council of Ephesus when Mary was finally pronounced *Theotokos*, the Mother of God. The title was proclaimed inviolate and Mary became a fixed absolute recorded in unchallengeable dogma, at least for the orthodox mainstream. No longer considered a simple character in an interesting tale, Mary became a cult figure revered by the church fathers because of her obedience to God, her freedom from the stain of sin and most of all because she remained ever virgin.

On the Camino I found much to counter Mary's supposed and holy submissiveness. While much of the artwork does portray a serene Mary, sculptors, artists and story-tellers frequently depicted her in great passions, either of anger or ecstasy. To me it seemed the icy doctrinal Madonna was a creation of the church and appealed only to conservative laity. In medieval Spain people had come to envisage a Mary who was much more human. As I walked I always sought out the early Romanesque effigies, the mother usually seated with the child on her lap. In many Jesus was holding an apple or being offered one by the mother, establishing an obvious connection to Eve who, according to the church fathers, had been the original cause of human strife. Now, with the apple safely in Mary's grasp, a viewer may presume the Virgin had saved humanity from Eve's sinful ways. However, in these statues this theological conservatism is undercut by the rustic primitiveness of the work. By placing her feet so firmly on the floor, the sculptors nearly always conveyed a confident Mary certain of her own worth and unheeding of ecclesiastical authority.

Many of the statues had been unearthed in rural locations and often by simple folk who understood the discoveries as miraculous. William Christian claims many of these may have been hidden by the medieval peasantry upon the arrival of the invading Moors. The villagers, having either been killed or driven away, the hiding places were forgotten and their recovery a few decades later considered a miracle. I came across one such statue when I walked the Camino. In the eleventh century Don Garcia, son of King Sancho the Great, was out hunting in the vicinity of Nájera. His falcon was troublesome and would not return. Following the wayward bird, the prince was led to a steep cliff-face and into a deep cave. There he found an effigy so wondrous he had his father build a chapel on the side of the precipice to house the find. Later, the humble building was replaced by the Monasterio Santa Maria de la Real.

On my first visit to northern Spain I did not know of the statue, nor had I read the story. When I entered the cave at the back of the monastery church I was overwhelmed. The richness of the red limestone glowed in the subdued light and, possibly because of a flickering single candle, the Virgin seemed animated. Crowned, enthroned and seated upon her pedestal, she looked me straight in the eye and I, too, felt a miraculous sense of her presence. When I revisited the cave with Terence, he was also moved.

We found another startling statue in the austere Monasterio de San Paio in Santiago. It was approximately thirty centimetres in height, placed on its own in a little glass case and standing on a plinth away from the other monastery exhibits. In her left hand Mary was clasping a cringing Christ child. Her right wielded a substantial club. As the fearful child burrowed into its mother's neck Mary prepared herself to lop off the head of a winged monster rising from beneath her feet. The statue was vibrantly energetic and the viewer had no doubt that the Virgin would succeed. I felt this statue had been an apt acquisition for a monastery built for the specific purpose of protecting the shrine of James.

In Spain Mary is often portrayed as the saviour of children. We saw one painting where she again countered evil, this time in the form of a Devil, nasty and black and about the same size as herself. On this occasion she brandished a sword. The story accompanying this work told of a small boy of over-abundant energy who was driving his mother to distraction. She could no longer cope and exclaimed, 'Oh let the Devil take you'. To her horror the Evil One obliged. As he reached out to take the child, the mother sent a desperate appeal to Mary who instantly arrived. Wielding her sword, she repelled the Devil, welcomed the child under her mantle and then returned him to the distraught mother.

Mary was not always so accommodating. From the National Historical Archives in Madrid, William Christian unearthed this story. On April 20 1399 just outside Santa Gadea, a small medieval village in the vicinity of Burgos, a boy called Pedro was watching his father's flocks together with his friend, Juan. As the two boys ambled over the open countryside they found a bee hive in an old oak tree and they agreed that once the sheep were safely stabled in town for the commencement of Holy Week, they would come at night and gather the rich supply of honey. This they did. While they worked with the sticky wax, a group of people in white garments gathered round a nearby hawthorn tree. As the boys looked on, a wondrous Madonna appeared, faintly at first, then shining so brilliantly the boys had to look away. Of course there was heavenly music, chanting priests and a procession before the vision wafted heavenwards.

The following week Pedro was back with the sheep near the same tree. This time the still glowing Virgin again approached Pedro, but this time at ground level. She told the boy her son had sent her to enlist Pedro's help to correct a terrible wrong. In times now lost to the memory of the present villagers, there had been a terrible shedding of blood on the site of the hawthorn tree and many Christians had been gloriously martyred by the infidel because they remained true to their faith. Christ and Mary now demanded that Pedro tell the parish priest, the general clergy and the Council of Santa Gadea so that a church and monastery could be built to revive the memory of this forgotten event and placate the unresting dead. Pedro remained silent, afraid the town dignitaries would not heed a young boy. Two nights later the Virgin arrived in Pedro's bedroom with two men dressed as monks. Mary ordered these monks to beat the boy. Neighbours, hearing his terrible screams, arrived to berate the supposedly cruel father. The boy finally spoke out, telling all how he had been confronted by the Virgin who wanted the villagers to heed her request. Mary had her way and the church was built.

The Virgin's concern also extended to those in holy orders. One wayward nun, lusting after the visiting curate, had her passion deflated by a hefty smack on the jaw. Another cleric who had stolen some fabric donated to the church, said he had intended to have some undergarments made with the cloth so that he could 'cover his sinful parts'. That night as he slept he was jolted awake by a dreadful pain and found his legs had been turned completely upside down and both his heels were now pressing into his loins. The story claims that this distressing anatomical inversion was brought about by Mary's intervention.

While Mary was petitioned to right wrongs and generally expected to help with the affairs of the rural peasantry, Spain's elite also called on her for military and political help. In her text, *Mary, Mother and Warrior*, Linda Hall has traced Mary's participation in the Reconquest, the ongoing endeavour to wrest Spain from the Muslims. While James had been engineered to be the divine help, Hall claims he was only effective in the North. Elsewhere Mary was more successful. Hall lists how the various kings of the Reconquest had all claimed Mary as responsible for their military accomplishments.

Mary's most significant achievement was at the battle of Navas de Tolosa. Here, in 1212 King Alfonso VIII was finally able to turn the tide against the Muslims. At the start Alfonso was in a vulnerable position, his Castilian army sparse and unlikely to succeed. The king of France offered troops, as did the crowns of Navarre, Aragon and Portugal. However, those armies from the Iberian Peninsula began quarrelling among themselves though they eventually rallied, but the French contingent, finding Spain too hot and disagreeing with Alfonso's merciful treatment of the Jews and Muslims, pulled out altogether. Fearing the worst Alfonso allowed himself to be led into

261

the fray by two bearers, one carrying a cross and the other waving a banner of the Virgin Mary. The arrival of this standard was said to be the turning point of the battle. The king of Castile, seeing the image of Mary attacked by stones and arrows, redoubled his efforts and, utilizing the superhuman strength bestowed onto him by the Holy Mother, was able to rally his troops, becoming a formidable force. Faced with such wrath the caliph fled. The Mary of Spain meek and mild? I think not.

Finally I cannot leave the self-assured Mary I met on the Camino without a mention of the *Cantigas de Santa Maria* or *Songs of Holy Mary*. This is a collection of stories and poems, beautifully illustrated, set to music and dedicated to Mary. Supposedly a collaborative work, the songs are the creative inspiration of the learned King Alfonso X, also called The Wise. While incorporating all of Spain the *Cantigas* are associated with the Camino, Alfonso being king of Castile, León and Galicia, and many of the events recorded in the songs supposedly taking place in the towns along the Pilgrim Way.

The early compositions are, in fact, retellings of popular miracle stories known all over Europe. Although these marvels were often attributed to other saints, in particular James, Mary is always the wonder-worker in Alfonso's manuscript. The later songs deal with social and political issues specific to Northern Spain or with matters personal to Alfonso. Scholars claim the King is always the narrator as well as the main protagonist in the illustrations. Whatever the problem or political challenge, the Virgin is at the heart of each composition. During Alfonso's reign the Reconquest was at a halt and the King was responding to the ordeal of restructuring an expanded realm destabilized by inflation, population shifts and religious diversity. He claims he would never have coped with his troublesome kingdom without the help of the Virgin.

As well as a glimpse into the everyday life of medieval Spain, the discerning reader can also gain insight into the complications of reorganizing a complex social order made up of three distinct and competing faiths: Jewish, Islamic and Christian, and all without resorting to violence. While Alfonso was tolerant of the other religions, the ardent desire for Christian hegemony is easy to detect. His *Cantigas* are simultaneously a potent ideological set of documents as well as a poignant statement of Alfonso's devotion to the Virgin.

Where the European church fathers had constructed an austere woman who was ever virgin, the medieval Spaniards came to know someone much more vibrant. In all this Spanish story-telling and artistic expression the question of Mary's virginity never arises. Instead, the people were seemingly attracted to the image of a forceful woman prepared to combat evil and provide succour to her prayerful petitioners. When I asked Terence if, after visiting Spain, he had revised his opinion of Mary, he only grunted, too obstinate to admit that maybe he had been wrong about this celestial being.

Today many feminists condemn Mary because of her perpetual virginity. Carolyn Osiek maintains that for Catholic women the Marian model is an 'impossible ideal to which no woman can attain, with whom all women are invited to feel inadequate'. Marina Warner claims Mary's asceticism does no more than emphasize her somatic uniqueness and this 'excludes and damages the condition of the majority of women'. There are also derogatory male critics. Episcopal Bishop John Shelby Spong laments the Marian doctrine, understanding it as a device by which celibate men are able to 'universalize guilt among

263

women'. Once this tenet is accepted, Spong says, 'at one stroke woman was and still is rendered inadequate, incomplete, incompetent'. The Mary these critics refer to is an orthodox theological creation promoting the doctrine that she must forever remain chaste. These critics also accept Mary as a genuine historical being. As I read their objections I wondered why it had been so necessary for the church fathers to continue emphasizing her virginity. As sexuality is integral to humanity it is indeed cruel to deny this in someone. I also feel it is mistake to see Mary as an actual historical person and I wondered if granting Mary goddess status would change matters, but I soon realized a mythological approach would not work.

In her essay, 'The Virgin Mary: A Goddess?' Ann Matter points out how the church cannot allow Mary to be divine. She has to remain human in order to protect the doctrine of the incarnation of Christ. As we have seen, this was made clear at the Council of Ephesus. However, considering a mythic perspective made me thoughtful. In my understanding myths are stories that convey a 'truth' or the central concerns of a certain people at a certain time. In each culture mythological tales reveal unrealized desires or specific world views that help bring that particular social order to consciousness. If the gospel stories concerning Mary are read as myth, they reveal more about the people who wrote them than the protagonist of whom they write. Naturally the authors were men and it is strange that those church fathers who approved of Mary's virginity also took upon themselves the same sexual self-denial. What was the foundation of this renunciation?

In order to trace the role sex has played in history, I consulted Reay Tannahill's *Sex in History*. As an anthropologist she starts her account by speculating on pre-historical sensibility when it was probable that there would have been little difference between humans and animals. With the glimmerings of awareness, humans would then have realized they were not only distinct from the animals, but also from each other, males separating themselves from females. It is Tannahill's contention that this differentiation is based largely on the fact that women bleed. Palaeolithic humanity would probably have made basic assumptions about life and death, understanding that in life blood was a vital energy. She provides ample anthropological evidence to show the importance of blood and how it had been used in a variety of ways: in magic rituals and in various cults dealing with an assortment of gods and spirits.

Tannahill then speculates on the conundrum of menstrual blood. For the females of that time from whom it issued, it contradicted the understanding of blood as a powerful force vital to life. It leaked out for no apparent reason and the women losing it did not weaken or die. It also flowed only in women, never in men, boys or young children. Associated only with the post-pubescent female, menstrual blood was strange and inexplicable and, as Tannahill correctly points out, the inexplicable is always potentially fearful. In the case of the menses, the fear would be a masculine burden. It is not therefore surprising that these monthly flows came to be associated with the arcane and the forbidden and seen as the domain of wicked witches and those who intend harm. While she accepts the ban against incest was in all probability the first taboo, it is her opinion that the prohibition of the menstrual woman came close on its heels. It is of little wonder that even in the present day the topic of menstruation is still shunned and associated with the unspeakable.

I found H.R. Hays' *The Dangerous Sex* a crushing read. Chapter after chapter catalogues an horrendous variety of ways in which men have victimized and segregated women on account of their menstrual cycles. Hays claims the basis of this tyranny is a fundamental and ongoing masculine insecurity which he attributes to all males in all historical eras. It begins at birth with the disruption of unconscious uterine bliss. Hays says women, with their potential to experience the giving of birth, are able to get over this anxiety. Seemingly men never do, instead projecting their angst onto the perplexing mystery of woman. According to Hays the woe of both men and women is insurmountable. I think maybe the early church fathers, stridently advocating celibacy, may have supported Hays' argument had they the chance to read this text.

Bettina Bildhauer's essay, '*The Secrets of Women*: A Medieval Perspective on Menstruation', was the most helpful in understanding the church fathers' angst. Though *The Secrets of Women* was published in the thirteenth century, too late to have been read by the likes of Augustine and Jerome, the ideas it contains would have been circulating in earlier times. The unknown author not only presents menstrual blood as upsetting the wider cosmic balance, but also claims it threatens men generally because of its capacity to endanger life.

The document is heavily influenced by Aristotle who aligned women with cold matter and associated men with the warmth of intellect, spirit and form. *The Secrets* also accepts both genders as fluid. The fluid of a female is negative because it seeps out of her in the form of menstrual blood. Male fluid as semen is controllable. (It is hard to believe the author knew nothing of wet dreams!) Semen, too, is said to be coherent and almost solid and so is positive and, according to the author, ardently desired by women. With a 'rapacious appetite', and supposedly driven by their leaky menstrual fluids, women 'steal semen by sucking it out with their vaginas during intercourse, depriving men of their precious hot, moist fluid'. Men's health then apparently deteriorates and they die early. As well, polluting menstrual blood can seep out of the 'pore holes' in women's eyes, putting babies at risk as they sleep in their cradles. Men, too, are unsafe. If a man's voice goes hoarse it is known he has been in 'the unclean air' of a menstruating woman. And so the text goes. It is little wonder the early church fathers wanted to remain celibate. By establishing Mary as ever virgin they can be understood as attempting to keep her ever pre-pubertal and uncontaminated. It seems the feminine was only acceptable to these deluded and vulnerable men if she was forever without taint. While, at this point, they had no wish to venerate Mary, they could well have been squeamish about Christ's close connection to polluting female genitals.

Consideration of the city of Rome in late antiquity also provides insight into the early church fathers' excessive misogyny. The disarray of the general social order brought about by the slow decline of the Roman Empire, the invasion of the barbaric tribes, the extraordinary rise of Christianity and the political and social instability wrought by these changes, is well documented. However, in the opinion of Reay Tannahill, one of the greater causes of the Roman disintegration was the changing status of women. Where, in classical times, females had been no more than the chattel of their menfolk, dominated as though with an iron rod, legal changes within the Roman marriage laws altered this rigid control.

The change was insidious and not by female instigation. In an effort to delay the paying of a dowry and the handing over to the prospective husband the daughter's various assets, a new form of marriage was introduced which allowed the betrothed pair to live together for one year as though on trial. If the relationship was deemed good, the bride's father relinquished his rights over his daughter and handed over her properties. She then became the husband's possession. While legally binding, the contract could be dissolved if there was a lapse of more than three days in the yearlong association, a delay that, with a little ingenuity, was easy to arrange. In this way a woman could almost indefinitely postpone the moment she became legally subject to her husband. Because the father as well as his daughter benefited, this kind of marriage contract became popular. Notionally still in the hands of the father, the daughter was no longer under his eye and many of Rome's daughters were at large to indulge in activities which no doubt horrified the stolid, staid and conservative church fathers.

In the contemporary Western world we are knowledgeable of female biology, much more comfortable with bodies generally and no longer concerned with the dictates of the early church fathers. Nevertheless Spain continues to idolize and venerate Mary. I wanted to know how it was she was able to arouse such devotion. Michael P. Carroll's text, *The Cult of the Virgin Mary*, provided me with a promising explanation. Carroll offers a psychoanalytical perspective based on Freud's Oedipal Complex. The argument, as far as it goes, is thorough and well supported but prejudiced in that it is really only relevant to men.

Carroll first summarizes Freud's theory of the Oedipal, a concept which refers to very early emotions and ideas that the mind represses in the unconscious. It is Freud's claim that at the start of life both girls and boys desire to sexually possess the mother. The small boy in the throes of this complex soon realizes his father is his competitor in his claim for the mother's attention and so has murderous intensions towards him, but fearing he might lose his penis, evidenced by his mother's and sister's lack of this appendage, decides to side with the father until such time as he is big enough to effectively take on the father. By that time the incest taboo is well established and the adolescent seeks a mate elsewhere. He has also forgotten or repressed his anxiety about castration. Because the complex works at a subliminal level and cannot be proven, a large number of people reject the dynamic. Many are also hostile because they refuse to associate little children with sexuality. This may be because they do not fully understand Freud's sexual theory.

Freud's use of the term 'sexuality' refers to desire and pleasure generally. He saw sexuality as a libidinal energy that gradually accumulates and then needs to be released in some way. The release comes with a diffuse sense of physical pleasure. This is not only brought about by sexual intercourse, but also by touching, holding, caressing, crooning and by simply being in the company of the loved one. That children crave such attention, are comforted by it and seek it out cannot be doubted. Because at the start of life it is usually the mother who offers this comfort, in Freudian terms, the child can be said to be sexually attached to her. In a boy this attachment must be repressed so the boy can identify with the father. It is Carroll's assertion that in Spain and southern Italy these Oedipal desires, and their repression, are particularly intensified and influence the way people in these two Latin countries respond to the Virgin Mary.

Carroll uses the term 'Machismo complex' to support his claim, contending that in these two countries this complex has particularly strong roots. Machismo, an ideology which encourages masculine pride and an exaggerated sense of power and sexual prowess, is understood as a compensatory response to a conflict experienced by males and brought about by an early extended and exclusive association with the mother. The family situation which fosters this sensibility Carroll calls 'father-ineffective'. Driven by unemployment and poverty fathers in many Spanish and southern Italian families were all too often called away to seek work elsewhere and the authority in the home was in the sole hands of the mother. Boys raised in such families identify only with the maternal. As they mature they discover that the larger social order expects them to act like males and their early feminine identification makes them feel insecure about their masculinity. Carroll contends in such family structures Oedipal desires are intensified.

Oedipal rivalry in the 'father-ineffective' family is also altered. Because the father, too, is a victim of paternal deprivation, he is strongly under the sway of the Machismo complex and so continuously libidinal. Even though he may not act on this in front of his son, the son can, at some level, feel the repressed sexual drive. It is Carroll's assertion that this intensifies the son's castration anxiety. The father-ineffective family is therefore characterized by uncertainty and hostility and, because of the father's frequent absences, the son's sexual attachment to the mother intensifies. Because of the incest taboo and the influence of the Catholic Church, the son's desire will not only be strong, but also strongly repressed. Agreeing with Freud, Carroll contends that these stifled tensions must always be discharged, but only in an acceptable way. In Spain and southern Italy fervent devotion to Mary on the part of these highly-charged males is the means by which this energy can be dissipated. As a replacement for the forbidden mother, Mary, made legitimate by the church, can be ardently and passionately revered.

Carroll extends his argument to say that Mediterranean men with strongly repressed desires are also subject to guilt because, at some level, the superego knows the ardour for Mary is also a transgression of the incest taboo. The guilt that arises from this subliminal contravention can generate another desire, a desire for expiation. The way to atone and overcome guilt is through punishment. Carroll asserts that men with strongly repressed desire for the mother will all too often exhibit masochistic behaviour. Carroll provides ample evidence to support this claim.

I can agree with Carroll's argument about the masochistic nature of Christianity. I have often wondered why Christians are so fixated on the crucifixion. After death, Christ was resurrected and then ascended into heaven, yet in every Catholic and High Anglican church one always finds graphic statutory of a broken and bleeding man on prominent display. The cross always has precedence, never the resurrection or ascension. Carroll addresses this morbid focus by offering a psychological interpretation instead of the official orthodox view which sees Christ only as a being sent to earth by a father so that humanity can be redeemed through his crucifixion. Carroll extends this reading by proposing Christ as son who experienced bodily mutilation and death at the instigation of the father. This horror can be read as castration anxiety realized. Carroll then says if Spain and southern Italy produce sons who have a strong but strongly repressed desire for the mother, a desire which is preserved and perpetuated through the veneration of the Virgin, such a son will find relief for his need for punishment through identification with the cross. Christ becomes the son's symbolic fulfilment.

All this may seem a bit over the top and I have to admit that Carroll's thesis is seriously flawed. For instance, in the nineteenth and twentieth centuries the Western social order generally had established males as bread-winners and separate from the home which was now considered the domain of the female. Many of these men also had to leave home in order to search for work to support their families, not just those from Spain and Italy. Most Western families of this time could thus be classed as 'father-ineffective'. Carroll also does not provide a convincing argument explaining how the 'father-ineffective' family increases the daughters' desire and why women too, engage so intensely with Mary. He does mention penis envy and the need to bear children, but this can be applied to all women everywhere. Also ignored are the upper classes whose family life was not unsettled by unemployment. My research and experience on the Camino indicate that people of all classes engaged in Marian veneration. And all Christians who reverence the cross, female as well as male, can be seen to engage in masochism, not just Spaniards and Italians. To me these are serious flaws, almost enough for me to consider discounting Carroll's text were it not for something that Terence and I witnessed in León.

Mid-way through our trip, Terence had been out exploring León his own. Lost but drifting homewards, he came across an old-fashioned print shop and small attached gallery. Impressed by the etchings in the window, he returned to our pension and invited me to go out with him once again to view the art. As we wandered round the city hunting for the gallery (Terence has an appalling sense of direction), we passed a small church and entered. The interior was unremarkable except for a life-size statue standing to one side of the nave depicting a black Christ wearing a thick crown of thorns. The face was expressionless, his hands demurely folded. Standing before the statue one made direct eye contact with this dark figure. I found it sinister and was glad to leave.

We eventually found the print shop and chose and purchased an etching. As the kindly proprietor, who also happened to be the artist, wrapped our picture, sealed the package with hot wax (it really was an old-fashioned shop), we ambled round his establishment. It was reminiscent of William Blake and made me feel as though I had stepped outside my time frame. Then, exacerbating the eerie feeling, we came across a large framed picture of the black Christ we had just left, propped up in a far corner. The proprietor, approaching with our parcel and sensing our interest, invited us into the back of his workshop and pulled out a large poster. It presented a night scene, a full moon shining on an extraordinary procession of people dressed in long purple robes and wearing very tall conical hats which completely covered their faces. Only their eyes were visible, glittering uncannily through slits in the dark purple fabric and strangely reflecting the moonlight. The shock I felt was visceral. How could this seemingly benign, friendly man be mixed up with the Ku Klux Klan? I was speechless.

When we got back to our pension I seriously considered returning the etching. I am glad I did not. We found the artist to be a man of some repute whose etchings had been displayed in the Vatican. Framed, our small print looks well on the wall. Once home Terence also discovered the meaning of the poster. It was a promotion for the *Semana Santa*, the Spanish Holy Week. In Spain during Easter, males garb themselves in penitential robes, don the cone-shaped hat and, all through the night, process the streets with their faces covered. While they look bizarre, the costumes are lawful and the ritual sanctioned by the church. The strange hat is modelled on the *capirote*, a very tall cone the Spanish Inquisition once

273

forced condemned heretics wear as a mark of their guilt and shame. Its height singled them out as they walked the streets on their way to execution and exposed them to public humiliation. Now, five hundred and thirty years after the inauguration of the Spanish Inquisition, thousands of men still engage in this walk of humiliation.

Easter penitential processions take place all over Spain. They are formal affairs organized by various religious confraternities. In León alone there are sixteen such brotherhoods, the largest boasting over four thousand members, differentiated by some small detail in the costume. These are no mere fancy-dress robes, but beautifully tailored outfits complete with leather gloves and correct shoes. The reason for the full flowing costume is now lost. The tradition dates back to the sixteenth century and combines religious devotion with art, evidenced by the exquisitely sculptured and decorated floats depicting graphic and gruesome aspects of Christ's passion. The black Christ we saw in the church and in the print shop was on prominent display. The floats, carried on the shoulders of the brothers, are processed at night through the streets to the slow accompaniment of a strange rhythmic tattoo pulsed out on drums and bugles. Often playing for nine hours at a stretch, the drummers frequently finish with bleeding hands, wounds of which they are proud.

Ostensibly these ritual processions provide men an opportunity to repent the sins committed in the past year. It is easy to recognize in the *Semana Santa* Carroll's psychoanalytical assertions. The ritual is exclusively male. The desire for punishment is evident, some men walking barefoot, others wearing shackles or carrying chains. Self-flagellation is also common. Other men carry a heavy life-size wooden cross. The floats they bear are extremely heavy, but those who take on this burden accept the weight as an honour. In León the most solemn point in the procession takes place in the central square in the form of an encounter between two statues, the Virgin as *La Dolorosa* (the Lady of Sorrows), and Saint John, Christ's beloved disciple. It is a formal moment called 'The Meeting'. As the two statues come together, the two penitents carrying them move in such a way that the statues seem to dance together. In other parts of Spain this meeting is between the Virgin and her son.

I have not had the privilege of witnessing a Spanish Holy Week, but I can imagine it would be an arcane experience for those taking part—the shadowy cold night, the strange mysterious music, the rhythmic beat of drum and stomp of feet and the anonymous men in bizarre costumes. Penitent but libidinal the men could well be in the thrall of maternal love. Even if the lover is not a flesh and blood woman, the generosity of Mary is offered as a sweet indulgence. Other-worldly and remote from every-day reality, the *Semana Santa* night processions could well give rise to the expression of a deep but little understood phenomenon. While Carroll's argument might seem extreme for some people, I cannot help but feel in Spain it has some merit.

Carroll has also provided yet another reason to explain Mary's disassociation from her sexuality, the issue that has been my main concern in this chapter. He claims, if a ritual or devotional practice is to be used to dissipate sexual energy, it must be disguised. Depriving Mary of the possibility for sexual intercourse will effectively mask what is really going on at a deep unconscious level. I am sure there are many who will be horrified by these explanations.

In spite of this obscure psychoanalytical interpretation the Virgin remains for so many Spanish a figure of iconic focus, a beloved holy mother, close-by and always available. Where church doctrine has Mary fall asleep so she could be bodily assumed into Heaven, the people have claimed her as a vibrant living force providing perpetual and unconditional love, the perfect mother who never disappoints her child, sees only the best in each human and who never judges, an impossible feat for both God the Father as well as flesh and blood mothers, no matter how ardently they try.

Works cited in this chapter

Bildhauer, Bettina, '*The Secrets of Women*: A Medieval Perspective on Menstruation' cited in Andrew Shail & Gillian Howie, eds. *Menstruation: A Cultural History*. New York, NY: Palgrave Macmillan. 2005. pp. 65-75.

Carroll, Michael P. *The Cult of the Virgin Mary: Psychological Origins.* Princeton, NJ.: Princeton University Press. 1986.

Christian, William A. *Apparitions in Late Medieval and Renaissance Spain*. Princeton, NJ: Princeton University Press. 1989.

'The Protevangelium of James' & 'The Gospel of Pseudo-Matthew' cited in Elliot, J.K., ed. *The Apocryphal New Testament*. Oxford: Clarendon Press. 2005.

Hall, Linda B. *Mary, Mother and Warrior: The Virgin in Spain and the Americas*. Austin, Texas: University of Texas Press. 2004.

Hays, H. R. *The Dangerous Sex: The Myth of Feminine Evil*. London: Methuen & Co. 1966.

Keller, John & Annette Grant Cash. *Daily Life Depicted in the Cantigas de Santa Maria*. Lexington, Ken.: The University Press of Kentucky. 1998.

Lowney, Chris. *A Vanished World: Muslims, Christians, and Jews in Medieval Spain*. Oxford, UK: Oxford University Press. 2005.

Maunder, Chris, ed. *The Origins of the Cult of the Virgin Mary*. London: Burns & Oates. 2008.

Olson, Carl. *The Book of the Goddess Past and Present: An Introduction to her Religion.* New York, NY: Crossroads. 1983.

Osiek, Carolyn. *Beyond Anger: On Being a Feminist in the Church.* Dublin: Gill & Macmillan. 1986.

Shail, Andrew & Gillian Howie, eds. *Menstruation: A Cultural History.* New York, NY.: Palgrave Macmillan. 2005.

Tannahill, Reay. *Sex in History.* Great Britain: Abacus. 1993.

Warner, Marina. *Alone of All her Sex: The Myth and Cult of the Virgin Mary.* London: Vintage. 2000.

9

Trilling Wire in the Blood

I had returned to Spain with Terence because I wanted to understand medieval sensibility and the nature of pilgrimage. Why had this walk and my encounter with the remnants of medieval Spain been so significant? At home again after this second visit, I was still without this insight. I resorted to books. Of those I read with regard to pilgrimage walking, the explanations offered by Victor and Edith Turner were the most satisfactory, particularly with regard to my own experience.

The Turners define pilgrimage as both a physical process and transformative rite. Their anthropological text, *Image and Pilgrimage in Christian Culture*, expands these definitions, describing the pilgrimage ritual as a dynamic performance that can only be physically experienced. While there is usually a general established rubric with regard to conduct, procedure and destination, underlying the journey, the Turners see significance that goes beyond institutionalize dictates. Today not many pilgrims walk according to a fixed rite controlled by an established religious order. Instead, the Turners claim many unconsciously step out because of unformulated esoteric reasons possibly related to a more ancient oral tradition now lost to memory. This motivation is nebulous and felt rather than cognitively understood. No matter the pretext, and having made the commitment to walk, pilgrims will still find themselves at the mercy of the elements, as well as their senses. Pilgrimage is thus an existential experience.

As a pilgrim it is as though one stands in an undefined metaphorical gap and, in spite of possible authorities back home, usually the church, the pilgrim is offered a chance to relinquish conventional and religious conditioning. Liberated from everyday reality and seemingly free and out in the open, a contemplative pilgrim gets an opportunity to reinterpret personal reality. For those who are able to accept this challenge, the journey becomes a momentous rite of passage, the participant moving from one psychological reality to another. For others not yet ready for such radical change, the focus of the walk will be on nature and body, or spirit and soul.

To explain this indeterminate and potentially subversive 'gap' that is both temporal and mental, the Turners use the word 'liminal', a term that establishes the actual pilgrimage journey as one taken in a tenuous space.[25] While there is a specific physical trail that is now very clearly signposted, the way is enigmatically experienced as seemingly enchanted and sandwiched between two specifically defined actualities belonging to the *status quo* (home before embarking and home upon return). As the pilgrim walks, this reality remains remote for the duration of the experience.

The Turners expand on the potential profundity of pilgrimage by using another Latin term, '*communitas*', this word translating as 'fellowship'. In the liminality of the pilgrimage trail the Turners understand the bonding experienced by pilgrims as potentially subversive, the interaction and rapport unlike ordinary, everyday

---

[25] This is the same term used by Arnold Van Gennep and cited in Chapter 7 to describe the act of dying as a nebulous place situated between life in this world and the afterlife on the other side.

communication which is generally structured and hierarchical. Instead, pilgrim relationships are always spontaneous and direct. They are also undifferentiated, pilgrims paying no heed to social class, age or creed. Not even language differences impeded my sense of comradeship. The Turners claim *communitas* as a sensibility that 'does not merge identities but liberates them from conformity. It is a mode which strains towards universalism and openness'. They describe it as seemingly 'magical' and richly charged with affects, mainly pleasurable. This is an insight I can wholeheartedly endorse. It also goes a long way to explain the medieval exhilaration described by Jonathan Sumption, Peter Brown and Patrick Geary: the euphoria, the miraculous healings, the general hysteria and the cacophony generated by the passionate veneration of old bones.

The experience of *communitas* is also often associated with marginality and taboo because control is no longer in the hands of those who favour the *status quo*. However, on the trail walkers experiencing this sensibility are unlike the socially marginalized back home who are usually disempowered and shunned. This is because pilgrims are not only in control but also feel powerful. The effects can therefore be far-reaching. For this reason authorities who value structure and order understand *communitas* as dangerous. Certainly when I reached Santiago, a number of the pilgrims I had got to know along the way were promising themselves major changes when they again reached home.

Many of the pilgrims with whom I walked arrived in Santiago euphoric and triumphant, but when I reached the city I felt inordinately sad. I now understood why. Not only had I revelled in what had seemed an enchanted realm, but I had also enjoyed the open-hearted generosity of my fellow walkers. I was now reluctant to return to far-away Australia and my mundane life. In part, my decision to research the medieval Camino was an endeavour to overcome this sense of loss.

And what of medieval sensibility? Walking the Camino, one cannot doubt that the Western world had been dominated by Christianity. Now, so claim some historians, the rise of secularism has left us unable to experience or fully appreciate medieval sensibility. From primary sources such as legal manuscripts (wills, transfer of land, court judgements, registers, as well as ecclesiastical records documenting papal bulls, episcopal appointments, decrees and declarations), one can put together certain facts that tell us a great deal about medieval times. However, such information will not provide insight into the medieval mentality, a sensibility so different from that experienced in the twenty-first century. Carolly Erickson, a twentieth century author, helped me to understand the difference.

For Erickson one of the major ways the medievals differed from us today was because these folk were in possession of what she calls 'visionary imagination'. This meant they could easily conjure up images and scenarios. At this time God, his angels, the saints and the Devil, were understood as real. They existed in the ether and were acknowledged as much more powerful than mere human beings. Even in learned theological writing, bodiless beings had a secure place. Erickson quotes Saint Jerome who wrote, 'Compared to the multitude of supernal and angelic beings the mass of humanity is as nothing'. For Isidore of Spain demons were real, 'unsettling the senses, stirring the low passions and disordering life'. Saint Aquinas found in angels 'a level of creation which made the whole of creation comprehensible'. Medievals did not doubt the unseen and believed in the images their imaginations were able to evoke. In those times the social order was multiform, never one-dimensional.

Other realms also existed: heaven, hell and purgatory. For the ancients these realities meant their mental lives could become unrestrained. Where we today have inserted boundaries between the material world and that which is other to it, the medievals were more unquestioning and their imaginative visions often sanctioned by the church. To authenticate reality most moderns use sense perception, but medievals were able to juxtapose imagination and factuality, the one always able to inform the other. Their world, the real and the imagined, was undifferentiated, allowing these people to assemble a reality from historical fragments and geographical certainty melded with biblical lore, myth and hagiography, composing mystical scenarios that the logical and scientific mind of today would not permit.

Because they also believed the force of divine creation was unleashed by sight, the arcane visions the medieval mind was capable of creating were understood as revelation and truth that was aligned to the mind of God. Sight was therefore not a passive recording of experience as it is for many today, but a form of creative energy. Erickson accepts that while such a vision would probably terrify a medieval, it would not challenge his or her understanding of the world. Instead it would reinforce it. In the Middle Ages visions defined reality. An unexceptional person from the twenty-first century, similarly confronted, would stand in abject horror, their expectations of reality shattered. From our point of view visions not only separate one from reality but also imply mental instability and possible psychosis.

For Erickson the medieval visionary imagination puts a basic perceptual barrier between us and the past which, she claims, we rational beings can now never cross. I tend to agree. Walking the Camino, I was often confused. On the one hand I found it incredible that the whole of Western humanity in medieval times could live not only in fear of a cranky bloke said to reside in the sky, but one who had to always to be constantly placated. At the same time, the 'Evil One' from down below had also to be avoided. With Western twenty-first century scientific knowledge, the existence of such a being is, for most, no longer a feasibility. On the other hand I often felt bereft because I could not reach out to the benevolence this supposed cranky bloke was able to grant.

Visiting the wondrous cathedrals, witnessing the outpouring of faith and devotion in the artwork and treasure and realizing this was (for most visitors) a thing of the past, I was saddened. It felt as though something wondrous had been lost, a mysterious beauty I badly wanted to regain. However, the scepticism of the Enlightenment, science, technology, the destruction of meta-narratives and Nietzsche's strident proclamation that God is dead have all seriously reduced the possibility of reaching beyond the here and now making, for the vast majority in the Western world, a return to medieval sensibility an impossibility.

To fill the gap vacated by God's demise, and with no over-arching narrative to hold the social order together, theorists have been at large to search elsewhere for meaning. Even though many scientists claim Darwinian Theory has proved that life is accidental and without purpose, psychoanalysts suggest we can replace God with a heart-felt search for self-realization. Moral philosophers have written numerous texts calling people to the 'Good Life'. Following the catastrophes of the twentieth century such as World Wars, genocides, Hiroshima and the Chinese Cultural Revolution, these writers assert we need to pursue and practice virtue if we wish to live meaningfully. Phenomenologists suggest we live in the present moment, finding meaning in the small things of life. These writers call on poets, artists, writers and musicians who, adopting this stance, have indeed found sufficiency in brief moments of sublime bliss.

Others simply accept life as diminished and reality impossible to formulate. For some the problem stems from language which, they claim, always lets us down, vocabulary never quite able to reach that seemingly intuitive knowing that lies just beyond the reach of consciousness. 'There always seems to be better words', says Simon Blackburn, 'if only we could find them, just over the horizon'. Contemporary poets, eschewing the rationalists, take a different view. For instance Rainer Maria Rilke maintained we have to engage in a very real 'struggle to name' that extended reality, the one not of the ordinary every day. It was Rilke's contention that we can no longer do this because of Christianity which, because of its focus on the afterlife, had created a rift between humans and nature, a divide that had stopped us from experiencing and articulating the earth as fully as we might.

These two stances: the one where the speaker accepts the divide and gives up the search, while the other is prepared to struggle in order to find appropriate words and phraseology, can be seen as a difference between two world views. On the one hand there are those who take a literalist scientific approach, using language to verify empirical reality. On the other, there are those who respond to the world intuitively or emotionally, believing it is possible to rouse and engage with subliminal knowledge at the edge of consciousness. It has been suggested that in past times this hidden knowing may well have been accepted as the domain of the divine. To verbalize this mystery and provide insight, one needs a different kind of language, one that utilizes metaphor, metonymy, symbolism and allegory. This is poetic language. Not only will it articulate concepts, it will also illustrate and evoke feeling. As well as effective words, poets, utilizing this kind of language, will also communicate through metre, pace, flow, tone, alliteration, repetition and sometimes nonsense, verbal wanderings or fuzziness. These are poetic tactics which perform within language and extend our knowledge of the literal world through implication and allusion, offering deeper understandings and new possibilities. An attempt to access that which remains subliminal in a direct rational way will always fail.

I am not a poet or a philosopher. When I walked the Camino I did not consciously engage with the profundity of 'being' or try to express my experience in expressive language. Nor did I think about how I could live meaningfully. I simply walked. It was when I returned to Spain with Terence that I remembered my experiences and formulated some ideas. Like the medievals who believed God revealed himself though sight, I gleaned my ideas from looking. Initially I observed art works. While we did see gruesome compositions that, in their own way, made a profound impact, we also found many pieces of exquisite beauty, painted canvasses as well as sculptures. I have discussed my response to sculpture in Chapter 7 when elaborating on Spanish mausoleums. In Chapters 6 I offered insight into painting from the perspective of 'presence', a concept offered by George Steiner and Hans Gumbrecht.

Presence for Steiner and Gumbrecht refers to the abstruse meaning that can be communicated through beauty and which these two academics see as grounded in the transcendent. For both, this nebulous, un-locatable 'presence' is capable of revealing an intuitive and unshaped knowledge that can shake the complacent observer out of his or her sense of stasis. Where Rilke would struggle to find words to describe such an epiphany, Gumbrecht and Steiner, neither of whom is a poet, suggest we do no more than recognize the sublime moment and appreciate it so that it may enrich our lives.

I am happy with such silence, finding profound things remain profound if unarticulated. Unless one is a talented poet, the pursuit of words can never reach the intuitive insight and the experience is indeed reduced. Steiner understood these silent moments as an unarticulated 'dialogue' between the observer and the observed in which beauty and truth become linked and provide a profound sense of sufficiency. It is a truth which is not logically thought out but something we participate in. Gumbrecht understood such an experience as a 'surrogate religion'.

I accept these insights, but decided this sort of meaningful 'truth' need not be limited to artistic works, literature or music as suggested by Steiner, but can also be gleaned from the natural world. Like a painting, nature, too, offers itself for contemplation. I recalled poplar groves in Spain and the manner in which sunlight made the leaves sparkle and dance, and standing on a cliff top with Terence, intrigued and mesmerized as mysterious ropes of mist twirled their way up a mountain slope. I remembered walking through the vast acres of northern Spanish wheat fields when I was on my own. The grain had just been harvested and, in the early morning sunshine, the remaining stubble was a glowing yellow. The tracks made by the mechanical harvester were still evident and filled the entire landscape with a wonderful sense of movement. It was as though some magician had reached down from the sky with an enchanted paintbrush and, in bold Van Gogh style, splashed gold paint over the entire landscape. Elated, I did a Dervish twirl in the middle of the dirt track and, to my astonishment, the fields began to dance. It was a moment of pure exalted joy.

I cannot say what such imagery 'means'. I can only report that, when surprised by scenes like these, the experience is profoundly significant. In Eliot's poetic words, it is like the feel of 'trilling wire in the blood' that somehow makes life momentous. On the Camino I kept such moments to myself. At that point, to share them with other pilgrims would have undermined the vision. Without poetic talent to give form to such moments, it is best to remain with one's uncritical solitude and in non-judgemental silence.

Now at a remove from Spain and having delved into the thoughts of others, I can ask, were these instants in the wheat fields and on the foggy mountain slope transcendental? Where do such unexpected moments come from? Does something animate the world in some way allowing Steiner's dialogue between the observer and the observed? Many poets write of such moments, offering up their insights. The more contemporary ones are wise never to mention God. However, when I hear of this being's demise I receive the news with serious doubt, but I, too, say nothing.

And the medievals who had straddled that terrible bind—the 'Evil One' on one side and the obligation to placate the 'cranky old bloke' on the other—to my way of thinking these beings have now been replaced and by something that is not visual, needs no explanation, is ineffable and is, at least to me, authentic and much more satisfactory.

Works cited in this chapter

Bull, Marcus. *Thinking Medieval: An Introduction to the Study of the Middle Ages.* Hampshire, UK: Palgrave Macmillan. 2005.

Caillois, Roger, trans. Meyer Barash. *Man and the Sacred.* Urbana, Ill.: University of Illinois Press. 2001.

Erickson, Carolly. *The Medieval Vision: Essays in History and Perception.* New York, NY: Oxford University Press. 1976.

Gumbrecht, Hans Ulrich. *Production of Presence: What Meaning Cannot Convey.* Stanford, Cal: Stanford University Press. 2004.

Steiner, George. *Real Presences.* Chicago, Ill.: University of Chicago Press. 1991.

Turner, Victor & Edith Turner. *Images and Pilgrimage in Christian Culture.* Oxford: Basil Blackwell. 1978.

Turner, Victor & Edith Turner. *Images and Pilgrimage in Christian Culture.* Oxford, UK: Basil Blackwell. 1978.

Watson, Peter. *The Age of Atheists: How we have sought to Live since the Death of God.* New York, NY: Simon & Schuster: 2014.

Selected Bibliography

Atienza, Juan Garcia, trans. Federico E. Rodriguez Guerra. *The Knights Templar in the Golden Age of Spain*. Rochester, Vermont: Destiny Books. 2006.

Attwater, Donald. *The Penguin Dictionary of The Saints*. England: Penguin Books. 1980.

Bahrami, Beebe. *The Spiritual Traveler. Spain: A Guide to Sacred Sites and Pilgrim Routes*. Mahwah, NJ: HiddenSpring. 2009.

Barber, Richard. The *Knight and Chivalry*. Woodbridge, UK: The Boydell Press. 2000.

Barton, Simon. *The Aristocracy in Twelfth-Century Léon and Castile*. Cambridge, UK: Cambridge University Press. 1997.

Bell, Adrian R. & Richard S. Dale. 'The Medieval Pilgrimage Business'. *Oxford Journals Humanities & Social Sciences, Enterprise & Society*. Vol 12 Issue 3. pp. 601-627.

Bernard of Clairvaux, ed. Emilie Griffin. *Selected Works*. New York: HarperOne. 2005.

Binski, Paul. *Medieval Death: Ritual and Representation*. London: The British Museum Press. 1996.

Brierley, John. *A Pilgrim's Guide to the Camino, 7th Edition*. Scotland: Camino Guides Findhorn Press. 2011.

Brodman, James William. *Charity and Welfare*: *Hospitals and the Poor in Medieval Catalonia*. Philadelphia, Penn: University of Pennsylvania Press. 1998.

_____. *Charity & Religion in Medieval Europe*. Washington, D.C.: The Catholic University Press. 2009.

Brooke, Christopher. *The Structure of Medieval Society*. London: Thames and Hudson. 1971.

_____. *The Age of the Cloister: The Story of Monastic Life in the Middle Ages*. United Kingdom: Sutton Publishing. 2003.

Brown, Peter. *The Cult of the Saints: Its Rise and Function in Latin Christianity.* Chicago, Il: Chicago University Press. 1982.

Bull, Marcus. *Knightly Piety and the Lay Response to the First Crusade.* Oxford, UK: Clarendon Press. 1998.

_____. *Thinking Medieval: An Introduction to the Study of the Middle Ages.* Hampshire, UK: Palgrave Macmillan. 2005.

Burgess, Glyn, trans. *The Song of Roland.* London: Penguin Books. 1990.

Butcher, Carmen Acevedo. *Man of Blessing: A Life of Saint Benedict.* Brewster, Mas: Paraclete Press. 2012.

Byrne, Joseph P. *The Black Death.* Westport, Conn: Greenwood Press. 2004.

Carroll, Michael P. *The Cult of the Virgin Mary: Psychological Origins.* Princeton, N.J.: Princeton University Press. 1986.

Charny, Geoffroi de, trans. Elspeth Kennedy. *A Knight's Own Book of Chivalry.* Philadelphia, Penn: University of Pennsylvania Press. Reprinted 2005.

Charles, Victoria & Klaus H. Carl. *Gothic Art.* Vietnam: Parkstone International. 2012.

Christian, William A. *Apparitions in Late Medieval and Renaissance Spain.* Princeton, NJ: Princeton University Press. 1989.

_____. *Local Religion in Sixteenth-Century Spain.* Princeton, NJ: Princeton University Press. 1989.

Coffey, Thomas F Linda Kay Davidson & Maryjane Dunn, eds. *The Miracles of Saint James.* Translated from the *Liber Sancti Jacobi.* New York, NY: Italica Press. 1996.

Defourneaux, Marcelin. *Daily Life in Spain in the Golden Age,* trans. Newton Branch. London: Allen & Unwin. 1970.

Davis, R.H.C. *The Medieval Warhorse: Origins, Development and Redevelopment.* New York, N.Y.: Thames and Hudson. 1989.

Dunn, Maryjane & Linda Kay Davidson, eds. *The Pilgrimage to Compostela in the Middle Ages.* London & New York: Routledge. 2000.

Edwards, John. *The Inquisitors: The Story of the Grand Inquisitors of the Spanish Inquisition.* Gloucestershire: Tempus. 2007.

Eire, Carlos M. N. *From Madrid to Purgatory*. New York: Cambridge University Press. 1995.

Ellis, Havelock. *The Soul of Spain*. Westport, Conn: Greenwood Press. 1976.

Erickson, Carolly. *The Medieval Vision: Essays in History and Perception*. New York: Oxford University Press. 1976.

Escohotado, Javier Pérez, trans. Jennifer Brooke Hoge. *St. Domingo de la Calzada: Engineer of the Land*, trans. Jennifer Brooke Hoge. Logroño, Rioja: Ediciones. 2009.

Fakhry, Majid. *Averroes: His Life, Works and Influence*. Oxford, UK: Oneworld. 2001.

Fernández de Castro Cabez, Sister Maria del Carmen. *The Life of the Very Noble King of Castile and León, Saint Ferdinand III*. New York, N Y: The Foundation for a Christian Civilization, Inc. 1987.

Fletcher, Richard. *The Quest for El Cid*. London: Hutchinson. 1989.

Frale, Barbara. *The Templars: The Secret History Revealed*. New York, N Y: Arcade Publishing. 2004.

Fremantle, Anne, ed. *The Age of Belief: Medieval Philosophers*, New York, N.Y: A Meridian Book. 1982.

French, Roger. *Medicine before Science: The Business of Medicine from the Middle Ages to the Enlightenment*. Cambridge, UK: Cambridge University Press. 2009.

Frewer, Ian. 'Weird and Wonderful: Witchcraft in Spain' *Expatia*. March. 2005.

Frey, Nancy Louise. *Pilgrim Stories on and off the Road to Santiago*. Los Angeles, Cal: University of California. 1998.

Frieder, Braden. *Chivalry and the Perfect Prince: Tournaments, Art, and the Spanish Habsburg Court*. Kirksville, Miss: Truman University Press. 2008.

Geary, Patrick J. *Furta Sacra: Thefts of Relics in the Middle Ages*. Princeton N.J.: Princeton University Press. 1990.

_____ . *Living with the Dead in the Middle Ages*. Ithaca, N.Y.: Cornell University Press. 1994.

_____ . Ed, *Readings in Medieval History Volume II*. Peterborough, Ontario: Broadview Press. 1998.

Gitlitz, David M. & Linda Kay Davidson. *The Pilgrimage Road to Santiago*. New York, N Y: St. Martin's Press. 2000.

Gregory, Bishop of Tours, trans. Ernest Brehaut. *History of the Franks*. New York, N Y: Octagon Books. 1965.

Gumbrecht, Hans Ulrich. *Production of Presence: What Meaning cannot Convey.* Stanford Cal: Stanford University Press. 2004.

Hall, Linda B. *Mary, Mother and Warrior: The Virgin in Spain and the Americas*. Austin, Tex: University of Texas Press. 2004.

Hays, H. R. *The Dangerous Sex: The Myth of Feminine Evil.* London: Methuen & Co. 1966.

Hemingway, Ernest. *Death in the Afternoon*. London: Jonathan Cape. 1958.

Holland, Tom. *Millennium: The End of the World and the Forging of Christendom*. Great Britain: Abacus. 2011.

Icher, François. *Building the Great Cathedrals*. New York, N.Y.: Harry N. Abrams, Inc. 1998.

Kaeuper, Richard W. *Chivalry and Violence in Medieval Europe.* Oxford, UK: Oxford University Press. 1999.

Keen, Maurice. *Chivalry*. New Haven, Conn: Yale University Press. 1984.

_____. *Nobles, Knights and Men-at-Arms in the Middle Ages*. London: The Hambledon Press. 1996.

Keller, John & Annette Grant Cash. *Daily Life Depicted in the Cantigas de Santa Maria*. Lexington, Ken: The University Press of Kentucky. 1998.

Kerr, Julie. *Monastic Hospitality: The Benedictines in England.* Woodbridge, UK: Boydell & Brewer. 2007.

_____. *Life in the Medieval Cloister*. London: Continuum. 2009.

Kevin, Tony. *Walking the Camino: A Modern Pilgrimage to Santiago.* Melbourne: Scribe. 2008.

Konstan, David & Kurt A. Raaflaub. *Epic and History*. Sussex U.K.: Wiley-Blackwell Publishing. 2010.

Krüger, Kristina. *Monasteries and Monastic Orders*: *2000 Years of Art and Culture*. Potsdam: Ullman Publishing. 2012.

Laffi, Domenico, trans. James Hall. *A Journey to the West. The Diary of a Seventh Century Pilgrim from Bologna to Santiago de Compostela*. Leiden, The Netherlands: Primavera Pers. Reprinted 1977.

Lawrence, C.H. *Medieval Monasticism*. London: Longman. 2001.

Leclercq, Jean, trans. Catherine Misrahi. *The Love of Learning and the Desire for God: A Study of Monastic Culture*. New York, N Y: Fordham University Press. 1998.

Lemay, Helen Rodnite. *Women's Secrets: A Translation of Pseudo-Albertus' De Secretis Mulierum* (with Commentaries). Albany, NY: State University of New York Press. 1992.

Levack, Brian P. *The Witch-Hunt in Early Modern Europe*, Third Edition. Great Britain; Pearson Education Ltd., Longman. 2006.

Lindberg, David C. *The Beginnings of Western Science*. Chicago, Il: The University of Chicago Press. 1992.

Llull, Ramon. *The Book of the Order of Chivalry*, trans. Noel Fallows. Woodbridge, UK: Boydell Press. 2013.

Lowney, Chris. *A Vanished World: Muslims, Christians, and Jews in Medieval Spain*. Oxford: Oxford University Press. 2005.

Maalouf, Amin, trans. Jon Rothschild. *The Crusades Through Arab Eyes*. New York, NY: Schocken Books. 1985.

Mâle, Émile, trans. Dora Nussey. *The Gothic Image: Religious Art in the Thirteenth Century*. London: The Fontana Library. 1961.

Marsh, Richard. *Spanish and Basque Legends*. Dublin: Legendary Books. 2010.

Maunder, Chris, ed. *The Origins of the Cult of the Virgin Mary*. London: Burns & Oates. 2008.

Melczar, William, trans. *The Pilgrim's Guide to Santiago de Compostela*, New York, N Y: Italica Press. 1993.

Merwin, W.S., trans. *Spanish Ballads*. Port Townsend, Washington: Copper Canyon Press. 1961.

Moore, R. I. *The First European Revolution c. 979-1215*. Oxford, UK: Blackwell. 2000.

Morris, Jan. *Spain*. London: Faber & Faber. 2008.

Mullen, Robert. *Call of the Camino: Myths, Legends and Pilgrim Stories on the Way to Santiago de Compostela*. Scotland: Findhorn Press. 2010.

Nardo, Don. *Life on a Medieval Pilgrimage*. San Diago, Cal: Lucent Books. 1996.

Nicholson, Helen. *The Knights Templar: A New History*. Gloucestershire, UK: Sutton Publishing. 2004.

Nooteboom, Cees. *Roads to Santiago*, trans. Ina Rilke. London: The Harvill Press. 1997.

O'Callaghan, Joseph F. *A History of Medieval Spain*. London: Cornell University Press. 1975.

Olson, Carl. *The Book of the Goddess Past and Present: An Introduction to her Religion*. New York, NY: Crossroads. 1983.

Paxton, Frederick S. *Christianizing Death: The Creation of a Ritual Process in Early Medieval Europe*. Ithaca, NY: Cornell University Press. 1990.

Peers, Allison E. *The Mystics of Spain*. Mineola, NY: Dover Publications. 2002.

Penny, Nicholas. *Mourning: The Arts and Living*. London: Her Majesty's Stationary Office. 1981.

Pérez, Joseph. *The Spanish Inquisition: A History*, trans. Janet Lloyd. London: Profile Books. 2004.

Rabe, Cordula, rans. Gill Round. *Camino de Santiago: Way of Saint James from the Pyrenees to Santiago*. Munich: Rother. 2007.

Rodríguez-Velasco, Jesús D. *Order and Chivalry: Knighthood and Citizenship in Late Medieval Castile*, trans. Eunice Rodríguez Ferguson. Philadelphia, Penn: University of Pennsylvania Press. 2010.

Rudy, Charles. *The Cathedrals of Northern Spain*. Boston, Mass: Colonial Press. 1905.

Sallis, John. *Stone*. Bloomington, Indiana: In University Press. 1994.

Scott, Robert A. *The Gothic Enterprise: A Guide to Understanding a Medieval Cathedral.* Berkeley, Cal: University of California Press. 2011.

Shail, Andrew & Gillian Howie, eds. *Menstruation: A Cultural History*. New York, NY: Palgrave Macmillan. 2005.

Simpson, Lesley, trans. *The Poem of the Cid*. Los Angeles, Cal: University of California. 1957.

Solnit, Rebecca. *Wanderlust: A History of Walking*. New York, NY: Penguin Books. 2000.

Southern, R.W. *Western Society and the Church in the Middle Ages*. Middlesex, England: Penguin Books. 1976.

Stamm, James R. *A Short History of Spanish Literature*. New York, NY: New York University Press. 1979.

Steiner, George. *Real Presences*. Chicago, Il: University of Chicago Press. 1991.

Stemp, Richard. *The Secret Language of Churches and Cathedrals*. London: Duncan Baird Publishers. 2010.

Strafford, Peter. *Romanesque Churches of Spain*. London: dlm Publishers. 2010.

Sumption, Jonathan. *Pilgrimage: An Image of Medieval Religion*. London: faber & faber. 2002.

Swaan, Wim. *The Gothic Cathedral*. London: Elek Books. 1969.

Tamburello, Dennis E. *Bernard of Clairvaux: Essential Writings*. New York, NY: Crossroads Publishing. 2000.

Tannahill, Reay. *Sex in History*. Great Britain: Abacus. 1993.

Torres Villarroel, Diego de. *The Remarkable Life of Don Diego*. London: The Folio Society. Reprinted 1958.

Turner, Victor & Edith Turner. *Images and Pilgrimage in Christian Culture*. Oxford: Basil Blackwell. 1978.

Vattimo, Gianni. *Beyond Interpretation: The Meaning of Hermeneutics for Philosophy*. Stanford, Cal: Stanford University Press. 1997.

Watson, Peter. *The Age of Atheists: How we have Sought to Live since the Death of God*. New York, NY: Simon & Schuster: 2014.

Warner, Marina. *Alone of All her Sex: The Myth and Cult of the Virgin Mary.* London: Vintage. 2000.

Wentworth, Webster. *Basque Legends*. London: Griffith & Farran. 1877.

Whitehill, Walter Muir. *Spanish Romanesque Architecture of the Eleventh Century*. Oxford, U K: Oxford University Press. 1968.

Whyte, Florence. *The Dance of Death in Spain and Catalonia*. Baltimore, Ml: Waverly Press. 1977.

Williams, Hywel. *Emperor of the West: Charlemagne and the Carolingian Empire*. London: Quercus. 2011.

Williams, John & Alison Stones, eds. *The* Codex Calixtinus *and the Shrine of St. James*. Germany, Tübingen: Gunter Narr Verlag. Reprinted 1992.